JUDITH MILLER
A CLOSER LOOK AT
ANTIQUES

JUDITH MILLER
A CLOSER LOOK AT
ANTIQUES

MARSHALL PUBLISHING • LONDON

JUDITH MILLER A CLOSER LOOK AT ANTIQUES

Conceived, edited and designed by
Marshall Editions Ltd
The Orangery
161 New Bond Street
London W1Y 9PA
www.marshallpublishing.com

MARSHALL EDITIONS LTD

Editor	Nina Hathway
Copy Editors	Caroline Bingham, Christine Davis, Sarah Halliwell, Gwen Rigby
Managing Editor	Liz Stubbs
Designers	Flora Awolaja, Anne Fisher, Caroline Hill, Thomas Keenes
Art Director	Dave Goodman
Editorial Director	Ellen Dupont
Editorial Coordinator	Ros Highstead
Picture Research	Pernilla Pearce
Editorial Assistant	Victoria Cookson
Production	Anna Pauletti
Specialist Consultants	Alexis Butcher (Silver)
	Jeanette Hayhurst (Glass)
	Gordon Lang (Ceramics)
	Jeremy Smith (Furniture)
	Nicholas M. Dawes (USA)
Writers	Jill Bace, Frankie Leibe, Sarah Yates
Illustrators	International Artworks Ltd
Photography	A & J Photographics
	Terrence McGinniss
	Graham Rae
	Steve Tanner

Cover
Photograph of Judith Miller by Adrian Weinbrecht
Front cover tr CC/ME, cr ST/JH, bl CC/ME,
br AJ/S; back cover t CC/ME, bl AJ/C, bc CC/ME, br AJ/AL.

Originated in Singapore by Pica
Printed and bound in Italy by Milanostampa

1 84028 320 3

Contents

Ceramics

Foreword

This Regency ebonized and painted, triple chair-back sofa is typical of furniture made in England during the early 19th century. Details such as the trelliswork back, the caned kidney-shaped seat, and the turned, tapered legs are all indicators of period and style. [H]

Value Codes

Every caption describing an antique in this book has a value code, a letter, at the end to give a broad indication of its value. For example, the 'H' above, means that this sofa is worth between £2,000 and £3,000. Full details of all value codes are given on p.205.

My initiation into the world of antiques was inauspicious. My parents were part of the 1950s 'Formica generation' who were determined to ditch all of their inherited antiques – 'second-hand furniture' according to my mother – and replace them with the wonderful new post-War designs that were becoming all the rage. So I am not one of those experts who grew up surrounded by fabulous antiques. In fact, I think the way I approach collecting was helped considerably by the fact that I came to everything with a fresh, enthusiastic eye. I was, however, fascinated by history from an early age and found myself drawn to the many junk shops near the flats I inhabited as an impoverished student at Edinburgh University during the late 1960s.

My first passion was 'china' (as all ceramics are known to the uninitiated) and I was very excited to find heaps of inexpensive old plates in these shops crammed full of dusty bargains. Delighted with my purchases, I determined to find out more about them. Even to my untutored eye each plate looked quite different: some glinted white, some had creamier background colours, others a distinctive grey tone. The decoration was also confusing. Why did Chinese sages dally in European landscapes, and why didn't their eyes have an oriental slant? Did the 18th-century clothes some figures wore indicate the date of the plate? And could I rely on the marks on the base to identify the maker?

To satisfy my curiosity, I set about looking for the humble plates' origins in all the books I could lay my hands on but, frustratingly, no information appeared in any of them. Indeed, all my research accomplished was to raise many other questions about identifying antiques. For example, how can you recognize alterations or additions, and – that perennial puzzle – how do you know whether that coveted piece is genuine, or actually a fake? And of course, how do you establish what an antique is really worth?

I then started to attend auction sales, where I could view the items and read their catalogue descriptions, although such material was so riddled with disclaimers that a great deal of the authentication was left to the would-be buyer. There was also the strange behaviour of the regular auction attendees to come to terms with. When unaccustomed to it, the novice can be bemused, if not terrified, by the rituals that dealers and collectors perform. Drawers were pulled out of chests and stroked. The backboards of bureau-cabinets were minutely inspected. The stretchers on chairs were compared from all angles. Porcelain bowls were pinged – and then licked! Glass goblets were stroked delicately with a knowing thumb, and silver teapots were 'huffed' on. I copied everything, but at first had no idea what I should be feeling, hearing or seeing.

My next step was to befriend accommodating dealers, and I must say that over the years I have been helped immensely by many of them. Nevertheless, it was, and is, unfair to expect a professional dealer to share years of experience and expertise with an enthusiastic amateur. So I tried other tacks as well. I visited museums and collections to look at the best examples of pieces that interested me. I also went to as many antiques fairs and shows as time allowed ... and, gradually, I began to develop an eye for materials, methods and dates of manufacture, countries or regions of origin, specific makers, styles of form and decoration, and a feel for changing market values. However, the most important thing I learned was that each antique contained a number of vital clues to its identification, as well as a fair sprinkling of red herrings. To spot these, antiques have to be touched and, in the case of glass and ceramics, the sound they make 'listened' to, not just looked at. In other words, to be an efficient detective you have to employ most of your senses.

I have now spent some 30 rewarding years collecting, solving mysteries and enjoying all the new discoveries that the world of antiques has to offer. In *A Closer Look at Antiques* I've concentrated on four of the most popular collecting areas that I have learned about during that time: Furniture, Ceramics, Silver and Glass. By putting each one into its historical context, by examining influential types, styles and makers, and then by dissecting key examples to divulge their crucial characteristics, the aim is not just to pass on what I know. Rather, the primary purpose of this book is to empower you with the basic techniques of identification and other tricks of the trade that will enable you to collect with confidence as an antiques expert in your own right. Happy hunting!

This English silver tankard was made by Alice and George Burrows in 1815. Always check the piece is fully marked on the body and lid. [I]

The moment you spot a figure with such exceptionally lively movement, fine detailing and strong colours, you can probably assume it is a Meissen figure from the mid-1740s. [H]

Baroque Style c.1620–1700

Allegory of the Sense of Hearing
by Jan Brueghel and Hendrick van Balen

THE BAROQUE STYLE ORIGINATED *in Italian painting, sculpture and architecture in the 1620s. Characterized by elaborately decorated and complicated shapes, the style reached its height in France at the court of Louis XIV where a wealth of decorative arts were made by the finest craftsmen.*

The grandeur of Baroque sculpture and architecture was reflected in the decorative arts, especially in furniture. The style incorporated architectural and sculptural elements, with the use of pediments (triangular gables), heavy scrolls, and swags (garlands), but it also used bulbous shapes, elaborate moulding, carving, gilding, and intricate floral marquetry (decorative wood patterns). Luxurious materials were preferred, including rich velvet, brocade and damask upholstery, semi-precious stones and ivory.

The increase in trade between China and the West during the 17th century, greatly influenced the style. It led to a demand for lacquerwork panels and furniture, and, especially, blue-and-white porcelain. The French Baroque style also spread new ideas throughout Europe in the 1670s and 1680s through the production of engraved ornament by leading French designers such as Jean Le Pautre and Jean Bérain, and through the emigration of Huguenot (Protestant) craftsmen from France fleeing religious persecution. Many Huguenots eventually settled in England, where the style was favoured by William III and Mary II.

After 1700, the strict formality, heaviness and symmetry of the Baroque was replaced in France by the lighter Régence.

Note the heavy mouldings, faceted ball stopper and lobed decoration on the foot of this glass goblet and cover, made at Potsdam (c.1730). All typify German and Bohemian Baroque glass. [H]

This English blue-dash charger reflects the late 17th- and early 18th-century desire for blue-and-white ceramics. [D]

Louis XIV

During the reign of Louis XIV (1643–1715), France led the way in the manufacture of luxury wares. A key factor was the king's employment of leading craftsmen to create magnificent decorative schemes at the royal palace of Versailles. Carved marble panels, decorative paintings, tapestries, gilding and mirrors were all used to emphasize the monarchy's power.

Louis XIV of France by a 17th-century French artist

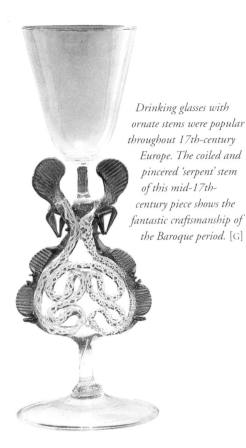

Drinking glasses with ornate stems were popular throughout 17th-century Europe. The coiled and pincered 'serpent' stem of this mid-17th-century piece shows the fantastic craftsmanship of the Baroque period. [G]

A northern European faience tulipière (flower pyramid), combines the European fashion for chinoiserie (European imitations of Chinese art) evident in its hexagonal pagoda form and blue-and-white style. [C]

Recognizing Style

■ Dominant motifs include acanthus, pediments, swags, masks, lion's-paw feet, cut-card work, chinoiseries and finely modelled figures.

■ Use of luxurious and expensive materials: *pietre dure* (semi-precious stones), marquetry and velvet upholstery.

■ Forms are heavy and sculptural, often curving or bulbous, but with formal and symmetrical decoration.

'MAROT' CHAIR BACK

BAROQUE MOTIF

DOUBLE-SCROLL LEG

Ornate cabinets-on-stands were fashionable pieces of Baroque furniture. This late 17th-century cabinet (with a stand from c.1830) is inlaid with 'seaweed' marquetry and pietre dure *panels.* [A]

Huguenot silversmiths introduced new, sophisticated silver shapes into England, such as tureens, sauceboats and wine-coolers. This richly embellished helmet-shaped ewer (1701), with cut-card work, was made by David Willaume. [A]

Rococo Style c.1720–60

La Lecture de Molière (1730)
by Jean-François de Troy

EMERGING IN FRANCE *in the early 18th century, the Rococo style was a reaction to the excessive formality and heaviness of Baroque classicism. Designers took a notably lighter, more exotic and frivolous approach to decoration and ornament. The style was very popular in Europe in the 1730s.*

Rococo style was initiated in France by designers such as Jean Bérain during the later years of the reign of Louis XIV. It continued to develop under the Régence (1715–21) and under the subsequent reign of Louis XV (1721–74).

Fuelled by a desire for a lighter, more informal style of decoration, early Rococo designers made much use of delicate repeating patterns, scallop shells and light scrollwork, while retaining much of the classical symmetry of earlier Baroque ornament. However, from the 1720s, Rococo became more extravagant, exotic and assymetrical, employing combinations of scrolls, foliage, chinoiserie, Turkish and Indian figures, monkeys, abstract forms of *rocaille* (shell and rock forms) and cartouches (framed panels) – the latter often surrounding allegorical figures and pastoral imagery.

Fashionable throughout much of Europe from the 1730s, the Rococo style made relatively little impact in the American colonies, except in furniture. However, although superseded by Neo-classicism during the second half of the 18th century, it enjoyed notable revivals on both sides of the Atlantic between c.1820 and 1860, and provided considerable inspiration for the Art Nouveau style.

A Louis XV amaranth and marquetry bombé *commode by Jean-Charles Ellaume. Rococo features include cabriole legs, inlaid floral bouquets and foliate ormolu mounts.* [F]

This silver tea-kettle, stand and lamp (1738) by George Wickes, and tray by Robert Abercrombie has characteristic elements of the Rococo style, including shells, scrolled feet, flowers, masks and latticework. [D]

Made in Philadelphia, this mahogany side chair (c.1770) has C- and S-scroll forms respectively, in the pierced splat (centre chair back) and toprail. The cabriole legs end in ball-and-claw feet, and shell motifs feature on the top- and seat rails. [B]

Commedia dell'arte

As personifications of drama and frivolity, the characters from the traditional form of Italian theatre, *commedia dell'arte*, were particularly suited to Rococo ornament. They were used in marquetry and lacquered furniture, and in Chippendale's designs for a chimneypiece and pier glass. Most notably, they were used for a series of porcelain figures by factories such as Nymphenburg and Meissen. Favourite characters included Harlequin, Pierrot, Mezzetin and Captain Spavento.

Modelled by Franz Anton Bustelli, this Nymphenburg porcelain figure of Capitano Spavento (*c.*1763) displays the stylized pose and subtle sense of movement typical of Bustelli's figures – qualities enhanced by the flowing scrolls of the base. [C]

The intricately carved frame of this giltwood chinoiserie mirror (c.1755) mainly comprises a series of interlaced foliate C-scrolls surmounted by a Chinese pagoda, which is flanked by smaller oriental dwellings. [E]

The duchesse brisée typifies French Rococo furniture. This Louis XV giltwood example has a gently scrolling, moulded frame, stands on cabriole legs, and is ornamented at intervals with twin flower-heads and scrolling foliage. [F]

Recognizing Style

■ Considerable use made of curvaceous, assymetrical forms – especially of elaborate combinations of C- and S-scrolls.

■ Main motifs include *rocaille* shapes, naturalistic flowers and foliage, grotesques and chinoiseries.

■ Thematic imagery includes theatrical and pastoral figures, as well as scenes and personifications of the seasons.

■ Preference for lighter (often pastel) colours, lighter woods and gilding.

FAUTEUIL A LA REINE CHAIR BACK

COMMODE LEG

PIERCED HANDLE

A Rococo Revival Derby porcelain shepherd candelabra (c.1830). The bocage (wooded background) framing the figure is less delicate than backgrounds found on 18th-century Derby. [M]

Neo-classical Style c.1760–1800

Entrance hall of Osterley Park House, Middlesex, England, by Robert Adam

NEO-CLASSICISM WAS THE REVIVAL OF *interest in Greek and Roman antiquity. It developed in the 1750s partly as a reaction to the frivolity and sentimentality of Rococo, and as a result of 18th-century excavations of Roman cities, such as Herculaneum and Pompeii. The Grand Tour – a trip around Europe's ancient classical sites, particularly the antiquities in Rome – also provided inspiration for the decorative arts, being undertaken by many English designers.*

From the mid-18th century, designers, architects and artists were inspired by numerous publications of archaeological discoveries. This led to a fashion for motifs taken from Greek and Roman architecture: Vitruvian scrolls (scrolling waves), guilloche (interlaced bands), fluting, columns and palmettes (stylized palms) began to appear. Furniture became austere and rectangular in form, and classically inspired urn and two-handled vase shapes were used in silver and ceramics.

By the 1760s and 1770s the discovery of the wall decorations at Pompeii had created a vogue for this style. Delicate grotesques, festoons, husks (stylized buds), ribbons and medallions were introduced.

The leading exponent of the Neo-classical style was the English architect and designer Robert Adam. He also introduced a distinctive variant of Neo-classical decoration known as the Etruscan style, inspired by the designs and colour schemes used on ancient Italian vases. These also influenced Josiah Wedgwood's production of black basalt and *rosso antico* wares from the late 1760s.

By the 1790s, Neo-classical shapes, particularly in furniture, were becoming simpler and more austere. A more archaeologically exact style developed in the early 19th century as the new Regency style.

Recognizing Style

■ Distinctive motifs include guilloche, egg-and-dart (egg and 'V' shapes) moulding, anthemions (honeysuckle flowers), grotesques and festoons.

■ Forms are simple and austere – including urn, tripod and vase shapes – with sparing use of decoration. Imagery is dominated by mythological subjects.

■ Colour schemes are pale and sober, apart from the red, black and white decoration of the Etruscan style.

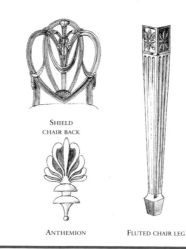

SHIELD CHAIR BACK

ANTHEMION   **FLUTED CHAIR LEG**

The strongly architectural character of Neo-classical furniture is evident in this 18th-century Irish mirror made by John and William Booker. The gilded frame, with a scrolled pediment topped with an urn, fluted frieze (decorative band) and Corinthian columns, imitates the shape of a classical temple. The mirror's border is edged with ribbonwork, rosettes and egg-and-dart ornament. [B]

Classical excavations

The 18th-century revival of interest in classical art and architecture was stimulated in particular by the rediscovery and excavation of the ancient Roman cities of Herculaneum and Pompeii. The former was discovered accidentally in 1709 by labourers. In 1738, Charles VII, King of Naples, initiated excavations there that uncovered a wealth of Roman domestic artefacts. At Pompeii, where excavations began in 1748, the most startling discoveries were the richly coloured wall decorations of grotesques (scrolls incorporating fantastic creatures) and intricate branched motifs. These excavations were instrumental in popularizing classical motifs and decoration.

First Discovery of the Temple of Isis at Pompeii from Campi Phiegraei (1776) by William Hamilton

Bright-cut decoration was often used on English Neo-classical silver. It comprises shallow engraved motifs such as swags and husks, as seen on this teapot (1780) by Hester Bateman. [J]

Wedgwood's most notable commission came from Catherine the Great, Empress of Russia, for a creamware dinner service. Made in 1773–4, each piece is painted with an English scene and a green frog crest, since it was made for her palace outside St Petersburg called Grenouillère (French for frog). [E]

The restrained carving of laurel leaves, acanthus and medallions on this French Louis XVI giltwood armchair (c.1775) is characteristic of French Neo-classical cabinet-makers. This is in marked contrast to the curvy Rococo style. [E]

Federal Style c.1776–1815

Federal Chillman Parlour, Museum of Fine Arts, Texas

THE FEDERAL STYLE, *which can be seen in late 18th- and early 19th-century American architecture and decorative arts, took its name from the establishment of the federal constitution in 1789. As a variant of Neo-classicism, this style was especially popular since it reflected links between the ancient republic of Rome and the modern United States of America.*

The Federal style was particularly evident in furniture and, to a certain extent, silver, but less so in glass, ceramics and textiles. Federal furniture is generally light, elegant, and made from mahogany. Inspiration for the style was taken from books by the English cabinet-makers Thomas Sheraton and George Hepplewhite, and pieces typically carry Neo-classical ornamentation, such as carved or inlaid paterae (oval shapes with fluting and/or rosettes), ribbonwork, swags, baskets of fruit, fans and urns. Tables, chairs and sideboards were made with sabre legs, while the lyre was a favourite motif for chair backs and as a support for card, work and sofa tables. Painted topographical views of Baltimore and New York were also popular.

The leading Federal cabinet-maker was Duncan Phyfe; others included Stephen Bedlam, John Seymour, John Finlay and Hugh Finlay, Elijah Sanderson and Jacob Sanderson. A French influence was also present through French-trained cabinet-makers. Their work is characterized by rich ormolu (gilt bronze) mounts, often imported from France, white marble and brass banding.

In silver, Neo-classical urn and two-handled vases and square bases were typically used for tea- and coffeepots. Decoration was kept to simple reeding or banding around the rim.

Heavier forms and detailing were used after about 1810: this is sometimes referred to as American Classical style.

The lyre pedestal on this work table made in Philadelphia (c.1810–15) is a characteristic element of Federal-style furniture. Note the richly figured bird's-eye maple and maple veneer. [C]

Duncan Phyfe

Duncan Phyfe (1768–1854) was the most influential, prolific and successful cabinet-maker of the early 19th century in the USA. He was also the leading exponent of the Federal style in American furniture. He emigrated from Scotland in the early 1780s and, a little later, set up a cabinet-making business for wealthy clients in New York.

Phyfe's work features imitations of classical furniture designs, rich veneers, claw and paw feet on brass mounts, lyre-shaped backs and sabre legs. Such was his reputation, New York Federal-style furniture is often described as 'Phyfe school'.

Duncan Phyfe probably made this upholstered mahogany sofa (c.1800–1815). The toprail is finely carved with sheaves of wheat. [A]

This fine mahogany sideboard (c.1780–1800), with its serpentine front, richly grained veneer, and inlaid quarter fans, husks and paterae is attributed to the New York cabinet-maker William Whitehead. [B]

Recognizing Style

■ Light and elegant shapes, with sparing use of ornament, were adapted from English Neo-classical designs.

■ Prevalent motifs include delicate scrolls, husks, urns, festoons, shells, and fans. Also, the American eagle.

■ Influence of the French Empire style is evident in the use of ormolu mounts and brass banding.

■ Use of mahogany is combined with indigenous woods, such as maple.

PATERA HANDLE

HEPPLEWHITE CHAIR BACK

AMERICAN EAGLE MOTIF

Ornate mirrors based on patterns by the English cabinet-makers Thomas Sheraton and George Smith were popular in the USA. The eagle on this mirror (c.1810–20) is a distinctively American Federal motif. [A]

Note the slender proportions, tapered, reeded legs, inlaid ovals and graceful leaf-scrolled cresting of this Sheraton-style mahogany inlaid secretary-desk, made (c.1800–15) in Boston, Massachusetts. [A]

The simple urn form and finial, beaded rim, square base and scroll spout of this coffeepot (c.1795) by James Musgrave of Philadelphia are all features of Federal silver. [D]

The shield-shaped back of this chair (c.1795) made in Connecticut is adapted from designs by Hepplewhite. A carved urn motif dominates the splat and sits on a plinth carved with rosettes. [FOR A PAIR A]

Regency Style c.1810–1830

Mr and Mrs Samuel Hoare in their Study at Hampstead Heath (c.1820)

THE REGENCY STYLE, *named after the regency (1811–20) of George, Prince of Wales, later George IV, King of England (1820–30), was principally a late development of the Neo-classical style. Shapes became heavier, larger and more richly ornamented. A growing taste for the exotic meant Turkish, Indian and Egyptian motifs were often used.*

Regency style was largely influenced by the development of the Empire style in France, which reflected the military victories and political ambitions of the empire of Napoleon Bonaparte. Characteristic was a demand for copies of classical artefacts, prompted by the increasing number of archaeological publications and by Napoleon's desire to associate his empire with ancient Rome.

In England, this approach was taken up by the designer and collector Thomas Hope, who created rooms in his London house filled with antique reproduction furniture. Similarly, leading silversmiths, such as Paul Storr, created copies of antique vases and other classical shapes.

Mahogany remained the most popular wood, but the vogue for richer decoration led to the use of woods, such as rosewood and satinwood, often combined with brass inlay. Motifs included classical palmettes, anthemions, winged lions, eagles and guilloche – all similar to those used in the late 18th century but often larger and more elaborate. Empire pieces can often be distinguished from their English Regency counterparts by the use of motifs such as bees and swans.

Alongside the continuing fashion for classical forms came an interest in exotic fashions that anticipated the diverse styles of the Victorian period. Turkish, Indian, Egyptian and chinoiserie motifs were all popular. Most favoured was Egyptian, and hieroglyphics, scarabs, stylized lotus flowers and sphinxes were widely used.

This Coalport dinner service (c.1815–25) is decorated with a pattern adapted from Japanese Imari porcelain. [E]

Regency furniture is often very opulent, as is evident in this rosewood sofa (c.1815) with its floral damask padded upholstery, turned, reeded legs, brass inlay and gently scrolling shape. [H]

Regency glass is heavy and elaborate in style, with intricate cutting: this rummer (c.1815) has fine flute cutting on the bucket-shaped bowl that simulates feathers. [S]

The curving 'boat' shape, fluting and gadrooning (lobing) around the base and rim, and the swan-necked spout of this teapot (1813) by Paul Storr, are typical of Regency silver teaware. [H]

This type of dining-chair is known as a 'Trafalgar' chair, since it first appeared in 1805, the year of Admiral Nelson's victory at the Battle of Trafalgar. The classically inspired lyre motif on the splat is commonly seen on Regency seat furniture. [L]

Recognizing Style

■ Shapes are generally classical, but heavier, curvier and more solid than the late 18th-century Neo-classical style.

■ Use of rich materials, such as brass inlay, ivory and ebony handles, and woods such as rosewood and ebony.

■ Typical motifs include palmettes, winged lions and griffins, anthemions (honeysuckle), paterae and guilloche.

■ A continuing popularity of exotic styles and motifs.

LION-MASK HANDLE

ROPE-TWIST CHAIR BACK   ROPE TWIST LEG

Thomas Hope

A member of a wealthy Dutch banking family, Thomas Hope (1769–1831) was the leading advisor on Regency taste in England. From the 1780s he travelled widely in Europe and the Near East, amassing a spectacular collection of items from ancient Greece, Rome and Egypt.

At home, Hope was concerned that his furnishings should complement his collection, and so he designed furniture, silver and textiles that echoed classical designs. Hope's Greek 'Klismos' chair, for example, was adapted from domestic scenes on Greek vases, and set in a sculpture gallery decorated with fluted Greek Doric columns.

Hope's simple designs, were popularized by the cabinet-maker George Smith and widely copied in the early 19th century.

Illustration from Thomas Hope's *Household Furniture and Interior Decoration* **(1807)**

Victorian Style 1837–1901

Three Ladies in a Drawing Room Interior
(*c.*1850) by Pieter Christoffel

THE REIGN OF QUEEN VICTORIA *(1837–1901) was dominated by the growth of industrialization and the mass production of goods for the expanding middle classes. A greater emphasis on comfort and display led to more richly upholstered furniture and a profusion of ornament.*

The 19th century saw a succession of revivals of historical styles, together with a fashion for realistic depictions of nature. In addition, different styles were often combined in a single piece. This was all driven by new industrial techniques that made inexpensive reproductions of historical styles and natural forms possible.

The principal historical revivals were the Gothic, Renaissance and Rococo. In Britain, the Gothic Revival came to be regarded as the 'national' style after it was used for the Houses of Parliament (1836).

Closely linked to the Gothic was the Renaissance Revival, but neither was as popular as the revival of the 18th-century Rococo style, particularly in furniture and ceramics. However, the curving shapes, carved scrolls and rich gilding were more sinuous and elaborate than before.

After 1850 there was a reaction against historical styles and the poor quality of industrial goods. This was led by Sir Henry Cole, who helped to organize London's Great Exhibition of 1851. Cole encouraged the employment of leading painters and sculptors as designers for industry. The South Kensington (later the Victoria and Albert) Museum was also established to improve design standards.

Glass manufacturers in Stourbridge, Worcestershire – where this late 19th-century ewer was made – were innovators in the production of glass in a huge variety of colours. [M]

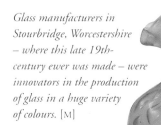

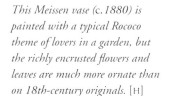

This Meissen vase (c.1880) is painted with a typical Rococo theme of lovers in a garden, but the richly encrusted flowers and leaves are much more ornate than on 18th-century originals. [H]

This sofa was made by John Henry Belter, the leading exponent of the Rococo Revival in American furniture. Belter used new techniques to produce his laminated rosewood pieces, adorned with scrolls, birds, flowers and fruit. [A]

Exhibitions

The expansion of world trade in the early 19th century encouraged the development of international exhibitions. These were showcases for industrial products, featuring the most up-to-date trends in design and technology.

The first, and most important, was the Great Exhibition of the Products of Industry of All Nations held at the purpose-built Crystal Palace in London in 1851. Selected objects from the exhibition were bought to form the basis of the collections in London's Victoria and Albert Museum.

The India Hall at the Great Exhibition from Dickinson's *Picture of the Great Exhibition*

The shape of this Stourbridge candelabrum (c.1880) was inspired by 17th-century Venetian glass. Gas lighting meant that many Victorian candelabra were more decorative than practical. [1]

Tiffany & Co., the leading manufacturer of Art Nouveau glass in the USA, produced this iridescent glass 'candlestick lamp' (c.1910). Its shade, slender stem and spiral detail are influenced by the curving forms of the Art Nouveau style. [1]

Interest in medieval and Renaissance ceramics in the 19th century led to a revival of the use of tiles for fire surrounds or wall decoration. Some had abstract patterns derived from Persian or Turkish ceramics. This American tile is decorated with an image by the English designer, Walter Crane. [Q]

An American shelf clock (c.1855) by Jerome & Co., shows the influence of the Gothic Revival style in its pointed gable, pinnacled side pillars and painted 'window'. Often known as 'steeple' clocks, these were mass produced by American clockmakers in the second half of the 19th century. [P]

Recognizing Style

■ Shapes are generally large, curvaceous and liberally ornamented.

■ Motifs from historical revival styles, such as Rococo scrolls, Gothic pinnacles and Renaissance strapwork (intertwined bands), were often combined.

■ Use of new industrial techniques, such as lamination and electroplating.

■ Realistic depiction of animals, birds, fruit and flowers, especially in large-scale centrepieces made for exhibitions.

GOTHIC REVIVAL CHAIR BACK

BALLOON CHAIR BACK

CARVED LEG

Arts & Crafts Style c.1860–1910

Arts & Crafts dining room designed by
M.H. Baillie Scott (1901)

THERE WAS INCREASING CRITICISM *during the 19th century of the poor quality of mass-produced goods. Small groups of designers, writers and craftsmen – who formed what was later known as the Arts & Crafts Movement – began seeking to improve standards of design and workmanship.*

The leading figure of the Arts & Crafts Movement was the British designer and theorist William Morris. Following the socialist ideas put forward by the writer and art critic John Ruskin, Morris believed that a return to medieval standards of craftsmanship, a rejection of machine production, and the use of good materials would improve the quality of life for both craftsmen and those who used their products. Morris's lead was followed by many other designers, including Gustav Stickley and Charles Rohlfs in the USA.

While designers developed distinctly individual styles and motifs, all Arts & Crafts pieces are characterized by simple forms with restrained ornament and an emphasis on revealing the beauty of materials.

This fall-front desk (c.1900) was made by Charles Rohlfs, a key exponent of the Arts & Crafts style in American furniture. The emphasis on exposed construction, seen in the decorative nailheads and hinges, is typical. [A]

Fine handcrafted ceramics were produced throughout the USA from the 1880s to c.1920. This simple bowl, with restrained floral decoration and a flat, matt glaze, was made by Artus Van Briggle, a leading producer of art pottery who founded a workshop in Colorado Springs. [Q]

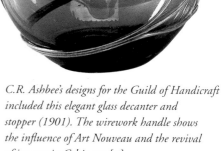

C.R. Ashbee's designs for the Guild of Handicraft included this elegant glass decanter and stopper (1901). The wirework handle shows the influence of Art Nouveau and the revival of interest in Celtic art. [D]

Look out for hammered finishes on metalwork, cabochon stones in silver and jewellery, and exposed dovetail and mortise-and-tenon joints in furniture.

Closely allied to Arts & Crafts was the Aesthetic Movement, which promoted the ideal of 'Art for art's sake' in an effort to reform design. It was strongly influenced by the simple forms of Japanese art.

Despite the movement's socialist philosophy, Arts & Crafts pieces were expensive and were bought only by the wealthy middle classes. In the early 20th century, many craftsmen were forced out of business by commercial imitation of their wares.

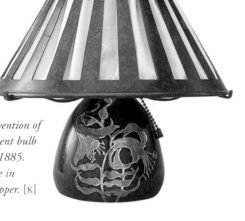

The production of electric table lamps, such as this piece made by Heintz Art Studios (c.1910), flourished after the invention of the incandescent filament bulb by Thomas Edison in 1885. Lamp bases were made in bronze, pewter and copper. [K]

An electroplated tureen, cover and ladle (1880), was made by Hukin & Heath. Its designer, Christopher Dresser, was noted for his geometric designs. He was heavily influenced by the restrained styles of Japanese art. [F]

The simple form and handcarved floral decoration on this vase (c.1900) are characteristic of the work of William Grueby, who established a pottery specializing in hand-thrown wares in Boston, Massachusetts, in the 1890s. Grueby was one of the pioneers of the use of subtle green, brown, yellow and ochre matt glazes. [A]

Recognizing Style

■ Most pieces are handcrafted, with an emphasis on exposed construction and restrained ornament.

■ Textiles and wallpapers use flat, repeating patterns of stylized birds, animals, flowers and plants.

■ Preference for relatively inexpensive materials, such as copper, pewter, semi-precious stones and indigenous woods.

■ Use of simple forms inspired by country furniture and Japanese art.

PIERCED HANDLE   FLORAL MOTIF

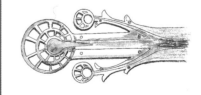

DOOR HINGE

William Morris

William Morris was responsible for the development of the Arts & Crafts philosophy. A gifted poet, designer and propagandist, he first became interested in medieval art while studying at Oxford University, where he met the painter Edward Burne-Jones. Disenchantment with the standards of machine production led him to establish, with Burne-Jones and others, the firm of Morris, Marshall, Faulkner & Co. (1861). They aimed to produce handcrafted furniture, textiles, wallpapers and stained glass, all strongly influenced by medieval designs. Among the firm's products were the 'Morris Adjustable Chair', and Morris's textile and wallpaper designs featuring repeated patterns of stylized birds, flowers and plants.

The 'Morris Adjustable Chair'(c.1866) was one of the most successful pieces of furniture produced by Morris, Marshall, Faulkner & Co. [I]

Art Nouveau Style c.1880–1910

Art Nouveau Interior (1900)
by Georges du Feure

THE ART NOUVEAU STYLE *is often considered the first truly 'modern' style, although it was strongly influenced by a variety of historical precedents. Its most identifiable feature is the use of sinuous patterns and shapes inspired by natural forms. This style reached its peak in 1900.*

Art Nouveau took its name from the 'Maison de l'Art Nouveau' gallery, which opened in Paris in 1895. The gallery showed work by a wide range of leading designers, including the Belgian Henry van de Velde and the American Louis Comfort Tiffany. Other designers strongly associated with the style were mostly French, and included René Lalique, who designed glass and jewellery, and Emile Gallé, who specialized in glass, ceramics and furniture.

The style was popular throughout Europe and the USA and was known by a variety of names: *Jugendstil* in Germany and Austria, *Stile Liberty* in Italy, *Modernismo* in Spain and the Tiffany Style in the USA.

Nature was the main inspiration for all Art Nouveau designers: dominant motifs included sinuous, curving and elongated forms inspired by plants, exaggerated asymmetry, and stylized floral and leaf motifs. Figures of women with dreamlike expressions and flowing hair and clothes were also popular subjects.

Like the craftsmen of the Arts & Crafts Movement, Art Nouveau artists and designers placed considerable emphasis on good materials and fine craftsmanship. However, unlike the followers of Arts & Crafts, many successfully produced designs for both handcrafted luxury goods and commercial mass production.

This cabinet by Louis Majorelle was shown at the World Exhibition in Paris in 1900, the showcase for the Art Nouveau style. The fluid ornament, use of exotic woods and pleated silk back panels are all characteristics of Majorelle's handcrafted furniture. [A]

The iridescent 'Favrile' glass, produced by Tiffany & Co. of New York from c.1900, is one of the most distinctive products made in the Art Nouveau style. The fluid shape of this 'Jack-in-the-pulpit' vase is modelled on natural plant forms. [D]

Naturalism

During the mid-19th century, scientific advances encouraged the development of a realistic representation of nature in the decorative arts. This naturalism was aided by new industrial techniques. However, Art Nouveau designers reacted against this, preferring a more abstract representation of nature. This led to the widespread use of fluid forms inspired by plant stems and tendrils. Stylized birds, flowers and insects (especially dragonflies) were favourite motifs.

Etagère (*c.*1900) by Gallé,
inlaid with catkins,
primroses and tulips. [F]

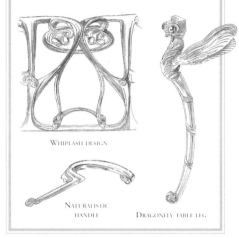

Iridescent glass produced by the factory of Johann Loetz-Witwe, near Vienna, is distinguished by the use of streaking, or 'oil spots', as seen in this gourd-shaped vase (1900) combining green, gold and copper iridescent patterns with blue. [D]

Art Nouveau designs were widely used on advertising posters that appeared from the 1860s. This poster of 1898 (below) typifies the work of the Czech-born designer Alfons Mucha. It depicts a woman with flowing, medieval-style garments and flower-laden hair.

Recognizing Style

■ Widespread use of fluid, elongated shapes inspired by plant forms.

■ Common motifs include female figures with flowing hair and garments, whiplash curves, stylized flowers, birds and insects (especially dragonflies).

■ Materials used include exotic hardwoods for marquetry, iridescent glass, silver and semi-precious stones.

■ Austere designs were produced by the Glasgow style of Mackintosh.

WHIPLASH DESIGN

NATURALISTIC HANDLE

DRAGONFLY TABLE LEG

Artists of the Glasgow style, led by Charles Rennie Mackintosh, produced individual variations of the Art Nouveau style. This high-back oak chair (c.1900) with a carved apple motif is a typical Mackintosh design. [A]

Among the more successful commercially produced wares were the domestic pewter and electroplated pieces manufactured by the German Württemberg Metalwork Factory. An example is this four-piece tea and coffee set with tray (1906). [H]

Edwardian Style c.1901–1910

Edwardian Interior (c.1910)

Royal Worcester

From the 1860s the Worcester Royal Porcelain Co. produced both domestic tableware and high-quality ornamental vases and figures in a wide variety of styles. Designs were copied directly from Japanese and Islamic ceramics, as well as from Indian ivories. However, simple ovoid (egg-shaped) vases with twin handles – vaguely classical in form – and fine hand-painted decoration are among the company's most notable early 20th-century products. Subjects include delicate floral sprays or scenes of Highland cattle in mountain landscapes.

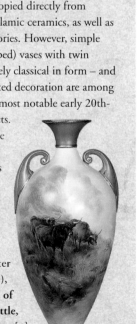

Royal Worcester vase (c.1909), with a scene of Highland cattle, by John Stinton. [G]

THE EDWARDIAN STYLE HERALDED *a trend for a lighter style of furnishings, influenced in part by the 19th-century design reform movements, such as Arts & Crafts and Art Nouveau. This new fashion was particularly apparent in the revival of the elegant forms of late 18th-century Neo-classicism in furniture and ceramics.*

The first indications of a revival of Neo-classicism came in 1862 at the International Exhibition in London. While the revived fashion appeared in silver and jewellery, it was most evident in furniture. The 18th-century designs of Thomas Sheraton and George Hepplewhite were especially influential; even their books on design were reprinted in 1897. Many late 19th- and early 20th-century Sheraton Revival pieces were made of pale woods, such as satinwood and satin-birch, and decorated with classical motifs.

During the Edwardian period, the classical forms of the Queen Anne period (1702–14) also inspired designers to use such elements as broken pediments (triangular gables open at the base) on sideboards and turned baluster legs on tables and chairs. Most pieces of furniture were mass produced.

The added influence of the Arts & Crafts and Aesthetic Movement to the style is seen in the decorative tiles for Edwardian washstands and fireplaces, as well as wickerwork furniture.

In the USA, the revived classical style was known as Colonial Revival. The use of Federal-style motifs was popular following the centenary of the founding of the United States in 1876.

The painted satinwood and cane-filled arms and back of this Edwardian armchair (c.1910) illustrate the move away from the heavily upholstered furniture of the mid-19th century. [I]

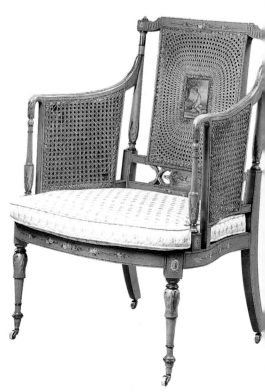

This magnificent mahogany, glass and mirrored cabinet (c.1910) would have been the most expensive and luxurious piece of furniture in a middle-class Edwardian home. The curved legs and richly carved decorative scrolls are inspired by 18th-century Chippendale furniture. [J]

Recognizing Style

■ Characteristic forms are simple and elegant, often imitating the restrained forms of Neo-classicism.

■ Prevalent use of motifs such as shells, palmettes, ribbonwork and floral sprays.

■ Common themes for painted decoration include flowers in delicate shades and lovers in landscapes.

■ Fashion for lightweight and pale-coloured materials such as canework, satinwood and satin-birch.

MARQUETRY DESIGN

SHERATON-REVIVAL LEG

The rectangular shape, decorative oval veneers and simple turned legs of this early 20th-century glass-fronted display cabinet imitate the forms and decoration of Thomas Sheraton's late 18th-century furniture designs. Manufactured by leading English firms such as Maples, and Waring & Gillow, these pieces remained popular well into the 1930s. [J]

The Neo-classical designs of Robert Adam influenced the semicircular shape, light-coloured wood, turned baluster legs and floral garland decoration of this light and elegant side table (c.1910). The legs of Edwardian imitation tables, such as this example, are often thinner and longer than on the 18th-century originals. [F]

Modernist Style *from* 1918

Study designed by Louis Sognot (*c*.1920)

MODERNISM WAS DRIVEN *by the technological changes and growth of consumerism that occurred after the end of World War I in 1918. The result was an unprecedented diversity of forms, styles and motifs. Although quality craftsmanship was still valued, the period also saw a growth in designs intended for mass production.*

Modernism is a loose term that embraces a collection of different styles. In the early decades of the 20th century the designers of the Vienna Workshops were among those who maintained the Arts & Crafts emphasis on simple forms and fine craftsmanship. Some British designers also adhered to this. And after 1945, Scandinavian design received acclaim for its organic forms, natural finishes and quality workmanship. Meanwhile, the studio pottery movement (which included Bernard Leach, Lucie Rie and Hans Coper) revived handmade pottery as a reaction against the standardization of industrially produced ceramics.

Yet while some designers of the period chose to reject machine production, others

welcomed it: the German Work Federation, a group of artists and industrialists, actively promoted design for mass production. This was taken up from 1919 by the German Bauhaus school of design. Bauhaus designers aimed to break down the barriers between art, craft, design and architecture. They advocated function over decoration, as was evident in their geometric designs lacking ornament.

With the 1950s and 1960s came a reaction against the austerity of modernism, that revealed itself in the use of sculptural, organic forms, bright colours and psychedelic patterns. Industrial designers also began to experiment with new materials, including plastics and tubular steel, to create affordable, stylish and highly flexible furnishings.

This 'Wassily' club chair 'B3' (1927–8), designed in 1926 by Marcel Breuer and produced by Standard-Möbel Lengyel & Co., Berlin, is one of the earliest pieces of mass-produced furniture made from chromium-plated tubular steel. [C]

The plain cylindrical form and spherical ball ornament of this ashtray (c.1935) by Belmet Products Inc., New York, are characteristic of the American Art Deco style. [N]

From the 1930s, the Wedgwood ceramics firm produced a popular range of tableware with designs by the illustrator Eric Ravilious. This bread-and-butter plate (c.1940) in the 'Travel' series combines a traditional form with a typical 1930s semi-abstract design of a steam train. [R]

The geometric shapes of the French Art Deco silversmith Jean Puiforcat strongly influenced the plain, faceted shape of this American silver dish (c.1930) by the Watson Company. [O]

After World War II, glassmakers began to experiment with colour, surface texture and organic shapes. These two vases were designed by Geoffrey Baxter for the Whitefriars Glassworks in England (both 1967–80). [S]

New Materials

Throughout the 20th century, designers experimented with new materials. In the 1930s Alvar Aalto patented a method of bending and laminating plywood to produce light and durable stools and chairs. Others favoured chromium-plated tubular steel, first developed in the 1880s. However, it was the development of plastics, such as Perspex, polythene, fibreglass and polyurethane, that revolutionized the development of affordable and disposable furniture in the 1950s and 1960s. People welcomed the variety of colours and the relatively cheap cost of these items.

A stacking chair in moulded and laminated plywood, designed in the 1930s by the Finnish designer Alvar Aalto. [M]

The sculptural form of this Italian 'Handkerchief' vase, made by the Venini glassworks in the 1960s, makes full use of the malleable qualities of glass. [L]

Recognizing Style

■ Widespread use of new materials such as fibreglass, plastics, moulded and laminated plywood, and chromium-plated tubular steel.

■ Form, colour and design, rather than applied ornament, were emphasized.

■ Abstract, stylized motifs were generally favoured over naturalistic ones, especially during the Art Deco period.

■ Use of bold primary colours.

STYLIZED DEER MOTIF

ART DECO HANDLE

EGYPTIAN LOTUS MOTIF

Stepped rectilinear forms and geometric ornament and handles, as on this desk (c.1928), are distinctive features of American Art Deco furniture. The fashion for elegant Asian shapes, black, red or green lacquered finishes, often embellished with geometric patterns in silver or gold leaf, were particularly favoured by American furniture designers such as Paul Frankl and Donald Deskey. [F]

Furniture

SINCE MARKS OF ORIGIN and dates of manufacture are conspicuous by their absence from many pieces of furniture, collectors must almost always rely on other means of identification. Usually they must evaluate characteristics associated with different historical periods, countries or regions, and specific makers or designers. For example, various species of wood, notably oak, walnut and mahogany, have been popular at different times, as have techniques of construction such as pegging and dove-tailing. Much can be learned from the different marks left on wood by hand-sawing and machine-cutting, and by the presence – or absence – of screws and nails. Variations in the type and style of decoration are also highly significant, as for instance in the differences between marquetry used in the late 17th century and that used 200 years later. Above all, the collector must decide if a piece is 'right', which involves developing an 'eye' not only for detail, but also for the proportions as a whole.

French marquetry writing desk, late 17th century [A]

29

How to Look at Furniture

Painted chests such as this example (c.1800) were often made in pine or poplar by German and Dutch settlers in Pennsylvania. [A]

Although this is an original Chippendale dining chair (c.1770), many good copies were made in the late 19th century. [H]

You can tell this card table (c.1850s) is made in the exaggerated Rococo Revival style by its S- and C-scrolled base. [I]

THROUGHOUT HISTORY, *furniture has been altered, extensively restored, made more fashionable, reproduced or quite simply faked. Consequently it has a greater need of the 'closer look' approach than any other category of antiques. I was alerted to this fact early in my collecting days when a dealer mentioned that there were many more 16th-century English oak refectory tables in homes around the world than there ever were houses in England to accommodate them.*

There have always been craftsmen well versed in traditional techniques, who, using old tools, could re-create a piece of antique furniture. I was initially surprised to see auction lots made up of bits of old furniture fetch large sums. It was only later, after visiting 'restoration' workshops, that I realised how valuable such lots are to the unscrupulous for altering furniture.

It is therefore vital to learn how to appreciate the correct proportions, colour, patination (the natural build-up of years of wax polishing, dust and dirt that gives antique furniture its rich lustrous glow) and the methods of construction used to make a genuine piece. Some fakers are highly skilful, but many cut corners owing to lack of time, knowledge or money.

The wood and the type of construction used should be correct for the period. As a general rule, the Oak period lasted from medieval times to the late 17th century; the Walnut period spanned *c.*1690–*c.*1735, the Mahogany period started from *c.*1735. In the later 19th century, there was greater use of exotic timbers, together with a return to using oak and walnut veneers.

Until the early 18th century. the most common form of construction was known as 'joined', using mortise-and-tenon joints held by dowels, or pegs. These pegs were handmade, irregular and the ends now usually stand slightly proud of the piece.

From the early 18th century, greater use was made of dove-tailing and gluing joints. Wood was still sawn by hand, and the edges, for instance, of drawers might display straight saw marks. With furniture dating from the early 19th century, the circular saw marks of mechanized cutting can sometimes be seen.

Evidence of real wear can tell you much about a piece, as fakers tend to over-do the distressing. Obvious places to check are stretchers (connecting bars between the legs of tables and chairs), doors and drawers. Look out for discolouration and build-up of dirt around the heads of screws, nails, hinges and handles. Any part exposed to sunlight should have a slightly lighter patina, while parts that are often handled, such as the arms of chairs, under drawer handles, and any crevices, deep carvings or mouldings, should be darker.

Beware the application of heavy wax polish, which may conceal alterations. Treat with caution early pieces that have been French polished, since the technique was not used much until the 19th century.

Aways suspect any plugged holes, evidence of wear when there seems to be no genuine cause, changes in the direction of the wood grain that are not consistent with the rest of the piece, and supposedly original carving that does not stand proud of the wood surface (incised or flat carving is almost certainly added later).

Re-veneering is another faker's trick. From the 19th century, fakers have often taken old veneer and applied it to unrelated, often oak, furniture. Old veneers were hand-cut, and are relatively thick and uneven. Later veneers were machine cut and uniformly thinner. So check that shrinkage splits on the carcass correspond to similar damage on the veneer.

CONSTRUCTION
The wood on both halves of a piece should match. At the back, check that the grain runs in the same direction on both top and bottom pieces.

COLOUR & PATINATION
These are two vital aspects to consider when checking a good piece of 18th-century furniture. The depth of colour should be the same on the whole surface of a piece – as should the patination.

DRAWERS
Furniture drawers reveal a great deal. Check that all the dove-tail joints in each drawer are handmade and identical. The runners under the drawers and the wear on the carcass should match. Many pieces have replacement handles; any plugged holes will indicate where they were originally fixed.

FEET
The most vulnerable parts on a piece of furniture are the feet. As a result of water damage or wear-and-tear, many feet will have been replaced over time. Always inspect the base and look for different woods and new additions. If these have been done sympathetically, it will not affect the price as dramatically as having feet of the wrong style.

A George III mahogany bureau bookcase (1760s), with a moulded cornice. Its hinged writing slope encloses a fitted interior. [E]

Furniture Styles Time Line 1700–1800

	1700–1720	1720–40	1740–60

Key Dates

● 1702 Queen Anne ascends English throne

1714–27 reign of George I

● 1730 Queen Anne style starts in the American colonies

1730–70 Age of mahogany

● 1748 Excavations at Pompeii

● 1715 Louis XIV dies

1715–23 Régence period in France

● 1738 Excavations begin at Herculaneum

● 1754 Chippendale first publishes *The Gentleman and Cabinet-Maker's Director*

Chair Backs

Daniel Marot

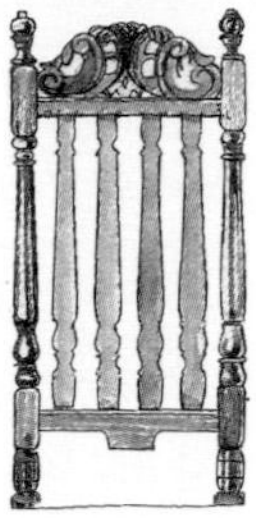

Provincial

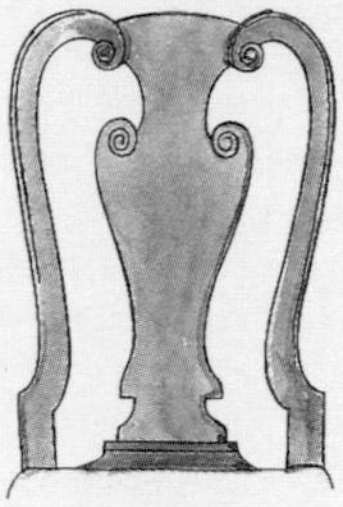

Fiddleback

Cartouche

Chippendale

Legs

Double scroll

Spiral twist

Key carved

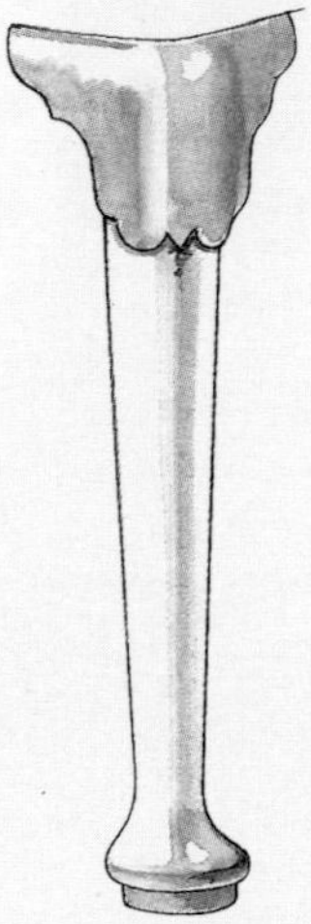

Turned

Block-and-spindle

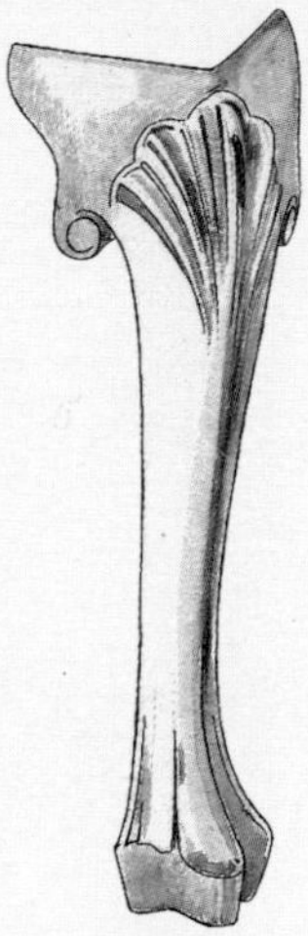

Cabriole

Cabriole

Feet

Ball

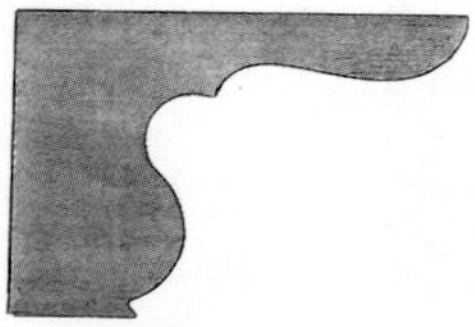

Bracket

Flattened bun

Pad

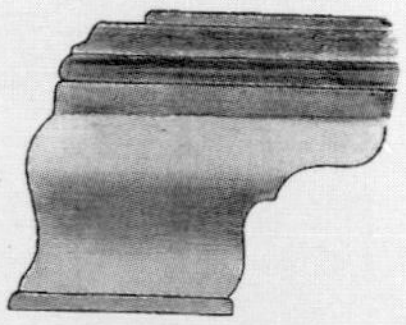

Ogee bracket

Handles

Drop

Ring

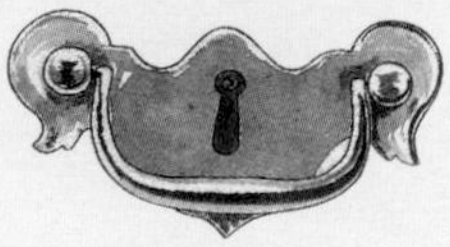

George I

Swan-neck

Pierced

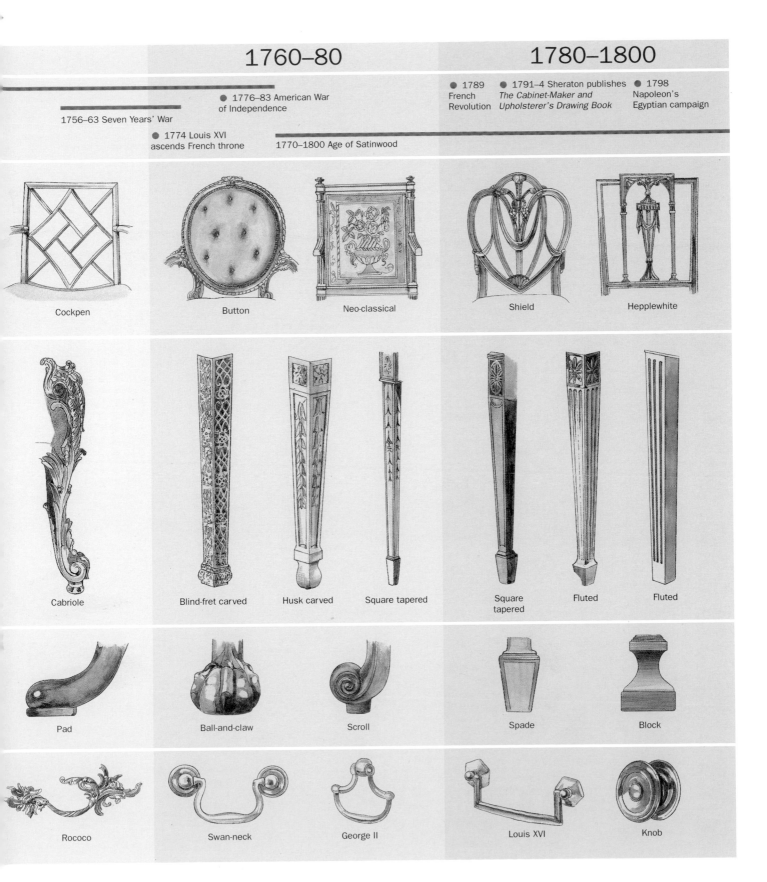

1760–80

1756–63 Seven Years' War

● 1776–83 American War of Independence

● 1774 Louis XVI ascends French throne

1770–1800 Age of Satinwood

1780–1800

● 1789 French Revolution

● 1791–4 Sheraton publishes *The Cabinet-Maker and Upholsterer's Drawing Book*

● 1798 Napoleon's Egyptian campaign

Cockpen

Button

Neo-classical

Shield

Hepplewhite

Cabriole

Blind-fret carved

Husk carved

Square tapered

Square tapered

Fluted

Fluted

Pad

Ball-and-claw

Scroll

Spade

Block

Rococo

Swan-neck

George II

Louis XVI

Knob

Furniture Styles Time Line 1800–1900

	1800–1820	1820–40	1840–60

Key Dates

1800–1820
- 1803 Charles-Honoré Lannuier arrives in New York
- 1807 Thomas Hope publishes *Household Furniture and Interior Decoration*

1811–20 English Regency period

1820–40
- 1830–50 Gothic Revival
- 1830 William IV ascends the throne
- 1837 Queen Victoria ascends the British throne
- 1836 Design for the Houses of Parliament, London

1840–60
- 1851 Great Exhibition in London

1847–58 J. H. Belter develops his lamination process

Chair Backs

| Greek key | Rope twist | Gadrooned | Gothic Revival | Balloon |

Legs

| Reeded | Waisted square tapering | Rope twist | Sabre/trafalgar | Baluster | Reeded | Ring turned |

Feet

| Splay bracket | Bobbin turned | Brass capping | Winged paw | Turned |

Handles

| Federal | Lion's-mask | Ring | Floral pull | Wooden knob |

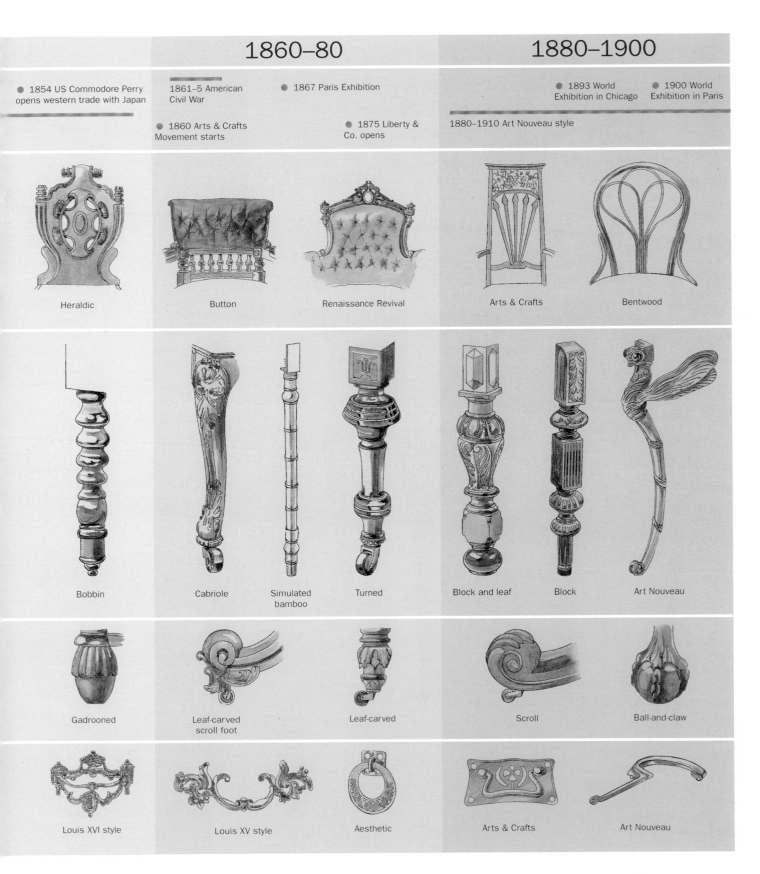

1860–80

- 1854 US Commodore Perry opens western trade with Japan
- 1861–5 American Civil War
- 1860 Arts & Crafts Movement starts
- 1867 Paris Exhibition
- 1875 Liberty & Co. opens

1880–1900

- 1893 World Exhibition in Chicago
- 1900 World Exhibition in Paris

1880–1910 Art Nouveau style

Heraldic

Button

Renaissance Revival

Arts & Crafts

Bentwood

Bobbin

Cabriole

Simulated bamboo

Turned

Block and leaf

Block

Art Nouveau

Gadrooned

Leaf-carved scroll foot

Leaf-carved

Scroll

Ball-and-claw

Louis XVI style

Louis XV style

Aesthetic

Arts & Crafts

Art Nouveau

Story of the Table

English oak refectory table, *c*.1600 [H]

OVER THE CENTURIES *the table has developed from a portable trestle (a horizontal frame with top) into the hugh variety of shapes and sizes that can be found today. The table's evolution mirrors the changing social habits that accompanied the growth of domestic comfort and leisure activities as well as the increasing informality of both social and domestic life.*

Joseph Highmore's illustration of the heroine of Samuel Richardson's Pamela, *published in 1749, shows her writing a letter while seated at a small tripod table.*

The English side table (c.1720) was designed to stand against a wall and would have been used as a writing or dressing table. The shaped frieze and the use of burr-walnut suggests that it was intended for a wealthy household; country or provincial versions were usually plainer and made in oak. [F]

Console tables were decorative pieces intended to be fixed to the wall. This English example, with a grey marble top supported by an eagle, was a popular pattern during the reign of George II; it may have been designed by William Kent. [D]

In the Middle Ages, what little furniture existed was the preserve of the upper classes, whose lifestyle demanded easily portable pieces. Early tables were simple planks of wood that rested on trestles and could be dismantled and moved at will. More settled communities, such as monasteries, had more permanent large, heavy, rectangular tables. Generally made of oak, they were used for eating and were named after the refectory, where meals were taken. In the 17th century, dining in a large hall was increasingly replaced by meals in a dining parlour. This more informal eating pattern demanded a more flexible table, often in the more compact form of the round or oval gateleg table with hinged flaps. Small round-topped tables were used as candle stands.

The increasing comfort of domestic interiors and domestic life in the 18th century coincided with the introduction of veneer. This encouraged the development of a whole range of smaller, lighter and more versatile side or 'occasional' tables, often with drop leaves and drawers and mounted on casters (wheels), that catered for such leisure activities as drinking tea, playing cards and other games, letter-writing and reading, but could also be used for light meals. The round-topped tables of the 17th century developed, in the 1730s, into the tripod table, often with a tilt top. In grand interiors, small side tables that once stood against the walls evolved into the elaborate, formal console table.

Mounted on casters and with a tilt top, this English mahogany breakfast table (c.1790) is both simple and practical. The edge of the table is crossbanded (decoration with thin strips of veneer cut across the grain) with rosewood and has a splayed base. Reproductions of this style can still be found today. [G]

Made c.1835, this imposing English mahogany serving table, with its ostentatious coat of arms, scrolling, leaves and pillars, would have formed part of a dining-room suite. Pieces of furniture such as this were intended to convey a sense of wealth and power. [C]

Dining tables with pedestal supports were introduced in the second quarter of the century, and the pedestal support table, often with additional leaves, remained a popular type.

Victorian households were full of tables for every occasion and use. The prosperous middle classes and their families ate in a dining room at one large central table that could be extended with leaves or flaps; imposing serving tables would often be set against the wall. In the 20th century, as domestic interiors shrank, so too did the size and variety of tables. New materials such as moulded plywood, tubular metal, glass and plastic were used to produce tables in versatile styles.

Charles-Honoré Lannuier

In 1803 the French cabinet-maker Charles-Honoré Lannuier (1779–1819) emigrated to New York. He came to play an important role as one of the first French cabinet-makers to enrich American furniture. Lannuier had an intimate knowledge of fashionable French furniture designs and decorative motifs, which he applied to Anglo–American-inspired forms in a style known as American 'Classical'. Lannuier's work is extremely rich and finely crafted, making use of exotic woods, brass inlays and detailed gilt-bronze mounts.

Rosewood card-table, 1810–20 [A]

Elements of Three Tables

The traditional way of constructing a table from two parts – a top and a base – has changed little over the centuries. Early table tops were made from several planks of wood that were not necessarily joined to each other, but simply pegged on to a base frame. Some tops were made from one solid piece of wood. The base usually consisted of legs connected at the top by a framework of rails joined by mortise-and-tenon joints (a rectangular opening in a piece of wood into which a projection, or tenon, fits) pegged with handmade pegs (dowels). On heavy tables of the refectory type, the legs were also joined at the bottom by stretchers .

The development of better and stronger glues in the early 18th century allowed pegs to be replaced with blocks of wood that were glued to the table top on one side and to the rails of the frame, or base, on the other. From the mid-18th century,

an alternative to pegging or glueing the table top to the frame was to join it with a screw sunk deep into the side rail.

The frieze just under the table top was not only a good area for carved decoration but could also be used to hold a drawer or drawers. The solid, often thick, timber used to create strong legs was another surface that could be decorated, either with handturning or handcarving, or both.

Furniture-makers met the demand for smaller, more versatile tables that could be moved around the room by introducing the gateleg table. The solid, pegged rectangular centre section had hinged leaves on either side – usually made of two pieces of wood – which could be raised. A 'gate'-shaped arrangement of legs and stretchers, which was hinged to the main framework, could be pulled out when necessary to support the leaves. Larger tables had double gatelegs. The more advanced

construction methods of the 18th century allowed the development of the dropleaf table, which did not require stretchers.

An alternative type of base, used with a circular top, was the tripod, where the framework of legs and stretchers was replaced by a central support, or column, ending in three legs.

A new type of joint introduced in the late 17th century was the dovetail, in which two pieces of wood were cut with matching interlocking elements that allowed the wood to be joined at right angles. Although primarily used for drawers, the dovetail was also a useful way of joining together the legs and support of the tripod base; these were often reinforced by a metal brace. Many tripod tables had a tilt-top, which fixed on to two parallel lopers, or bearers, that were hinged to the top of the pedestal support so that the top could be tilted to vertical for easy storage.

Refectory Table

*The **top** on an original table will comprise a single plank of wood or interlocking planks of wood. The surface should be uneven, particularly after many years of use. Old tops have often been replaced with flat, regular machine-cut timber.*

*If the **frieze rail** is on three sides only the table was probably originally designed to stand against a wall. Fine examples have inlaid friezes.*

Wooden pegs (dowels) secure the legs to the stretchers. These should stand proud of the surface on an original table.

***Size** is important; a 'small' refectory table may well have been reduced from a much larger table.*

*On late Elizabethan and Revival tables these **baluster legs** would be elaborately carved in the 'cup and cover' (deep cup with domed lid) style.*

***Stretchers** are almost always worn on the top and knocked or scarred on the outer side. Tables without stretchers, tend to be 19th-century copies.*

Gateleg Table

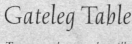

Tops on early examples will be thick and uneven

Frieze drawers may be missing or have been replaced; look for hand-finished drawer linings and replacement handles.

Each **baluster leg** will be slightly different in shape, if the table has been hand-carved.

Stretchers may be worn down by use.

Thumb-moulded edges/rule joints fit into the grooves on the leaves.

Drop leaves are vulnerable and tips and sections or entire leaves may have been replaced; the hinges have also often been replaced.

The **gateleg** is pegged at both ends, which allows it to pivot out and support the dropleaf.

Feet have often had new tips added to repair the ravages of damp and worm and to correct uneven wear.

Tilt-top Table

Lopers/bearers should extend across the table. Look carefully at the whole table underneath for filled-in holes, which show where they were originally placed.

The **'birdcage mechanism'** secures the tripod base to the top. The **wedge** in the centre locks it into position.

Knees are often carved. If the carving is very shallow, the piece may have been 'improved' in the 19th century.

Ball-and-claw feet should be crisply carved.

The **snapcatch** fits into the slot at the front of the birdcage.

The **circular top** should be in proportion to the diameter of the base. An original 18th-century example will be slightly oval where the horizontal grain of the wood has shrunk slightly.

Shaft/column

Knops are carved or left plain.

Tripod bases were usually supported by a metal brace underneath.

A CLOSER LOOK *Gateleg Table*

Gateleg tables typically have a fixed central section supported by four immovable legs joined by stretchers, and two hinged flaps supported on gatelegs that swing open. Smaller tables generally have single gatelegs; larger tables, such as the example looked at in detail here, have double gatelegs. The finest examples have handcarved legs. First developed as luxury furniture in the 16th century, gateleg tables became the staple of the country kitchen and hence were generally made of indigenous woods such as oak and elm. Early examples were usually made of oak and used mortise-and-tenon construction, which was pegged with oak or, sometimes, willow dowels (pegs). Until the 19th century dowels were handcut and were usually irregular; machine-cut examples have a more regular shape.

▲ You can see the fine quality of this table in the **'thumb-moulded'** edges of the fixed section that fit snugly into the **groove** on the leaves. The **hinges** are original – there are no marks nearby to suggest that they have been replaced.

▲ The top of the table is pegged with **handcut oak dowels**, which originally would have lain flush with the surface. Here you can see how over the years the grain has shrunk, leaving the dowels **slightly proud** of the surface.

Oak gateleg table, 17th century
This English table has acquired a superb patina over the years. It is generous in size, with a two-piece pegged top and two-piece leaves that need the support of double gatelegs with hand-turned barley-twist stretchers. [G]

▲ A drawer in the centre section was a common feature of late 17th-century tables. This well-worn example has **deep channels** running down the sides, which is another feature often found on late 17th-century drawers. The wire handle is more unusual.

Reproduction Tables

Copies of gateleg tables have been made since the late 19th century, but their machine-made construction clearly distinguishes them from their predecessors – as you can see in the example below. The major difference is the uniformity of machine-made pieces. A handmade surface, such as that on the table opposite, will be thick and uneven, in marked contrast to the flat, regular shape, texture and colour (produced by staining rather than patination) of a machine-made table, with mechanically turned barley-twist legs. The other major difference is the absence of pegged construction (later examples have glued mortise-and-tenon joints), the smaller size, and the use of a simple peg for a stop.

English oak gateleg table, 1920s [Q]

▼ Expect to see a **flattened section** on the **barley-twist stretchers** where many feet have worn them down over the years. This is an excellent sign of age.

▲ By turning the table upside down you can see that the underside is **lighter in colour**, with none of the patination found on the top. Patina is the surface colour caused by years of wear and polishing. You can tell that the **gateleg stops** are still in their original position because of the **wear** on the wood where the legs have been pulled out into place.

Types of Table

Triple-top table

Multiple-purpose tables were largely an English phenomenon and were mainly produced from *c*.1730–*c*.1770.

■ The folded top of this mahogany table can be unfolded to reveal a polished top for taking tea and then unfolded again to reveal a baize-lined top that was originally used for playing card games.

■ The quality of the carving on this example is particularly outstanding.

■ Most examples are made of mahogany.

Tea and games table,
***c*.1750** [D]

Pier table

Pier tables were designed to stand between two windows and often had a mirror placed above them. Purely decorative examples became fashionable in the 17th century and this type of semicircular form was introduced *c*.1760.

■ In this Neo-classical table you can see a number of features common to the type: the use of satinwood; exotic marquetry (inlaid wood); square tapering legs (often found in furniture made between *c*.1780–1810); and bell-flower motifs.

■ Marquetry is often found in pier tables made from *c*.1770.

■ The table's elegant decoration includes the use of exotic, and expensive, woods such as amboyna and harewood.

Satinwood pier table,
***c*.1785** [D]

Worktable

Worktables fitted with silk bags for storing embroidery or needle-work, and drawers for sewing accessories, were first made in Europe and the USA in the second half of the 18th century. They were subsequently made in a variety of styles.

■ The workbag, which in this example was designed to slide out, is particularly vulnerable to wear and tear. Don't be surprised to find examples where this has been replaced.

■ The clean lines and elegant proportions of this American mahogany example are characteristic of the Federal style.

■ Examples by known craftsmen can have a substantially increased value. This table has been attributed to John Seymour & Son of Boston.

Mahogany worktable,
***c*.1800–1810** [B]

Regency dining-table, early 19th century [D]

Dining-table

Mahogany dining-tables with three pedestal bases were introduced in the mid-18th century, during the reign of George II. The pedestals support leaves so that the table can be enlarged. This English example has two leaves.

■ The heavier proportions of these larger tables anticipated the more elaborate furniture of the mid-19th century.

■ Centre sections have often been removed from the table and made into separate tables – tell-tale signs include narrow proportions.

Nest of quartetto tables,
*c.*1810 [D]

Gothic Revival centre table,
*c.*1830 [D]

Quartetto tables

The nest of four tables (hence the name quartetto) was a popular type of furniture during the 19th century. The tables could be brought out when required, as for taking tea, and tucked away when not in use.

■ Early sets, such as this English rosewood example, are usually lighter and more elegant than later Victorian versions.

■ Rosewood, satinwood and mahogany were used for quartetto tables. This set has a brass inlay of stars within brass stringing (inlaid lines).

Centre table

This type of table was first introduced in the early 19th century.

■ Typical Gothic Revival features include the pointed arch frieze, the quatrefoils, the shaped scrolled trestles and the arched stretcher.

■ This centre table is a well-known and documented product of the firm of Joseph Meeks & Son of New York.

■ Look out for manufacturers' marks or paper labels, which may be on the underside of a table; these give details about the manufacturer.

'Boulle' centre table, *c.*1835 [E]

Saloon suite table,
*c.*1840 [I]

'Boulle' centre table

The late 17th-century decorative technique known as 'boulle', where brass inlay and marquetry are combined, saw a revival from *c.*1810–1870.

■ It is named after André-Charles Boulle, cabinet-maker to Louis XIV, who excelled at this type of decoration.

■ This red tortoiseshell- and ebony-veneered English table is inlaid with rich cut-brass decoration – a common combination.

■ Decoration on later examples can look rather mechanical.

Saloon suite table

In the mid-19th century, whole suites of matching furniture were made for the Victorian middle-class interior, both in Europe and the USA.

■ The decoration on this Dutch example – the shaped carving on the underside of the top, the moulded edge to the top, and the abundant carved and turned pedestal and legs – is the very height of the overblown Rococo Revival style.

■ Walnut was a popular wood used for 19th-century tables.

A Closer Look *Pembroke Table*

The Pembroke was just one of a range of small, versatile tables that developed during the 18th century to cater for the growing range of leisure activities of the wealthy. It is thought to have been named after the aristocratic lady who was the first person to commission one. These high-quality tables made their first appearance in the drawing-rooms and ladies' boudoirs of the late 1750s. They were often mounted on casters so that they could be moved around the room with ease. The tops were made in a variety of shapes – square, rectangular, oval, serpentine or 'butterfly' – and the flaps were supported on hinged brackets. Being such a compact item of furniture, which can be stored at one side when not in use, the Pembroke table has remained popular. Later copies tend to be of a more squat form than the originals.

▲ Decoration on Pembroke tables ranges from hand-painting to **inlaid borders**. On this table, the decoration comprises mahogany (the darkest wood), kingwood **crossbanding** (the thick edge), ebony strings (black lines) and boxwood (the thin light strips), surrounding an oval panel of satinwood with a fruitwood centre (seen in the main picture).

Pembroke table, c.1790
The bowed drawer of this elegant piece echoes the serpentine shape of the top and leaves. The tapered legs are mounted on brass casters. [D]

▲ The carcass of this Pembroke table is of beech, which is a cheap and lightweight softwood. The two small, hinged and shaped **fly-brackets** that support the leaves give an indication of the high quality of this piece. If you look at the underside of the leaves you can see signs of **scratching** and **discoloration** that show where the table has been handled over the years. It is very clear where the brackets have rubbed into the softwood when the table was opened and folded away. If the brackets still align with the wear marks, this indicates that the flaps have not been shortened.

The Age of Satinwood

Satinwood, a light yellow, tightly grained exotic timber from the West Indies, is so called because its figuring (pattern of the grain) resembles satin fabric. Being very expensive it was used largely as a veneer on high-quality furniture, from *c.*1770–*c.*1810. Satinwood from the East Indies, with a distinctive 'stripy' figuring, was introduced at the same time but used mostly on Sheraton Revival furniture (*c.*1870–*c.*1920).

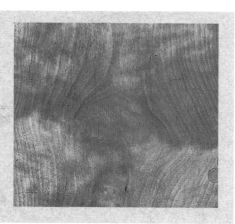

A CLOSER LOOK *Sofa Table*

In the late 18th century, the Pembroke table was joined in the drawing room by the sofa table – a new, slightly larger, type of occasional table. As the name suggests, it was designed to be placed directly in front of the sofa, where it was used for such ladylike pursuits as drawing, writing and reading. Like the Pembroke table, the sofa table has two flaps, or leaves, but they are set on the short sides of a straight-edged rectangular top. The table is usually veneered, and has two matching sets of drawers (either one long drawer or two short): a dummy set that faced into the room and a real set that faced towards the sofa. Earlier examples tend to have standard ends, more rarely legs at each corner, while those from the 19th century usually have a central support. Rosewood, with its lovely reddish colour and strong black figuring, was popular for sofa tables.

▲ At the side of the drawer you can clearly see the **dovetail joints** used in its construction and also the slight **ridges** along the sides made by years of opening and closing the drawer.

English mahogany sofa table, 1820
Many typical late-Regency features are evident in this English sofa table, in mahogany with a rosewood veneer top. These include rope-twist decoration on the pedestal, brass claw feet and inlaid decoration. [H]

▲ **Quarter beading**, seen in the corner of the drawer, was used from the early 19th century. Drawers were often made from oak or pine; the **mahogany-lined** drawers on this example are a sign of quality.

▶ If you pull out the drawer completely you can see the **ridges** on the inside of the carcass where the base of the drawer has rubbed. This type of wear is to be expected, and is a good sign that the table has seen consistent use for over 180 years.

▶ **Handles** are particularly vulnerable: they get damaged easily and tend to be the victim of changing fashions. They have often been **replaced**, as you can see here, where the hole for the original handle can clearly be seen beneath the **new fixing**.

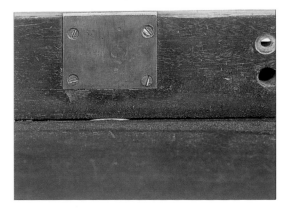

A CLOSER LOOK *Tilt-top Tables*

The tilt-top, or hinged top, was an ingenious device that allowed circular tables to double up as a firescreen or to be stored neatly and compactly when not in use. Small tilt-top tripod and centre tables were made in Britain in the early 18th century and the type soon became equally popular in the American colonies. By the late 18th century and during the 19th, the tilt-top was also used for taking breakfast and as a small dining table. A sophisticated 'birdcage' mechanism that allowed the top both to tilt and swivel was used on smaller English tripod tables between 1740 and 1760. The system, consisting of two platforms joined by four pillars, lingered on in the American colonies beyond this date. A comparison of the more modest mahogany English table with its grander American counterpart reveals a number of differences.

▲ The underside of a table can often tell you more than the top. Here you can see indentations from a needlework clamp and the **'halo'** effect created by handling – a good sign of age.

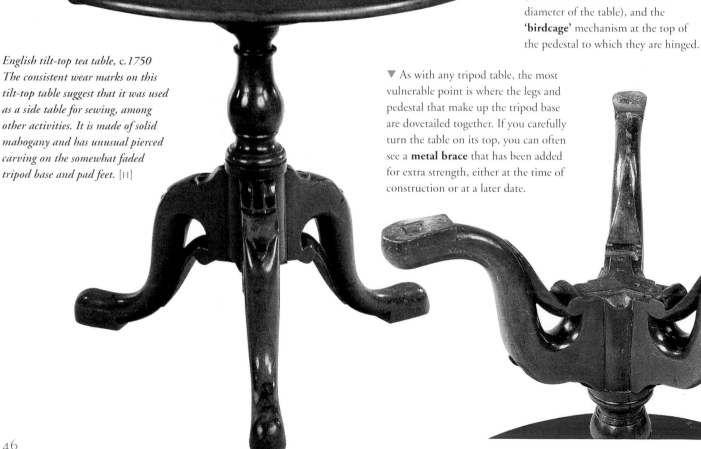

English tilt-top tea table, c.1750
The consistent wear marks on this tilt-top table suggest that it was used as a side table for sewing, among other activities. It is made of solid mahogany and has unusual pierced carving on the somewhat faded tripod base and pad feet. [H]

▲ When tilted, the elements of the construction can clearly be seen: the two parallel **lopers**, or bearers, on the underside of the table top (these should stretch across the diameter of the table), and the **'birdcage'** mechanism at the top of the pedestal to which they are hinged.

▼ As with any tripod table, the most vulnerable point is where the legs and pedestal that make up the tripod base are dovetailed together. If you carefully turn the table on its top, you can often see a **metal brace** that has been added for extra strength, either at the time of construction or at a later date.

▶ This brass **snap catch** was designed to fit into a slot in the centre of the birdcage to hold the table top in position when lowered. Although in the 18th-century style, the many **filled holes** around it suggests that the catch is not original to the table.

▶ By skimming your hands around the edge of the table top, you can feel the **'dished' top**. This is a sure sign of a more sophisticated table. The result was achieved by carving away a solid board of wood from the centre of the top to create a neat raised edge. Exceptional tea tables may have scalloped (also called 'piecrust') rims.

American tilt-top tea table, c. 1770–80 Made in the American 'Chippendale' style, with a tripod base ending in ball-and-claw feet, this fine example was produced after the second wave of immigrant craftsmen reached Pennsylvania and began to create furniture that incorporated both European and American features. [F]

◀ The **'birdcage'** mechanism shown here is typical of those found on American 'Chippendale' tea tables. The shaft, or column support, fits through the bottom platform and is fixed to the neck by a wedge.

▶ Another indication of the quality of this table is the bold shape of the legs, each of which have been carved from a solid piece of wood. The legs end in classic **ball-and-claw** feet. It can be identified as a Pennsylvanian table because of the slightly flattened shape of the bulbous ball.

Story of the Chair

TRADITIONALLY, THE CHAIR *was a symbol of status. The early Greek and Roman 'X-frame' chair was easily folded and transported and, when opened out, was used by a person of authority. The few chairs made before the 16th century were also the preserve of dignitaries, but by the 17th century more comfortable and democratic seating furniture was produced, including upholstered easy chairs and side, or dining, chairs.*

The curving lines and decorative motifs of the Rococo style have been incorporated into this giltwood Louis XV fauteuil (c.1750). With its padded back and seat, comfort is clearly an important consideration here. [H]

'Easy' or wing armchairs were originally designed to be used by the elderly and infirm. They were generally located in the bedroom rather than the drawing room. This wing chair, made from maple and mahogany, was produced in Boston, Massachusetts between 1750 and 1765. [A]

A View of a Drawing Room (1780). In this painting you can see how the chairs have been arranged around the side of the room; this was typical of grand interiors of the period.

Before the late 15th century, only the master of the house or important visitors would use an armchair. These early chairs were made of solid, indigenous woods. In the early 17th century, the back legs of the stool were elongated to provide a frame for an upright back, and the early side or dining-chair – without arms – was born. With the Restoration (1660), continental styles of chair reached Britain.

These included lighter chairs with caned backs and upholstered seats, and chairs with upholstered backs and seats. Such styles became increasingly common in London after 1666, when there was a demand for furniture to replace that lost in the Great Fire. A further demand for chairs was brought about by the change in dining habits during the 17th century, when the single large table was replaced by informal groups of smaller tables.

By the end of the 17th century, the side chair assumed greater importance as suites of chairs were placed against the walls to emphasize the architecture of the room. The comfortable armchair, or *fauteuil*, was

produced in a variety of new forms that suited a new era of intimacy and conversation. Upholstery became more generous and chairs became more comfortable, with flowing lines and cabriole (shaped) legs, giving rise to the armchair with upholstered sides known as the *bergère* in France and the 'easy' chair in England.

The early 18th century was a golden age for the English wing armchair, which at this time was usually made of walnut and upholstered with needlework. By the 1760s, the influence of Thomas Chippendale's *Gentleman and Cabinet-Maker's Director* (1754), which included designs for intricate Gothic-, Rococo- and Chinese-inspired chair backs, was felt in Britain and the American colonies.

From the mid-18th century, the Neoclassical style spread to England, where it was interpreted by Robert Adam, George Hepplewhite and Thomas Sheraton. They produced a variety of designs for light and elegant chairs with painted decoration, oval and shield-shaped backs, and straight-sided backs respectively.

The early 19th-century, French Empire style, which used decorative motifs and forms that celebrated the successes of

The shield-shaped chair back is a form that is particularly associated with the work of George Hepplewhite. This English designer made furniture for the Prince Regent, who became George IV in 1820. [G]

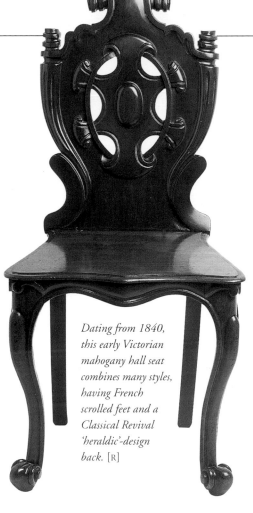

Dating from 1840, this early Victorian mahogany hall seat combines many styles, having French scrolled feet and a Classical Revival 'heraldic'-design back. [R]

Made in 1815, this Regency mahogany armchair, with sabre legs, formed part of a set of six dining-chairs. [M]

Developments in coiled-spring and upholstery techniques resulted in the Victorian button-back chair. This example, which was made in the 1860s, has a solid rosewood frame with a serpentine front and turned baluster legs. [O]

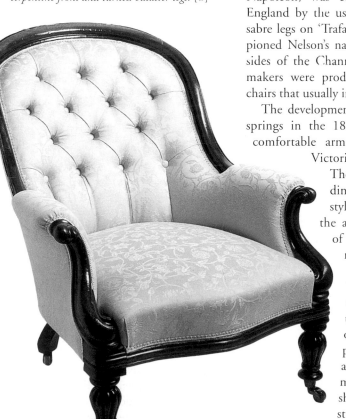

Napoleon, was countered in Regency England by the use of rope carving and sabre legs on 'Trafalgar' chairs that championed Nelson's naval victories. On both sides of the Channel, meanwhile, chair-makers were producing sets of dining-chairs that usually included two armchairs.

The development of coiled upholstery springs in the 1820s resulted in more comfortable armchairs, including the Victorian button-back chair.

The Victorian fashion for dining-chairs in revival styles ran in parallel with the anti-ornamental stance of William Morris and members of the Arts & Crafts Movement. The construction of chairs changed little until the development of moulded plywood, plastics, tubular steel and synthetic fabrics made a new range of shapes and types of construction possible.

Thomas Chippendale

Thomas Chippendale (1718–79) established his cabinet-making business in London in 1753. The following year saw the publication of his highly influential *Gentleman and Cabinet-Maker's Director*, which contained more than 161 plates of precise drawings and designs for a wide range of furniture. The book was to inspire countless versions of 'Chippendale' furniture, both in Britain and USA. His work and legacy is particularly associated with the Rococo style of the mid-18th century.

Mahogany 'ribbon-back' chair, *c.*1755, by Chippendale [E]

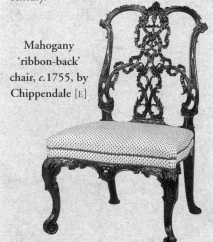

Elements of Three Chairs

Early chairs were usually made from solid timber, cut or sawn by hand and, where necessary, turned on a hand lathe. The glue available in the 17th century was not strong enough for structural joints, which were held together by a mortise-and-tenon joint in which the tenon (a protruding rectangular piece of wood) fitted into a rectangular hole known as a mortise. Mortise-and-tenon joints were particularly vulnerable, so the holes (generally two) were drilled through the joint and handcut wooden pegs (dowels) were driven into them in order to provide much needed strength.

By *c*.1715 in London (some 30 to 40 years later in rural areas), stronger and better glues meant that mortise-and-tenon joints could simply be glued, and stronger pegged joints were needed only in parts of the chair that were subjected to the most stress, such as at the top of the leg.

Legs had to be strong and were usually made from solid timber; stretchers between the legs provided added strength and were tenoned into position. The back legs extended to form the stiles (vertical uprights) and these and the splat (central part of the chair back) were joined to the horizontal toprail with mortise-and-tenon joints. In early chairs, the 'shoe' brace (bar) into which the bottom of the splat fitted was separate; in later chairs it became part of the back seat rail. On 18th-century armchairs, the arms were screwed to the seat rails and stiles.

Early seats were of solid wood, but by the end of the 17th century on the Continent and the early 18th century in England, there was a greater desire for comfort, and upholstered seats were introduced. Seats made of cane had a soft, feather, squab cushion. Padded drop-in seats fitted inside the seat rails; and in stuff-over seats, the fabric covering the horsehair stuffing came over the seat rails and was nailed underneath. Seat rails were often made of softwood, such as pine or beech, because they were concealed. A major innovation in the 19th century was the use of coiled-wire upholstery springs, which allowed deeper upholstery of the type seen on Victorian button-back chairs.

Another development in the construction of chairs was veneering, used on English chairs between *c*.1700 and 1720. Like other decoration, it was usually applied to the front of the chair – the part that would be seen – especially on side chairs, which were placed around the edge of the room, while the less visible back of the chair was left plain, with visible joints. Seat rails, in particular, which were often made of inexpensive softwood, were then covered with a veneer of a more impressive, expensive wood, such as walnut.

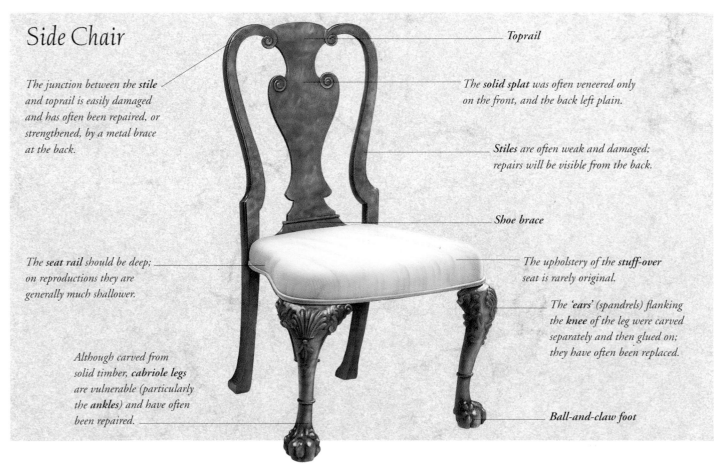

Side Chair

The junction between the **stile** and toprail is easily damaged and has often been repaired, or strengthened, by a metal brace at the back.

The **seat rail** should be deep; on reproductions they are generally much shallower.

Although carved from solid timber, **cabriole legs** are vulnerable (particularly the **ankles**) and have often been repaired.

Toprail

The **solid splat** was often veneered only on the front, and the back left plain.

Stiles are often weak and damaged; repairs will be visible from the back.

Shoe brace

The upholstery of the **stuff-over** seat is rarely original.

The 'ears' (spandrels) flanking the **knee** of the leg were carved separately and then glued on; they have often been replaced.

Ball-and-claw foot

Wing Armchair

'Wing'

*The **serpentine crest rail** is usually more highly arched on early 18th-century chairs.*

*The **covering** is rarely original, with the exception of a few chairs with needlework upholstery.*

*Vertical **cone-shaped arms** were used on New England chairs, while C-scroll horizontal arms were used on Philadelphia chairs.*

*The stuffed **'squab' cushion** is supported by a stuffed seat.*

*Raked **back legs** had to be strong; these are square and continue up to form the stiles. In the USA the legs were often made of maple.*

Seat rail with rounded front corners are typical of wing armchairs made in New England.

*Stretchers (here **block-and-spindle**) were usually walnut and continued to be used on New England wing armchairs after they were abandoned in Philadelphia.*

Ball-and-claw feet may well have been repaired or replaced.

Armchair

*Downswept **arms** were generally screwed to the seat rails and into the back stiles. Arms have often been weakened by lifting the chair and may have been replaced or repaired.*

*The interlaced scroll **splat** was tenoned and glued into the toprail, but only tenoned into the shoe to allow for shrinkage.*

Trefoil motif

Back stile/upright

*On **stuff-over seats** the seat rails have often been replaced; original rails often show signs of woodworm, discolouration and holes where previous upholstery was nailed.*

*The **seat** on an original 18th-century armchair will be about 2in (5cm) wider than that on a side chair; narrow proportions suggest a later 'upgrading' from side to armchair.*

Back legs will often be worn at the bottom, where the chair has been pushed back as the occupant stood up.

*The **cross stretcher** is particularly vulnerable and may well have been replaced; check for wear and colour match.*

A Closer Look *Early Chairs*

Although made during the reigns of George I and George II respectively, these English and American chairs share two characteristic features of Queen Anne furniture: the use of walnut and curving lines. These chairs would have been made as part of a set (usually six), and both have their numbers neatly carved on the seat frame. However, there are some interesting differences in construction. While the American chair is made from solid walnut, the burr-walnut on the English chair has been applied as a veneer to the oak splat (the central part of the chair back) and to the stiles (uprights) and seat rail. Although both chairs have drop-in seats, cabriole legs ending in ball-and-claw feet, and vase-shaped splats, some basic differences exist.

▲ The exceptionally fine **detailed carving** you can see on this **toprail** (also on the legs and the front rail) is common on 18th-century walnut furniture.

▲ On the back of this chair the **toprail** has been **pegged** into the splat with a horizontal join. This is typically English; on continental chairs the join was usually vertical or angled.

▲ Here you can clearly see the **pegs** that have been used to join the solid walnut legs to the back rail; on the front of a chair, pegged joints are often hidden by the veneering.

English walnut chair, c.1720
With its fine carving, stuffed drop-in seat and cabriole legs ending in ball-and-claw feet, this chair is a good example of an early 18th-century English side chair. [H]

▲ Remove the solid drop-in stuffed seat and you can see the **seat frame**, which alone would have been originaly supported it; the shaped **corner brackets** were added in the 19th century. The brackets are always screwed into the frame and glued for extra strength.

▲ Early **handcut veneering** was much thicker than later machine-cut veneering. In this detail you can just make out the thick veneer on the outside of the seat frame, which is riddled with **woodworm**.

▲ **Scallop shells** and **volutes** (scrolls), which you can see in an even finer form on the chair opposite, were one of the carved decorative designs most favoured by makers of Queen Anne furniture in Pennsylvania. The **patina**, seen on both of the chairs, shows that these are high-quality pieces.

American black walnut chair, c.1750
The Queen Anne style reached its high point in Philadelphia in the mid-18th century, when this chair was made. It features a curving top rail, cabriole legs with pad feet, and an intricately shaped and pierced splat. [A]

▲ A **metal brace** has been added at a later date to the back of the chair. This strengthens the area where the horizontal toprail joins the upright **stile**.

▲ The **rectangular seat support** is a particularly American feature. It has been cut from the solid frame and therefore additional corner supports for the seat are not needed.

The Age of Walnut

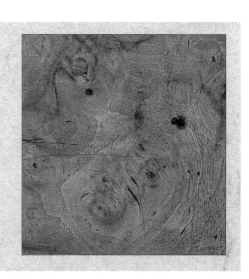

Walnut is a fine-grained timber that varies from honey coloured to red and includes the distinctive figuring of the highly prized burr-walnut. Furniture made from walnut became fashionable in Britain from *c.*1660. Initially, solid walnut pieces were made, but during the 'golden age' of walnut furniture (*c.*1690–*c.*1735), British furniture-makers used walnut as a veneer. In the severe winter of 1709 most European walnut trees perished and from the 1730s mahogany gradually superseded walnut.

▲ At the back of the chair you can see the **'through tenon'**, in which the seat rail pierces the stile. This is a common feature on Queen Anne chairs made in Pennsylvania.

Types of Dining-chair

Japanned chair

'Japanning' was fashionable from the late 17th to the early 18th century. It is used on this English dining-chair with cane back panels and seat.

■ The technique of japanning – where layers of paint and shellac (a type of lacquer) are painted on a piece of furniture – was developed in Europe in the 17th century in response to the huge demand for wares in the oriental style.

■ Japanned decoration can easily flake and chip, so check examples carefully for damage.

Japanned armchair, c.1730 [H]

George II side chair

This red walnut English side chair was made in a style first introduced in the early 18th century that remained in fashion for some 30 years.

■ The curved shape of the top-rail is a characteristic feature, as is the solid, unpierced splat and the deep seat rail for the drop-in seat.

■ Equally common at this period are the gently curved cabriole legs, with scroll-carved decoration to the knees, and the neat pad feet.

■ Stretchers on English chairs were generally abandoned from c.1720–35; the back stretcher on this example indicates that it is of provincial origin.

■ Red walnut was used for good-quality country furniture.

George II side chair, c.1730 [J]

'Chippendale' chair

Originally part of a set, this mahogany dining-chair has many of the decorative elements made popular by the publication of Thomas Chippendale's *Gentleman and Cabinet-Maker's Director* (1754).

■ The pierced, carved vase-shaped splat beneath the wavy top rail uses Gothic-style elements; other styles used Chinese motifs.

■ The broader overall proportions of the chair, with its stuff-over seat, chamfered (squared off) square legs and H-shaped stretchers, are typical of 'Chippendale' chairs.

'Chippendale' dining-chair, c.1760 [M]

'Sheraton'-style armchair

In this restrained English mahogany armchair you can see many characteristic features late Neo-classical furniture.

■ The rectangular, rather formal, chair back first came into fashion in the late 18th century.

■ The panelled, tapered square legs and spade feet are also associated with this period.

■ The shaped, downswept arms are a particular feature of late 18th-/early 19th-century chairs.

■ Chairs such as this would have been part of a large set of numbered dining-chairs.

'Sheraton'-style armchair, c.1790 [J]

Neo-classical dining-chair

The impact of Neo-classicism and the continuing influence of Thomas Sheraton's *The Cabinet Maker and Upholsterer's Drawing Book* (1791–4), can be seen in this mahogany dining-chair.

■ The influence of Sheraton is evident in the design of the splat, which is topped with a panel carved with drapery swags – a popular Neo-classical motif.

■ The turned tapering leg, first introduced in the late 18th century, was popular until *c.*1815.

■ Although this example has a gently serpentine stuff-over seat, drop-in seats were also popular at this time.

George III dining-chair, *c.*1790 [M]

Regency dining-chair

Simulated woods were a popular feature of Regency furniture. This dining-chair has been painted to resemble the exotic wood, coromandel. Rosewood was also often simulated during the Regency period.

■ Chairs such as this would have been made as part of a large set.

■ The sabre legs – curving outwards at the front and back – are taken from the ancient Greek 'Klismos' chair.

■ The cushion is in a style known as a squab cushion. It covers a cane seat, which was very popular at this time.

■ The use of gilt and painted decoration reflects the Regency love of the exotic. The decorative effect is enhanced by simulated stringing (thin inserts of wood).

Regency armchair, *c.*1815 [I]

William IV chair

The trend towards heavier furniture and use of historical influences, which reached its height during the Victorian era, is seen in this mahogany, William IV chair.

■ Gadrooning (carved rounded mouldings) and roundels are usually found on furniture made between 1825 and 1835.

■ This type of upholstered seat has coiled-wire springing, which was first developed in the late 1820s.

■ The Neo-classical elements – such as the formalized lyre-shaped, dished back and the gadrooning on the toprail – are much heavier than those seen on Regency pieces.

William IV chair, *c.*1830–37 [P]

Rococo Revival chair

The Rococo Revival that began *c.*1840 was just one of the many revival styles popular during the Victorian period, when this rosewood dining-chair was made.

■ The Rococo and Rococo Revival styles are synonymous with the use of the curving line, seen here in the cabriole legs, the serpentine seat rail and the top-rail, stretcher and stiles.

■ Rococo is a light and feminine style, which became popular during the reign of Louis XV (in the 18th century). Victorian interpretations of this style are often excessively decorated.

■ True 18th-century Rococo furniture made much use of gilt wood. However, on Victorian Rococo Revival furniture this was often replaced with rosewood.

Rococo Revival dining-chair, *c.*1845 [P]

A CLOSER LOOK *Dining-chairs*

Dining-chairs, or side chairs, did not become fashionable in Europe until the 17th century. Made without arms, they were originally designed to be placed around the walls of the room rather than in the centre. By the 19th century they were being produced in quantity, and both the English chairs shown here reflect the contemporary fashion for historical styles. In the early 19th century the excavations at Herculaneum (1738) and Pompeii (1748) fuelled an interest in classical antiquity, while the end of the century saw an interest in reviving the late 18th-century designs of Thomas Sheraton. The most obvious difference between the two pieces is in their colour and proportions: the mahogany Regency chair has a much more 'masculine' feel, with broader proportions. The Sheraton Revival chair is more 'feminine', made of light-coloured satinwood (popular at the time) with narrower proportions and a more slender back.

▼ If you turn the chair upside down, you can see how the **seat rail** has been strengthened with **corner braces**. These have been fitted into slots in the seat rails and glued into position – a type of construction that was frequently used from *c.*1740 to the early 19th century when it was replaced by the three-sided bracket (seen opposite).

◀ The distinctive shape of the **Grecian lyre** was a very popular **Neo-classical** ornament, which was frequently used on Regency chair backs. Here you can see how it has been combined with equally characteristic **reeding** (fine rectangular mouldings) on the top 'tablet' rail and down the stiles. The **good patination** on this chair indicates that it is a period piece.

▼ The **back legs** of a chair invariably bear the brunt of years of wear and tear. If you run your hand over the very bottom of a leg and foot you can feel how the back edge has been worn down. This is the result of the chair repeatedly being scraped against hard floors as it was pushed back when the occupant stood up. Irregular **scratches**, **dents** and **scars** are all good signs of authenticity.

Regency dining-chair, c.1810
This lyre-back hair is typical of English dining-chairs made in the early 19th century. The chair is made from a softwood frame with a mahogany veneer. Stuff-over seats are also typical of this period. [P]

▶ **Hand-painted** and **inlaid decoration** are features of Sheraton and Sheraton Revival furniture. Decoration on later examples is sometimes more mechanical and **stiffer** than on earlier examples.

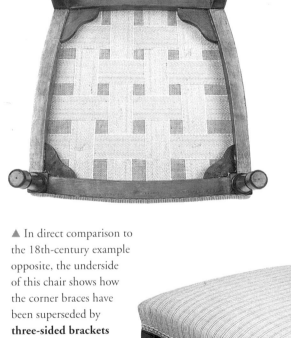

▲ In direct comparison to the 18th-century example opposite, the underside of this chair shows how the corner braces have been superseded by **three-sided brackets** with neat **serpentine fronts**. If you look closely you can see how each of these brackets has been **screwed** tightly into the seat rail – a type of construction that was used in the late 19th century.

Sheraton Revival

From the mid-19th century, the British middle classes played an important part in determining furniture design as they sought to furnish their homes. Their preference was for comfortable, smaller-scale pieces that would suit their smaller houses, and for styles from the past. Manufacturers responded by copying, and modifying, designs from, among others, *The Cabinet-Maker and Upholsterer's Drawing Book* (1791–4) by Thomas Sheraton. Sheraton Revival furniture was fashionable from *c*.1870 to *c*.1920. It included chairs in satinwood with painted floral and inlaid decoration, square backs and turned tapering legs, as well as many other furniture types, often in mahogany with satinwood crossbanding.

Sheraton Revival satinwood armchair with painted decoration, *c*.1910 [I]

Sheraton Revival dining-chair, c.1905
In order to match the smaller contemporary interiors of the Edwardian period (1901–10) this English satinwood chair has been scaled down in size. Compared with an original, you will usually find that a later copy has more slender turned tapering legs, a thinner seat rail, and a taller, more upright back. [P]

Types of Upholstered Chair

George II wing armchair

Wing armchairs were first made in England in the late 17th century. The deep 'wings' at the sides protected the sitter from draughts.

■ You will find that the upholstery on the seat-cushion and padded frame, which would have been made of fine needlepoint, is rarely original. If it is, it may be quite shabby.

■ Wing armchairs were made in walnut and mahogany. Mahogany examples tend to have more elaborate carving on the knees of the cabriole legs.

■ Legs on wing armchairs made before the mid-18th century are rarely joined by stretchers.

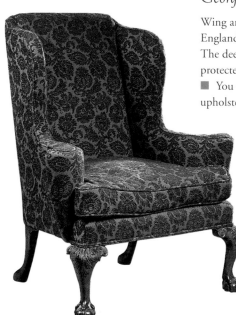

George II wing armchair,
***c*.1745 [D]**

Louis XV fauteuil

The *fauteuil* is a type of French open (without sides) armchair with a padded seat and back, that was often made as part of a suite for formal entertainment.

■ The shaped back, the serpentine front rail and cabriole legs typify the curving lines of the fashionable Rococo style.

■ Precise, detailed carving and an elaborately shaped front rail are all signs of good quality.

■ This type of chair would not originally have had casters; on this example they have been added at a later date.

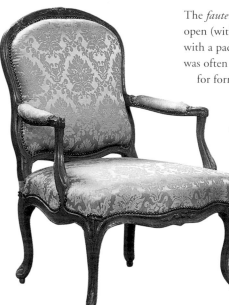

Louis XV *fauteuil*,
mid-18th century [I]

George III wing armchair

This type of wing armchair was made some 30 years later than the example above, and a comparison of the two shows the how the style developed.

■ In this example the padded back has a more 'waisted' shape, and the arms scroll up and over, with rounded tops, rather than outwards.

■ The legs are joined by H-stretchers, a feature found on English wing armchairs made between *c*.1750 and 1790.

■ This is the most commonly found type of wing armchair. It was made both with and, as shown here, without a loose seat.

George III wing armchair,
***c*.1780 [H]**

Louis XVI fauteuil

This type of *fauteuil* was introduced in the late 18th century and shows the changes brought about by the move from the Rococo to the Neo-classical style.

■ The straight lines of this chair reflect the newly fashionable classical influence.

■ The curved legs have been replaced by the straight, turned tapering legs used from *c*.1780–1800. The very upright back legs are a particularly French feature.

■ The superb carving, the lavish use of ornament and the printed silk upholstery are all hallmarks of luxury furniture.

Louis XVI *fauteuil*,
***c*.1780–1800 [I]**

Armchair en gondole

This type of armchair ('gondola') shows the influence of French furniture popular in the USA after the Restoration of the monarchy in France in 1814. Before this time, American furniture was mainly influenced by English designs. This example was made by Duncan Phyfe.

■ The carved lotus leaves on the arm supports are an Egyptian motif that was used on 19th-century French furniture following Napoleon's Egyptian campaign of 1798.

■ Although the upholstery has been replaced, it is in an appropriate style.

Armchair *en gondole*, *c.*1830 [B]

William IV armchair

The design of this rosewood armchair was never particularly popular and therefore remains quite unusual. These chairs were generally made in pairs for the libraries of middle-class homes.

■ You can see the classical influence of the Regency period in the X-frame supports.

■ This type of leg is particularly vulnerable and should be carefully checked for damage and restoration. The casters on this example are original.

■ More luxurious examples will have gilt mounts and finely carved detail; less desirable examples will be in simulated rosewood.

William IV rosewood armchair, *c.*1835 [H]

Gothic Revival armchair

You can clearly see the Victorian passion for historical styles in this armchair, which incorporates elements of the Gothic, Louis XVI and even Indian styles.

■ The introduction of coiled springs in 1820 resulted in the deeper, more luxurious upholstery seen in this example.

■ The chair's appeal lies in its ostentatious excess: the use of gilding and painted decoration; the carved, pointed finials on the chair back and arms; and the arcaded top, seat and arm rails.

■ Check carefully for any damage or restoration that will detract from the effect.

Gothic Revival armchair, *c.*1860 [H]

Liberty & Co. armchair

This upholstered armchair is typical of the late 19th-century designs by the firm of Liberty & Co. This famous London shop was well known for furniture in exotic styles that were fashionable in the late 19th and early 20th century.

■ The combination of velvet and tassels to the arms, back and seat rail is typically Victorian. This type of upholstery needs to be cared for.

■ Look out for pieces with surviving labels or stamps (usually underneath the seat), which can add greatly to the value of the piece.

Liberty & Co. armchair, *c.*1890 [J]

A CLOSER LOOK *Gustav Stickley Chair*

Gustav Stickley was one of the leading members of the American Arts & Crafts Movement. In 1898 he set up his own business in Syracuse, New York, and inspired by the philosophies of William Morris and John Ruskin, in 1900 launched a range of Arts & Crafts furniture. The design for the 'Morris' chair featured here was patented on 10 September 1901. It was produced during a particularly creative period for Stickley, who believed that furniture should be 'thoroughly practical, not too good for everyday use'. He increasingly emphasized the structure of his pieces, which became more 'angular, plain and severe'. Stickley's furniture is always of pleasing proportions and bold construction. His 'Morris' chairs can be easy to date because of the clues they give us and the way their construction developed.

◀ The back of the chair has five **slats**. Here you can clearly see the **movable pins** that support the back; these can be adjusted to suit the occupant. The pins on such early chairs as this have a **tapered rectangular shape**, while on later pieces they have regular rounded ends.

▲ Most Stickley furniture is marked, and the changing style of the mark helps with dating. This particular red **decal** (a type of transfer) with the **joiner's compass** on the underside of the arm and was used from 1902–03.

'Morris' chair by Gustav Stickley, 1902
This chair demonstrates Stickley's philosophy of 'returning to the plain principles of construction and making simple, strong, comfortable furniture'. The tapering brackets (known as corbels) under the arms are a particular Stickley detail; unlike most other craftsmen Stickley pinned these to the leg. [C]

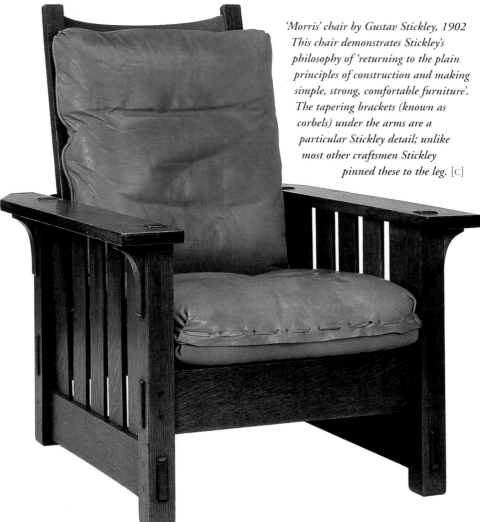

▲ Stickley saw the **mortise-and-tenon joints** as an important part of the character and aesthetic appeal of his reclining 'Morris' chair. Here you can see how the joints have been carefully secured using **dowels**. In order to emphasize the chair's construction, Stickley specified that the tops of the tenons should stand proud of the tops of the front posts (by 38mm/1½in) and should protrude through the mortise in the seat rails.

A CLOSER LOOK Windsor Chair

Windsor is a term used to describe chairs in which the legs, arms and spindles (back rails) are socketed into a shaped seat. Windsor chairs have been made in Britain since the mid-18th century. Although closely associated with the county of Buckinghamshire, in particular the town of High Wycombe, where by 1875 some 4,000 were made each day, the style was used for provincial chairs throughout Britain and also in the USA. The style of the legs can help with dating: earlier examples tend to have more slender legs and stretchers; these become chunkier in later mass-produced chairs. Windsor chairs were made from different types of wood, including ash and elm, and maple, ash and hickory in the USA. Chairs in hardwoods such as yew are much sought after, as are those made of mahogany. Examples are sometimes painted.

◀ One clue to authenticity is evidence of the number of people who have used the chair. Here, the 'saddle' seat has been **discoloured** from use, and the arm rests show **wear** from contact with numerous arms and sleeves.

▶ Most Windsor chairs are made of a combination of different woods. **Yew** has been largely used for this chair, including the legs; this hardwood is impervious to woodworm and has a **reddish parallel grain**. The less-visible parts, such as the stretchers shown here, are **elm**, which has a **wide, open grain**. The seat is also of elm, typical on English Windsor chairs.

Other Windsor Chairs

Although there are many different styles of Windsor chair, they fall into two major types: those with a straight, horizontal toprail, known as a comb back (often found on early chairs); and the more common variety with a rounded back and a bowed back stretcher (also known as a 'hoop' or 'crinoline' back). One of the most desirable, although rare, types of Windsor chair is the 'Gothic' style chair made in yew from the late 18th century.

Comb-back Windsor chair, early 19th century [I]

Windsor armchair, c.1850
Here you can see all the features characteristic of 19th-century Windsor chairs, such as the shaped 'saddle' seat, the bowed back, thick turned legs and stretchers. Because they have seen active service in the kitchen for so many years, you should expect surviving examples to have replacement legs, stretchers and armrests. [K]

Types of Settee & Sofa

English double
chair-back settee,
*c.*1720 [C]

Triple chair-back settee

The triple chair-back settee was a development of the double chair-back. Like many of the chair-back settees of the 1750s and 1760s, this mahogany example, with its stuff-over seat, follows the chair patterns popularized by Thomas Chippendale.

■ Pieces such as this show the influence of the 'Chinese' Chippendale style that was fashionable during the 1750s – the toprails are carved with pagodas and bells and the legs and stretchers are carved with geometric patterns (fretwork).

Triple chair-back 'Chippendale'
settee, *c.*1755 [C]

Double chair-back settee

The double-chair back settee was produced from the mid-17th century. The type shown here first appeared in the early 18th century and was often made of walnut, sometimes with burr-walnut splats.

■ The style echoes that of side chairs made at the same time (*see* p.52).

■ The cabriole legs, with carved shells on the knees, are an indication of the high quality of this grand sofa. A considerable amount of timber was needed to achieve the elegant curves.

■ This type of settee would have had a drop-in upholstered seat.

Camel-back sofa

This type of sofa is often known as a 'camel-back' because of the serpentine shape of the upholstered back. It came into fashion towards the end of 18th century.

■ The square front legs are typical of Chippendale seat furniture. So, too, are the squared, raked (sloping) back legs that are joined by plain rectangular stretchers.

■ This design is typical of the American 'Chippendale' style, which lasted from *c.*1755 to *c.*1790.

Regency 'bamboo' sofa,
*c.*1790–1810 [I]

Regency sofa

During the Regency period, chairs and settees were often painted to simulate another material such as bamboo, ebony or rosewood.

■ The seats were usually caned and often had a squab cushion – another feature that is common in Regency seat furniture.

■ The decoration was painted on an inexpensive softwood.

■ Always check for damage on such delicate furniture as parts can easily be broken (*see* above) and this can affect value.

American camel-back sofa, *c.*1780 [A]

**American 'Classical' sofa,
1820–40 [G]**

American 'Classical' sofa

American 'Classical' furniture evolved from the Federal style from *c.*1815 to 1830 and is particularly associated with New York. It is essentially an interpretation of the English Regency style (*see* p.16). One of the best-known cabinet-makers was Charles-Honoré Lannuier (*see* p.37).

■ This style of furniture is usually of monumental proportions.

■ Animal-paw feet are commonly found on this type of furniture and are inspired by designs from classical Greece. Other popular motifs included cornucopiae, dolphins, swans and rosettes.

■ In the example above, the arms scroll out and the crest scrolls down; this is another feature borrowed from classical Greece.

Chaise-longue

The light and elegant Regency chaise-longue was gradually replaced, from the 1820s, by a heavier and more florid style. This example is made from bird's-eye maple with parcel gilt (partially gilded) decoration.

■ Exaggerated carving was increasingly fashionable at this time, as you can see in the leaf-carved frame and the heavy, tapered legs.

■ The asymmetrical curves of the seat rail and the scrolled end have been emphasized in what, today, seems a rather heavy-handed manner. They are embellished with leaf-form carvings and parcel gilt.

**Victorian chaise-longue,
*c.*1840 [G]**

Rococo Revival sofa, 1850–60 [A]

Belter sofa

The Rococo Revival was fashionable in the USA between the 1840s and the 1860s. This rosewood sofa is attributed to John Henry Belter, one of the leading exponents of the style.

■ Belter is best known for laminated rosewood furniture made using his patented technique, developed between 1847 and 1858. Sheets of rosewood were glued together, steam-moulded into elaborate shapes and then pierced and carved with leaves, fruits and flowers.

**Louis XVI Revival sofa,
*c.*1870 [I]**

Canapé

The 18th-century Louis XVI style enjoyed a revival in France during the Second Empire (1852–70). The *canapé* (a type of sofa), was popularly made in the Louis XVI style.

■ This sofa employs many of the Classical motifs associated with the Louis XIV style, such as rams' heads and quivers of arrows. However, like many Revival pieces, it lacks the elegant proportions of the originals. The carved cresting is slightly too large, and the fluted legs slightly too short.

Story of Storage Furniture

Italian walnut *cassone*,
late 16th century [F]

BEFORE THE 17TH CENTURY, *the chest was used to store all household items. A major innovation was introduced in the mid-17th century when a drawer was incorporated within the chest. This useful addition was the forerunner of many variations in chests and drawers that were adopted over the centuries for different regional and national types of storage furniture.*

The chest was one of the earliest types of furniture. It had been used in Ancient Egypt for storing linen and valuables. By the Middle Ages, it was the most important type of furniture in many wealthy households, where it was used not only for storage but could also double up as a table, seat or even a bed. Construction and decoration varied from lidded boxes on legs to elaborate carved chests of frame-and-panel construction.

The difficulty of retrieving items stored at the bottom of a chest resulted, in the mid-17th century, in a major break-through in design when a drawer was incorporated into the base of the chest or coffer. By the end of the 17th century the

The two chests-of-drawers in this 19th-century painting by William Henry Hunt, Girl at Prayer, *are a reminder of their importance as storage furniture from the 17th century onwards.*

The chest-on-chest is often referred to as a double chest-of-drawers. Many of the finest examples of this type of storage chest were made in the USA. This walnut chest-on-chest (c.1760–80) is of very good quality and was made in Philadephia – an important centre of American furniture from the mid-18th century. [D]

This English oak chest (below; late 17th century) is of frame-and-panel construction and has been carved and inlaid. [J]

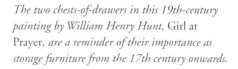

simple chest with a drawer had evolved into the chest-of-drawers. The other solution to the problem of storing the increasing quantities of household linen was the upright cupboard, known as an linen-press, or armoire. During the second half of the 17th century, this also developed – with distinct regional variations – and had shelves enclosed by two long doors and a heavy base that sometimes incorporated a storage drawer.

During the 18th century, new forms of storage furniture based on different combinations of chests and drawers evolved. These included the chest-on-stand, the chest-on-chest and smaller chests-of-drawers, such as the bachelor's chest. Towards the end of the century, the role of the early serving table was assumed by a new form of the sideboard. This combined a flat surface for the display of food

By the mid-18th century, the commode had an established place in the fashionable English household. This satinwood example (c.1910), with painted and inlaid decoration, is a copy of an 18th-century Sheraton original. [H]

and silver, with drawers and cupboards for storage. From the mid-18th century, under the influence of French furniture-makers, the straight-sided chest-of-drawers was transformed into a fashionable curvaceous commode. Although the curving lines were gradually replaced by the straighter Neo-classical shape, the commode remained popular.

During the 19th century, established types of storage furniture were produced in a wide range of Revival styles. The side cabinet enjoyed a golden age with the introduction of new types – such as the chiffonier and the credenza – and the revival of decorative techniques such as *pietre dure* (semi-precious stones) and boulle work. The wardrobe, meanwhile, evolved from the armoire and linen-press to provide a hanging space for clothes that had previously been folded for storage.

The heavy proportions of this armoire (c.1790) are typical of Dutch linen-presses of this period. [G]

Made in New York c.1795, this sideboard is a high-quality piece of Federal furniture – as can be seen from the fine proportions and the highly figured mahogany and satinwood veneers. [A]

Marquetry

The technique of marquetry has its origins in Renaissance Italian inlay work. It is a highly skilled craft whereby small, differently shaped pieces of coloured and exotic woods are arranged in pleasing designs and applied to a piece of furniture to form a decorative covering. It was one of the major forms of decoration used by Dutch and Flemish cabinet-makers. The high point of floral marquetry, inspired by contemporary Dutch still-life paintings, was between *c.*1660 and 1700.

English marquetry chest-of-drawers, *c.*1690 [C]

A CLOSER LOOK Oak Chests

One of the earliest types of furniture is the oak chest. By the 17th century, chests were largely made using the frame-and-panel construction. The front and sides of a frame-and-panel chest comprise top and bottom horizontal rails (the frames), which fit into vertical bars, or stiles, at each end; these often continue downward to form 'stile' feet. On the best examples, the panels, which were made of thin planks of wood, were shaped to fit into grooves in this framework. The panels were then secured in place by hand-shaped wooden pegs. The most common type of decoration was a simple carved design, used on the front panels only. From the late 19th century, oak chests were reproduced in large numbers.

▲ The vertical bar (known as a **muntin**) has been carved in a curve to fit the frame neatly. This is a sign of good-quality mid-17th century chests. **Handcut pegs** were used in furniture construction at this time; note how the heads of the pegs have been pushed out as the oak has shrunk.

▲ If you look at the back of the chest you can see the **hinges** on the back of the lid. The original wire hinges, which would have been subjected to considerable wear, have been replaced with more robust 18th-century metal hinges.

◀ On early chests, the carving was usually confined to the front panels. Here you can see the **depth** and **irregularity** of the **handcarving**. Early chests that were decorated at a later date tend to have shallower, more mechanical carving.

English oak chest, c.1650
The rich, dark colour (patination) of this chest identifies it as an early chest. Other signs of good quality include handcarving – arcading (linked arches) on the top rail, guilloche (figure-of-eight motif) on the bottom rail and stylized flowers on the stiles that run all the way down to the bottom of the feet. [G]

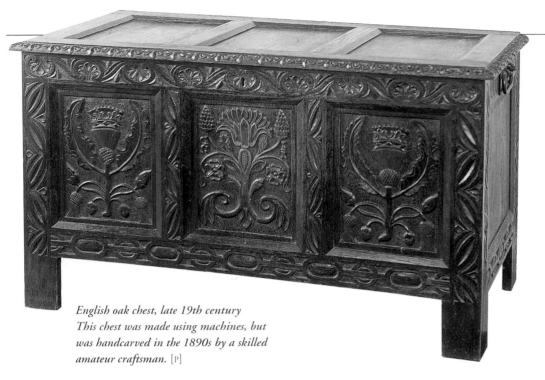

English oak chest, late 19th century
This chest was made using machines, but
was handcarved in the 1890s by a skilled
amateur craftsman. [P]

▲ Look out for **carving** on the **side panels**. This is a feature often associated with Victorian or later chests. However, on later chests you will not find the same build up of dirt in the crevices as in earlier examples.

◀ When you lift the lid, you can see that the lines of the **sides** are straight, flat and **uniform**. This confirms that the wood used to make this chest was **cut by machine** – it has none of the irregularities associated with handcut timber.

▶ Many plain 17th-century and even 19th-century chests were 'improved' by carving at a later date. In this detail you can see how the **muntin** has been **machine cut** to fit into the top and bottom rails. The most tell-tale sign of a later date, however, is the **crisp, sharp decoration** that has not been worn and softened by centuries of use.

The Age of Oak

Throughout the Middle Ages and up until the late 17th century, furniture-makers used mainly indigenous timbers. Oak was widely available in Britain and Europe and was the preferred wood for better-quality furniture because it was resistant to woodworm and rot. Although it was gradually superseded by walnut for fashionable furniture, oak continued to be used for country furniture and enjoyed a revival in the 19th century.

English oak chest with carved linenfold panels, mid-16th-century [G]

▲ Another clue to the 19th-century origins of this chest is the **carved edge** of the lid.

A CLOSER LOOK *Chest-of-Drawers*

The chest-of-drawers was a new form of furniture that was introduced in the late 17th century and developed from that time onwards. On early examples, you will notice that the joiners used the basic pegged, mortise-and-tenon joint construction that can be found on frame-and-panel chests and coffers (*see* p.66). By the 18th century, chests-of-drawers were being produced in some quantity and in different styles. One of these was the so-called bachelor's chest. Designed, as the name suggests, for a bachelor's apartment, this was a versatile piece of furniture that was used to store clothes, toiletries or writing materials. Chests-of-drawers were rarely made of solid wood. Most had a carcass (basic frame) made of a cheap indigenous timber, such as pine or oak, covered in a veneer of more expensive wood: walnut was most commonly used in England until *c*.1740, after which mahogany was preferred. One of the best-quality mahoganies is known as 'flame' or 'fiddleback' and its grain looks 'feathered'.

English bachelor's chest, c.1750
This chest is veneered in mahogany, but at
this time, it is not uncommon to find other
examples that are veneered in walnut. [G]

▶ Although the fronts of the drawers are veneered, the carcass is made of oak. See how the **grain** of the wood runs from the **front to the back** of the drawer; this is a typical 18th-century feature. On 19th-century drawers, it runs from side to side.

▲ Open the top drawer and you will see how versatile it is. Hidden at the side of the drawer is a **swing-out section** that may have been used for keeping an inkwell (look for tell-tale stains). The **different compartments** in the drawer were designed to hold writing accessories or toiletries. A pull-out slide covered in green baize would have been used as a desk or a surface for brushing and folding clothes.

▲ Pull out a drawer and look at it from the side. Here you can see the thick **veneered front**, the neat **dovetail joints**, and the slight **discoloration** at the front, the result of years of handling and exposure to light when the drawer was not fully closed.

▲ A good test of whether the drawers are original is to check that the irregular **ridged wear** on the **runners** and sides matches the wear on the main carcass, seen here. (Runners are fixed to the bottom of the drawers and can be seen in the photograph above.)

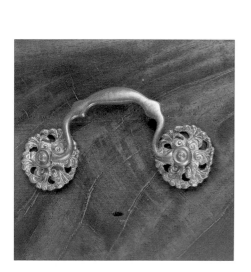

▲ This brass handle, although quite old, is actually a replacement. By lifting it up you can see where, over the years, the original handle has knocked against the wood, causing a distinctive blackish **'bruise' mark**. To check whether a handle has been replaced, you should also look inside the drawer for holes, which will show where the original handle would have been secured.

Veneering

The technique of veneering involves glueing a layer of expensive or exotic wood on to a carcass of less valuable timber. Veneers were first used in Britain at the end of the 17th century and by the early 18th century were widely employed . The handcut veneers of the 17th and 18th centuries are almost always thicker than the regular, machine-cut veneers of the 19th and 20th centuries, which are almost paper-thin. Sheets of veneer were arranged to form patterns ('oyster' veneering is an example of this) or cut into thin strips to trim drawers and table edges. The technique was also adapted for marquetry decoration (*see* p.65).

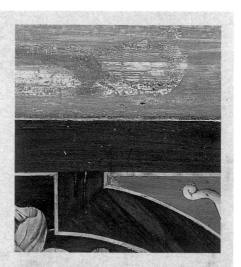

French veneering (early 18th century) on an oak carcass.

Types of Chest-of-Drawers

English chest-of-drawers, *c*.1695 [C]

'Seaweed' marquetry chest-of-drawers

The use of walnut, swing drop handles, bun feet and 'seaweed' marquetry (so called because it looks like seaweed) are characteristic of good-quality chests-of-drawers made in the late 17th and early 18th century.

■ Chests-of-drawers of this period have often had their bun feet replaced with bracket feet. Always check underneath chests-of-drawers for signs such as old holes, which indicate the position of the original feet.

■ Look for 'bruise' marks where the handles have hit the wood.

Commode

The term 'commode' is French for chest-of-drawers. This particular design was developed in the late 17th century.

■ This superb example, with parquetry (geometric-pattern marquetry) in exotic woods, has been attributed to Charles Cressent.

■ The bulging shape of the commode is known as '*bombé*'.

■ If you look inside the drawers of an early example, you will see that the carcass (basic frame) is made from oak or pine.

French Rococo commode, *c*.1730 [A]

Bachelor's chest

The bachelor's chest was one of the styles of chests-of-drawers that evolved during the 18th century. This example has the narrower proportions introduced *c*.1710, which were popular until the mid-18th century.

■ The rectangular fold-over top could be used either for folding and brushing clothes, or as a writing surface. When opened out, the top is supported on two pull stops at the front of the chest.

■ The typical drawer configuration on this type of furniture was two short drawers over three long drawers, as shown in this example.

■ Introduced in the early 18th century, the bracket foot was widely used until *c*.1750.

English mahogany bachelor's chest, *c*.1740 [E]

American highboy, 1760–80 [A]

High chest-of-drawers

High chests-of-drawers, or highboys as they are now known in the USA, were first made in England at the end of the 17th century. By the early 1730s, however, they had become almost exclusive to the American colonies.

■ Typically for the mid-18th century, this piece is made in two sections – an upper section with graduated drawers and a lower case standing on cabriole legs.

■ Specifically American features include the closed broken pediment (triangular gable) with turned urn finials, the elaborate shaped apron (ornamental 'skirt') on the base, and the slender legs.

■ The appeal of this example lies in the mellow patination of the figured walnut and its excellent condition.

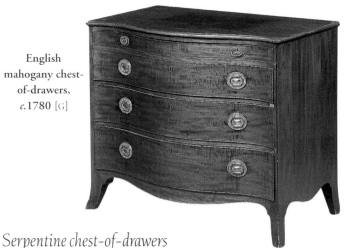

English mahogany chest-of-drawers, c.1780 [G]

American chest-of-drawers, c.1810 [F]

Serpentine chest-of-drawers

The 'serpentine' (gently bulging) front of this English mahogany chest of drawers was a common feature from c.1750 to the end of the 18th century. Here it has been echoed in the shaped apron at the bottom.

■ The shallow top drawer, which is fitted with a mirror and divisions, would have been used for storing trinkets and smaller items. The three long graduated drawers would have been used for larger items.

■ The splayed bracket feet are a typical late 18th-century feature.

■ Look inside the drawers to see if the handles have been replaced.

■ This style of chest is more desirable if it has serpentine sides – this example has straight sides.

Federal chest-of-drawers

With its light, delicate form and use of finely figured veneer, this chest-of-drawers is characteristic of the early Federal style, which lasted from c.1795 to c.1815, when it was replaced by the American 'Classical' style.

■ The colour contrast between the dark mahogany and flame birch veneer is a typical feature of good-quality Federal furniture.

■ The turned feet on this example are slightly taller than those found on similar English pieces of the same period.

■ Although the elaborate cast handles and escutcheons (ornamental plates around keyholes) are authentic, they are quite unusual; normally during this period these would be more Neo-classical in style.

Campaign chest

Thought to have been introduced during the years of the Peninsular War (1809–14), and made throughout the 19th century, campaign chests were constructed in two parts so that they would fit into a crate and could be moved about with their owner. This example can be dated to the mid-1830s by the style of the feet.

■ Campaign chests normally have inset flush handles – here in brass – and feet that can be unscrewed to facilitate packing and moving.

■ The top drawer in the centre includes a drop-front compartment for storing letters.

■ Teak examples are also relatively common.

English Wellington chest, 1845 [H]

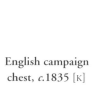

English campaign chest, c.1835 [K]

Wellington chest

Although allegedly invented by the Duke of Wellington, this type of chest closely resembles a kind of narrow French chest with seven drawers that was used to store linen for each day of the week. Introduced c.1820, it became a standard piece of furniture throughout the 19th century.

■ The number of graduated drawers varies – some examples have as many as twelve.

■ They usually have simple wooden knob handles and are invariably locked by one or both of the hinged right- and left-hand stiles (uprights).

■ This example is veneered with burr-walnut, but many different types of wood were used, including mahogany.

Types of Wardrobe & Linen-Press

Provincial armoire

The term 'armoire' is French for a type of closed cupboard used for storing linen and other valuables. This carved walnut armoire is typical of an early 18th-century French provincial piece.

■ The bun feet (often replaced) and carved roundels (round, carved ornament) are both early 18th-century features.

■ Provincial armoires were made in different local woods, but usually a type of fruitwood, such as walnut or cherry.

■ Good examples, have such ornament as ivory studs – seen here in the centre of the roundels.

French walnut armoire, early 18th century [F]

Louis XV armoire

This type of armoire, with a domed top and shaped frieze, was a common form from *c.*1730–770.

■ Unlike earlier examples, this type of armoire was not carved. Instead, decoration takes the form of 'quarter' veneering (where the veneers were cut into quarters) and crossbanding on the doors, together with applied ormolu (gilt-bronze) mounts.

■ More luxurious armoires have more elaborate inlaid decoration and a greater number of ormolu mounts.

French armoire, *c.*1750 [E]

Armoire

The waved moulding and carved decoration on the long panelled doors of this provincial armoire help to date it to the second half of the 18th century.

■ The shaped apron below the doors is pegged at the front and the sides.

■ These pieces were often made as wedding gifts and carved with doves, the couple's initials and a date.

■ This is a modest provincial piece, made in indigenous oak. More expensive armoires were made with elaborate veneers and ormolu mounts.

French provincial oak armoire, mid-18th century [I]

Linen-press

The linen-press is a two-piece combination of a closed cupboard with adjustable shelves over a chest-of-drawers. It was produced from the mid-18th century through to the early 19th, when it was gradually replaced by the more practical wardrobe.

■ Good-quality examples such as this will have a pull-out slide for brushing and folding clothes, drawers of graduated sizes lined with oak or mahogany, and often some decoration.

■ More modest provincial examples were made in oak or pine, with pine-lined drawers, and without the slide and carved decoration.

English mahogany linen-press, *c.*1755 [E]

Linen-press

Linen-presses made in the Low Countries were generally of huge proportions with a heavy cornice (horizontal top). This shape was used throughout the 18th and 19th centuries.

■ Characteristically Dutch features include extravagant floral marquetry and heavily carved walnut decoration.

■ Oversized linen-presses such as these were designed to come apart so that they could be easily reassembled if the owners decided to move house.

Dutch walnut linen-press, early 19th century [F]

Regency linen-press

Made in the early 19th century, this mahogany linen-press has the arched pediment and ebony inlay often found on pieces made from 1805 to 1830.

■ An unusual and attractive feature is the bow front – a straight front is more commonly found.

■ The well-figured veneered doors conceal sliding trays used for storing clothes; sometimes these have been removed.

■ The bow front, figured timber and restrained ebony inlay are typical of a good-quality piece; a more luxurious version would have a greater amount of elaborate inlay.

Regency linen-press, c.1810 [H]

Victorian wardrobe

Late 19th-century wardrobes, such as this example, are frequently a confused combination of styles and a mixture of decoration.

■ The mirrored door, hanging space inside and ornament are all 19th-century features. They are combined with 18th-century style decoration including Sèvres-style porcelain plaques and elaborate ormolu mounts.

■ Late 19th-century wardrobes were also made with plain doors. Check that the veneers match – a plain door may be a replacement for a damaged mirrored door.

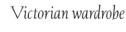

English mahogany wardrobe, late 19th century [G]

English satinwood wardrobe, c.1880 [E]

Sheraton Revival wardrobe

Furniture in the Sheraton Revival style was a popular choice for middle-class homes from c.1870–c.1920.

■ Two distinctly 19th-century features are the arched panels on the doors (18th-century panels had flat tops) and the central hanging space.

■ Much of the wardrobe's appeal lies in the marquetry decoration. The classical-style motifs include ribbon-tied urns, leaves and husks.

A Closer Look *Closed Dresser*

The type of dresser shown here evolved from the 17th-century side table with drawers. These began to be made with cupboards below the drawers and then, from the mid- to late 17th century, acquired a rack or set of shelves on top of the table. The rack was used to display pewter and ceramics. Such dressers were important pieces of furniture in rural areas, particularly in Wales, north-west and south-west England, where distinct regional types developed. Therefore, many variations exist, including some with spice cupboards set into the shelves and others with a central open space below. The closed dresser shown here, is so called because the shelves are closed in with a back. The break (protruding) front and T-drawer configuration, with a central bank of drawers beneath the side drawers, is common on dressers made in North Wales.

◀ Compare the **handles** and **handle plates** carefully, since often these **do not match** because, over the years, many have been replaced

◀ Pull out a drawer and you will see that **beading** has been nailed over the **dovetail joints** to conceal their construction. This is a particular feature of dressers from Wales.

▲ If handles have been replaced, you will notice empty **holes** inside the drawer – this is where the originals were fixed. In this example, you can see that the original **nut fixings** are still in place on the pine-lined drawers.

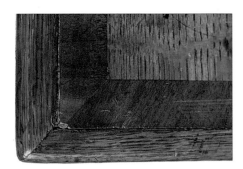

▲ Most Welsh dressers were made of oak. Another typically Welsh feature is the use of **mahogany crossbanding**, as shown here.

▶ See how the **crossbanding** carries through to the **back** of the dresser; this suggests that it may have originally been made without a rack. Crossbanding was expensive and would not have been used for an area that was hidden from view.

▲ The oak rack has been 'closed' at the back with **stained pine boards**. The backing is of a **tongue-and-groove** construction, which has been nailed into position.

Other Dressers

The style of a dresser is often a good indication of where it was made, although dating can be more difficult, since traditional designs were little influenced by contemporary fashions. Dressers made in North Wales and north-west England usually have closed racks above a base with drawers and cupboards; dressers made in South Wales and south-west England usually have an open base, with a pot board below, and an open rack of shelves above. Those made in mid-Wales often combine southern and northern features with closed racks above an open base with a pot board.

Oak and elm open dresser, 1750–75 [F]

Closed dresser, mid-18th century
This example from Gwynedd features the break front typical of North Wales dressers. [F]

Types of Cabinet

Cabinet-on-stand

This type of cabinet contains drawers for storing precious items. It was popular both in England and Holland between 1680 and 1720.

■ The superb quality of this cabinet lies in its floral marquetry decoration, influenced by Dutch examples.

■ On more modest pieces, the stand would have been less ornately carved. Here the barley-twists all turn the same way; on later examples they alternate.

■ The stands are fragile and have often been reduced in height. When full

English walnut cabinet-on-stand, *c.*1690 [D]

height, the top of the chest would have been invisible, and was, therefore, not veneered. Stands that have been reduced in height have often been veneered at a later date.

Cabinet-on-stand

Dating from the early 18th century, this type of cabinet is an imitation of a fashionable lacquer cabinet made in China for the European market in the late 17th or early 18th century.

■ European versions with japanned decoration were usually made in blue, black, dark green or scarlet.

■ The giltwood base, with shell-carved apron (decorative 'skirt' at the front), leaf-carved cabriole legs and pad feet, is pure early 18th-century English. Very often the giltwood bases have been damaged.

English cabinet-on-stand, early 18th century [E]

■ Look carefully to see if the decoration has been restored or is very chipped or worn, since this will largely determine the appeal and value of the piece.

Corner cupboard

The corner cupboard is an eminently practical, triangular standing corner cupboard that was introduced *c.*1750.

■ The glazing bars are unusual and elaborate – 13 octagonal panes are more usually found.

■ A sign of good quality is the inlaid sycamore stringing on the door, which also identifies the time of manufacture as the late 18th century. Earlier examples would have been plainer.

■ Standing corner cupboards were made in different woods. More luxurious drawing-room pieces, which were used to display precious objects or books, were made in mahogany.

English mahogany corner cupboard, *c.*1790 [G]

Chiffonier

Made from *c.*1800, this type of cabinet usually has a shelf supported by brackets and an enclosed cupboard or drawers beneath. Chiffoniers were often used as a type of sideboard.

■ Rosewood and mahogany were the most popular woods employed.

■ The panels of the doors could be of silvered glass or have pleated silk panels (which have often been replaced); on some, they are covered by a latticed brass grille.

Regency chiffonier, *c.*1820 [H]

■ Regency chiffoniers tend to have rectangular door panels, while those on Victorian examples are usually arched.

■ The craftsmanship on Victorian chiffoniers is generally not of the best quality and they have often been altered to look like Regency examples.

**English credenza,
c.1860 [H]**

Credenza

The credenza – a large D-shaped cabinet with storage or display shelves at either end – was named after a type of early Italian sideboard and was fashionable in the second half of the 19th century.

■ This walnut example has a straight front with bowed ends; pieces with serpentine fronts are even more sought after.

■ Other distinguishing features of more expensive examples are well figured veneers and good-quality porcelain plaques.

■ Check the veneer carefully because sometimes restoration work has been concealed by painted graining.

Cabinet-on-stand

Magnificent cabinets-on-stands were made in northern Italy in the late 19th century. These pieces are reminiscent of the very fine ebony-veneered Baroque cabinets that were made from the 1590s to the 1640s, particularly in Naples and Spain.

■ The quality of the ivory inlay – a typical Italian feature – and the luxurious decoration suggest that it was made for an international exhibition.

■ One important point that distinguishes this as a southern European piece is the drawer linings – these are always walnut or a softwood on Italian examples.

■ These cabinets often conceal hidden drawers and compartments.

Italian cabinet-on-stand, c.1880 [C]

Side cabinet

Ebonized (stained in imitation of ebony) cabinets of this type reflect the Japanese influence behind the Aesthetic Movement popular in Britain from the 1860s to the 1880s.

■ The decoration on such pieces is restrained and relies on contrasting decorative woods and Japanese-style gilt panels.

English side cabinet, c.1880 [K]

■ Ebonized wood was a particular hallmark of Aesthetic furniture. You should always check carefully for areas where the ebonizing has rubbed off, revealing a paler wood underneath.

■ Well-known manufacturers included Gillows of Lancaster and Lamb of Manchester; a manufacturer's stamp will add value and desirability.

■ Very exclusive cabinets of this type were made by E. G. Godwin.

Display cabinet

Designed for a middle-class drawing-room, this satinwood display cabinet is in the Sheraton Revival style that was popular in the late 19th and early 20th century. The top part would have been used for books or ceramics.

■ The narrower scale, suitable for the smaller Edwardian interiors, distinguishes it from an 18th-century original.

■ The inlay decoration on the cornice is a typical Sheraton Revival feature.

■ The figured satinwood veneers, oval inlay panels and elaborate glazing bars (carved with the Prince of Wales's feathers) are all signs of quality.

Satinwood display cabinet, c.1910 [G]

Story of Library Furniture

English walnut escritoire, c.1700 [F]

BEFORE THE 18TH CENTURY, *book ownership was largely the preserve of monasteries, universities and the upper classes. The private library – with its bookcases, writing desks, bureaux and chairs – developed largely during the late 18th and early 19th centuries. There was a corresponding flowering of library furniture at this time.*

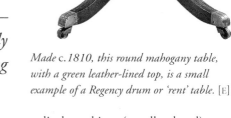

Made c.1810, this round mahogany table, with a green leather-lined top, is a small example of a Regency drum or 'rent' table. [E]

The domestic bookcase did not emerge until the 18th century, when the number of private people owning books increased. These bookcases varied from the large, grand break-front version, with a glazed upper section over drawers below, to a more modest bookcase element placed on top of a writing bureau. The top half of a display cabinet (usually glazed) was also used for books, with the bottom half kept for storage. In the 19th century, book ownership became increasingly common and further variations on book storage were introduced. These included revolving circular and rectangular bookcases, and open bookshelves mounted on casters.

Lili Cartwright's painting, Mr Cartwright's Study at Aynhoe, 1835, offers an insight into the different types of library furniture that had developed by the early 19th century. These included the pedestal desk, the rolltop desk and the library bergère with caned sides.

This magnificent break-front (protruding central section) mahogany bookcase, with a broken pediment and adjustable bookshelves, was probably based on a design from Thomas Chippendale's influential The Gentleman and Cabinet-Maker's Director *(1754). The panelled doors conceal further bookshelves. The bold architectural design was common on mid-18th century bookcases intended for grand libraries.* [B]

The writing table or desk has a longer and more complex history. The early portable writing box, with a sloping top, evolved into the escritoire – a writing cabinet on a stand – in which the flat front could be let down to form a writing surface, revealing small drawers and pigeon holes for storage. This feature is also found on the secretaire, which, after the early 18th century, gradually replaced the escritoire.

The bureau, like the escritoire, was another shape that evolved in France in the mid-17th century. This term is used for a flat-topped writing table with drawers, or a type of furniture with a sloping or curved lid to the writing surface. French furniture-makers were largely responsible for the many variations on both types. These included, in the 17th century, the *bureau Mazarin*, a writing table with eight legs and two banks of drawers flanking an open kneehole; and in the 18th century, the *bureau plat*, in which the banks of drawers were replaced by single drawers with a shallow drawer in the kneehole space. Also introduced at this time were the rolltop *bureau à cylindre* and the *bonheur du jour*, a lady's writing table.

Other new English types of writing table included the drum table, introduced *c.*1760, and, in the late 18th century, the light, elegant desk designed for and named after Carlton House – the residence of the Prince Regent. However, the pedestal desk remained popular during the 19th century and into the 20th, when it was interpreted in Art Nouveau and Art Deco styles.

Gillows of Lancaster

Founded in Lancaster *c.*1730, this firm of furniture manufacturers had by 1769 opened showrooms in London's Oxford Street. The factory made furniture for both the export and home markets, in particular for the wealthy middle classes of nearby Liverpool and Manchester. In the late 18th and early 19th centuries, Gillows was among the first to make and popularize new forms such as the Davenport desk and the quartetto nest of tables. The company's reputation for quality materials, fine construction and good workmanship allowed it to flourish, particularly during the era of historical revivals in the 19th century, when Gillows made furniture in Gothic Revival style after designs by members of the Arts & Crafts Movement.

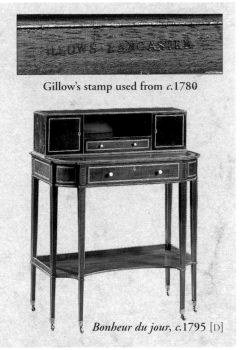

Gillow's stamp used from *c.*1780

Bonheur du jour, *c.*1795 [D]

This rosewood flat-topped library table was made c.1825, possibly by Gillows of Lancaster, since it is very similar to an 1823 design in the company's Estimate Sketch Books. [F]

The pedestal desk was first introduced into Britain in the first half of the 18th century, and is still in production today. It is both a practical and impressive item of furniture, which is at home in a grand library or a private study. The drawers, in moulded plinths, provide ample storage space. The large writing surface is covered with a tooled leather top. There is plenty of knee space, as well as writing space. This mahogany example was made c.1840. [F]

A Closer Look *Bureau Bookcase*

The bureau bookcase was a popular piece of library furniture from the mid-18th century onwards. This example is a 'marriage' of an 18th-century mahogany bureau – with its bracket feet, dovetail joints and construction typical of the period – with a late 19th-century mahogany bookcase. When you look at a bureau bookcase, check to see whether the two elements match: they should be made of the same type and quality of wood, which should be of the same colour and patination, and any mouldings and decorative details should also be the same. The bookcase here, made at the end of the 19th century, has been glazed with astragals in a pseudo-Gothic style. The interior of the 18th-century bureau has been pierced at a later date to give a 'Gothic' feel and match the style of the bookcase. A closer look at both elements reveals further discrepancies, providing overwhelming evidence that the bureau and bookshelves are a later marriage rather than an original coupling.

English bureau bookcase, c.1750 and later
Proportions are one of the first things to consider when you stand back from a piece of furniture such as this. Here you can see how the bookcase looks too squat for it to belong to the bureau beneath. [J]

◀ As with dressers, the shelves of bookcases were often a **later addition**. If you look at this bureau bookcase from the side, you can see how the bookcase **overhangs** the back of the bureau. This suggests that these bookshelves were not made at the same time as the bureau.

◄ The front of a drawer can give valuable clues as to whether the **handles** are original to the piece. Look carefully and you can see the **darkish outline** that shows where the old handle used to be. This is probably the result of a build-up of cleaning agents, polish and dirt that have become clogged around the edge.

▼ The bookcase can be removed from the bureau, allowing you to look underneath. Here you can see that the top of the bureau is **veneered** – further confirmation that this bureau was originally made without shelves. Had it been designed with shelves, the top would have been concealed and the veneer therefore superfluous.

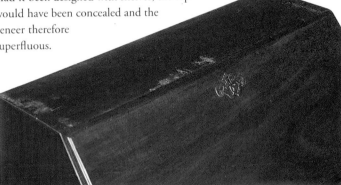

▲ The **backs** of furniture such as bureau bookcases are fairly basic, since they were not meant to be seen. In this detail you can see how the wood on the bureau runs **horizontally**, while that on the bookcase runs **vertically** – another clue to suggest that these two pieces of furniture were never intended for each other.

▲ The evidence for replacement handles on the front of the drawer is further confirmed when you look inside the drawers. In this detail you can see the **holes** where the original handles would have been fixed.

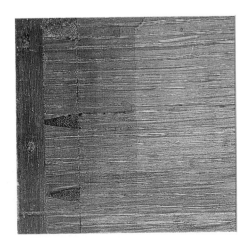

▲ Pull out the drawer and you can see the neat handmade **dovetail joints**, the thick **mahogany handcut veneer** and the **oak drawer lining**. These features are all characteristic of the Georgian furniture.

The Age of Mahogany

Although one of the most widely used woods in British furniture-making, mahogany is not native to Europe. The strong, fine-grained timber, which can vary in colour from pale to dark reddish brown, was imported into Britain from South America and the West Indies. Four main types, based on the country of origin, were used: Jamaican, San Domingan (often known as Spanish mahogany), Cuban and Honduras. Mahogany is highly resistant to woodworm and warping and ideally suited to high-quality, crisp carving. From c.1730, mahogany swiftly became established as a highly popular wood with both British and American furniture-makers, who used it to make solid furniture and as a veneer for a range of furniture types. It was not widely used on the Continent until the 1760s.

Bureau bookcase, c.1790 [F]

81

Types of Writing Desk

French *bureau Mazarin*,
late 17th century [A]

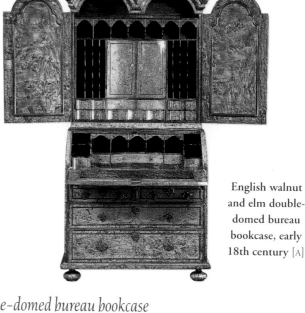

English walnut
and elm double-
domed bureau
bookcase, early
18th century [A]

Bureau Mazarin

Made from the late 17th century through to the early 18th, the
bureau Mazarin – named after the French cardinal and chief minister
of Louis XIV– was revived by manufacturers in the 19th century.

■ The superb quality of this example is evident in the use of boulle
work (a type of marquetry), with brass and red tortoiseshell inlay.

■ The mounts on the corners are exceptionally crisp and detailed.

Double-domed bureau bookcase

The double-domed top was introduced into English furniture *c*.1700.

■ The elaborate shaped cornice, fitted interior and serpentine-fronted
drawers would be found on only very expensive examples.

■ Check that the top and bottom were made at the same time. Tell-tale
signs include differently coloured woods and different drawer linings.

English tambour
desk, *c*.1790 [C]

Desk-and-bookcase

The combination of two
short drawers beneath a
glazed bookcase, seen here
on a Federal desk-and-
bookcase, is a typical feature
of American furniture.

■ Another American feature
is the protruding rectangular
secretary drawer, on turned
supports and with a hinged
flip-top writing surface.

■ The brass finials are also
common on American
pieces. Here they are both
original and in good
condition, which enhances
the value and appeal of this
piece of furniture.

Tambour desk

The tambour (roll front) desk was particularly popular between *c*.1770
and 1790. Copies were made in the later 19th century.

■ Outstanding features of this type of desk are marquetry decoration
and crossbanding.

■ The decoration continues on the back of the desk, an indication
that this piece was designed to stand in the centre of the room.

American mahogany desk-
and-bookcase, 1800–20 [F]

Secrétaire à abbatant

The *secrétaire à abbatant* was a popular French desk, introduced in the mid-18th century, in which the top section dropped down to reveal a leather-lined writing surface. This mahogany example is in the French Empire style, which was popular in Europe and the USA from *c.*1810.

■ As you can see here, the restrained, severe form relies largely on the use of well-figured veneer for decoration.

■ If you look inside some examples, you will find elaborately fitted interiors with small drawers, pigeon holes and bookshelves in the top section and larger drawers in the bottom section.

French *secrétaire à abbatant*, *c.*1810 [G]

Davenport

The Davenport was introduced *c.*1810, and was made throughout the 19th century.

■ Davenports were made in different woods; rosewood and mahogany were both used, but walnut was especially popular. This example is made in very desirable and beautifully figured burr-walnut.

■ Other signs of quality are the storage drawers, concealed by the leather writing flap, and the round escutcheons around the high-quality locks.

■ With a finished back, this desk was designed to stand in the centre of the room; those with unfinished backs stood against the wall.

English burr-walnut Davenport, *c.*1835 [G]

Kidney-shaped writing table

This type of delicate shaped writing table (a table with drawers in the frieze) was a phenomenon of the mid-19th century.

■ The quality of the neatly turned legs on this example adds to the appeal and value, as does the original inset leather top.

■ Always look out for pieces by well-known makers. This table has been stamped on the cedar-lined drawer with the name of Johnstone Jeanes & Co., who supplied furniture to the royal family.

English walnut writing desk, *c.*1850 [G]

French kingwood *bureau plat*, late 19th century [B]

Bureau plat

The *bureau plat* is a long, flat writing desk, usually with two or three drawers, which was popular in France from the late 17th century.

■ The proportions of 19th-century copies are often more cumbersome than those of the original desks.

■ This *bureau plat* is by François Linke, one of the greatest exponents of Louis XVI Revival furniture in the late 19th century. Any piece by Linke will be very expensive and highly sought after.

Ceramics

COLLECTORS OF CERAMICS are spoilt for choice, since both useful and decorative items have been produced in far greater numbers than any other type of antique, especially since the 17th century. Moreover, an enormous quantity of pieces has also managed to survive from ancient China and Egypt, classical Greece and Rome. They have been fashioned in a wide range of styles and shapes, making use of many different decorative effects. Identification of specific pieces, particularly those from more recent times, can often be achieved by reference to manufacturers' and decorators' marks, as well as company design books. More often, however, establishing the desirability and worth of a piece requires more sophisticated detective work. Essentially this involves developing a knowledge of how a piece was made and decorated as well as keeping abreast of market trends – a process that can be as rewarding as collecting itself.

Worcester basket, *c.*1770 [H]

How to Look at Ceramics

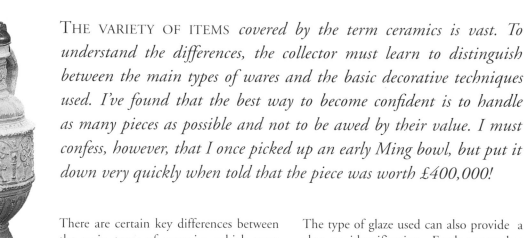

Siegburg was best known for its refined white stoneware, such as this tankard (1601). Many early wares will show some signs of everyday wear, but usually this does not affect their value. [H]

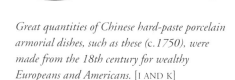

Great quantities of Chinese hard-paste porcelain armorial dishes, such as these (c.1750), were made from the 18th century for wealthy Europeans and Americans. [I AND K]

Majolica wares, such as this maple syrup jug (1880) made by Griffen, Smith & Hill, can now fetch very high prices at auction. [O]

THE VARIETY OF ITEMS *covered by the term ceramics is vast. To understand the differences, the collector must learn to distinguish between the main types of wares and the basic decorative techniques used. I've found that the best way to become confident is to handle as many pieces as possible and not to be awed by their value. I must confess, however, that I once picked up an early Ming bowl, but put it down very quickly when told that the piece was worth £400,000!*

There are certain key differences between the main types of ceramics, which most collectors can learn to recognize quite quickly. Earthenware is opaque, stoneware is usually opaque – although some rare examples are translucent. Porcelain is almost always translucent. Holding a piece up to a strong artificial light will help you determine the type.

It is also vital to get into the habit of studying the colour of the unglazed clay body. This is sometimes visible on the base or foot-rim, but, on pieces that have been glazed all over, the ceramics sleuth must look for a chip or crack.

As a general rule of thumb, the colour of earthenware bodies ranges from the off white of creamware, to the buff colour of Delft and the red-brown of Staffordshire slipware. Stoneware bodies range from off white to dark brown, while porcelain tends to vary from pure white to cream.

One of the hardest things to determine is whether a piece of porcelain is hard paste ('true') or soft paste ('artificial'). If a chipped area has a granular appearance, it suggests that the piece may well be made of soft-paste porcelain. Soft paste is also more absorbent, which means that, if the base is unglazed, it may appear dirty and discoloured. On the other hand, if a chip is smooth and glassy with a sharp flint-like edge, the piece is more likely to be hard paste. I also personally find that when I hold a piece of soft paste, it feels slightly warmer than hard paste. This can be especially apparent if it is held to the face.

The type of glaze used can also provide a clue to identification. Earthenware has been covered with many types of glaze, one of the most common being a thick, white tin glaze. Incidentally, the colour of tin glaze can also help identify where a piece was made. For example, a milky white glaze was used on one type of 17th-century London delftware, while a pale sky blue glaze was applied to some varieties of French faience at that time.

In the case of stoneware, one common way of glazing pieces was to cover them with a salt glaze, which often created a glittery, pitted surface, similar to orange peel. Hard-paste porcelain, however, has always been fired at such high temperatures that the glaze fuses with the body and is generally very thin and hard. Eighteenth-century soft-paste porcelain tends to be more flawed than its hard-paste equivalent. With this type of porcelain, look for a thick, sometimes greenish or bluish glaze, that has 'pooled' in crevices.

Decoration can provide useful pointers to a piece's date. As a general rule, early ceramics are decorated with simple scratched or incised motifs, while later wares, such as porcelain and high-quality earthenware, are often painted or printed. Many types of decoration can be felt with your fingers. Incised decoration, for example, is cut into the surface, while over-glaze enamelling stands proud.

Finally, the sound a piece makes when it is tapped can help determine whether it has been restored. A perfect piece gives a good ring, a restored one merely a dull 'thud'.

*Figures made by Johann
Joachim Kändler, the
chief modeller at
the Meissen factory in
Germany between 1733
and 1775, are quite rare
and extremely sought
after. This group of
figures was made
c.1740. [B]*

MODELLING

When assessing a porcelain group, look at
the overall modelling. Here the figures of a
gentleman and his companion are full of life
and movement. The couple strike a confident
pose and are painted in strong colours, which
all point to a mid-18th century date.

DETAILS

Hard-paste porcelain is renowned for its
finely wrought details. The detailing
on this group is very fine: from the well-
defined fingers to the realistically painted hair.
All indicate a group of figures from the 'golden'
age (c.1730–c.1760) of Meissen.

BASE

Often bases are very simple on early figures
and more complicated on later examples.
In a Meissen piece of this date, expect the
underside of the base to be unglazed.

GILDING

Extremely good, tooled gilding stands
proud of the surface and can be felt.
On this basin the warmish tinge
and high quality points to
18th-century Sèvres.

PAINTING

Look carefully at the quality of
the painted decoration. At Sèvres the
painting was extremely sophisticated,
resembling the best oil painting. In
general, painting carried out in
England is flatter, lacking the
same mastery of perspective.

*The bleu celeste
colour of this basin
(1780) was introduced as a
background colour at Vincennes
(later Sèvres) near Paris in 1752. [G]*

87

Story of Earthenware

Istoriato dish, Urbino, *c.*1520 [D]

IN COUNTRIES OF THE WORLD *as far apart as China and England, earthenware has played a significant role in the history of ceramics. From ancient times it has appeared in many guises, which can be identified mainly by regional differences in glazing and decoration. Italian maiolica, Dutch Delft, English delftware, French and German faience are but a few of the many types made.*

Earthenware is a coarse material that is fired at a relatively low temperature and remains porous. As a result, a glaze must be applied to prevent the body (the mixture from which the vessel is formed) from absorbing moisture.

Simply decorated earthenwares were produced during the Neolithic period in China. By the time of the Tang Dynasty (AD 618–907), ceramic production had become increasingly refined owing to developments in both production techniques and artistry.

Traders took these wares to Arab lands, fostering a pottery industry that was to influence the development of ceramics in the West significantly. Tin-glazed wares, lustrewares, where oxides of gold, silver, or copper are added to create a metallic surface, and blue-and-white wares came to Europe following the Arab invasion of Spain in the 8th century.

The decorative technique most used on European earthenware was tin-glaze. Known as maiolica in Italy, Delft in the Netherlands, delftware in England and faience in France and Germany, tin-glazed pottery was made in much the same way everywhere. Tin oxide was added to a lead glaze, which was then used to cover the earthenware surface with an opaque white layer, similar in colour to porcelain.

Maiolica advanced greatly in Italy during the 15th century. Important centres of production included Deruta, Gubbio, Urbino, Siena and Faenza. Italian potters took their skills to France in the early 16th century, and within a hundred years the style had been adapted to suit French tastes. Faience pottery centres included Nevers, Rouen, Strasbourg and Marseilles.

The Netherlands also played host to immigrant Italian craftsmen in the early

Chinese Sancai Wares

During the Tang Dynasty, potters fashioned a distinctive range of *sancai* (three-colour) figures and vessels from a fine, white earthenware. Created as funerary goods, *sancai* wares were decorated with runny lead glazes with added metallic oxides to produce green (copper) and brown or amber (iron), giving a streaky or mottled appearance. Many pieces, however, also had touches of black and blue.

Tang horse, AD 618–907 [A]

One of the most typical types of German faience, this mid-18th century tankard, known as a Walzenkrug, has been painted with bright enamel colours. Favourite decorations for these vessels included landscapes, birds and animals, figures and buildings, and chinoiseries. [J]

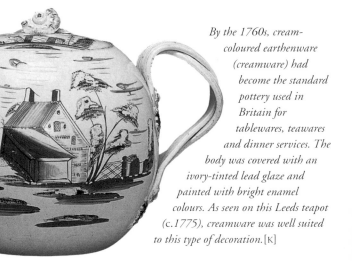

By the 1760s, cream-coloured earthenware (creamware) had become the standard pottery used in Britain for tablewares, teawares and dinner services. The body was covered with an ivory-tinted lead glaze and painted with bright enamel colours. As seen on this Leeds teapot (c.1775), creamware was well suited to this type of decoration. [K]

Created by Josiah Wedgwood as an improvement to his creamware, the body of pearlware was covered with a bluish white glaze. Pearlware was mainly used for domestic wares and were usually adorned with painted or printed decorations. This charming christening bowl (1837) was painted by the highly skilled artist William Fifield of Bristol. [K]

years of the 16th century. Dutch tin-glazed earthenware production flourished in Amsterdam, Haarlem and Rotterdam, but was led by the city of Delft. Wares included blue-and-white and later multicoloured tulip vases, drug jars, dishes and tiles. Dutch potters took this style to Germany, where a faience industry developed.

In Britain, delftware, which took its name from the Dutch town, was mainly produced in London, Bristol and Liverpool, until the late 18th century. Most wares imitated the blue-and-white chinoiserie style, a European imitation of oriental designs, although British themes were adopted from the late

17th century. British potters also developed distinctive types of wares in Staffordshire using imaginative lead glazes, among them slipware, agateware and tortoiseshell wares.

From the 1760s, competition from the more sophisticated creamware and pearlware types of earthenware contributed to the ultimate demise of the tin-glazed variety in Britain and on the Continent. Majolica (which is a corruption of the Italian term 'maiolica') wares were made by both British and American factories from the 1850s and have bright lead glazes and quirky designs.

Earthenwares were produced in the USA by the early colonists, but they never achieved the success of Britain's widely exported Staffordshire pottery. American potteries made distinctive domestic wares that included slipwares, spongewares and spatterwares.

In the 20th century, earthenware continued to be the material of choice for factory-produced wares. Royal Winton and Wedgwood made numerous ranges of tea and dinner wares, while Clarice Cliff produced striking, hand-painted tablewares and Carlton Limited, humorous 'walking' teapots and jugs.

Japanese art became fashionable from the 1860s in Europe and the USA. This English Minton majolica teapot (1891) is an example of a popular range of eccentric teapots in the form of oriental figures, boats and animals, such as this monkey. [K]

Most famously manufactured by the United States Pottery of Bennington (est. 1840s) in Vermont, wares known as 'Rockingham' were covered with a treacle-like glaze. Modelled in the form of a dog, this pitcher, (c.1880), has the streaky, lustrous finish common to such pieces. [O]

Since the 17th century, the French town of Quimper has been an important centre of faience production. The factory of Antoine de la Hubaudière produced wares such as this dish (c.1900), painted with bright colours. Decorations include rather stiff figures, rustic landscapes and sprays of flowers. [M]

A Closer Look Early & Late Maiolica

By the 16th century, Renaissance Italy was producing sophisticated maiolica of great artistic merit. This type of earthenware was so popular that by the 19th century, a thriving industry in high-quality reproductions had developed. Although wares made by accomplished potters of the time, such as Ulysse Cantagalli, could fool even connoisseurs, most copies of 16th-century originals can be identified if the piece is inspected carefully. The most obvious key to authenticity lies in the style of the painting, which is bold and accomplished in the hands of the skilful Renaissance artist, but less fluent and sometimes incompetent in 19th-century versions. Colour also provides a useful clue; while bold colours were used to decorate original maiolica, the colours are usually much softer and paler on later imitations.

Early maiolica dish from Urbino, c.1570
Portraying the biblical story of the Prodigal Son, this plate's bright blues, yellows and oranges are typical of wares from Urbino, one of the most important centres of maiolica production. [E]

▲ Note the **fluid style** of this **simple inscription** on the back of the dish, which bears the hallmarks of genuine 16th-century Italian script.

▶ Turn the dish over and look under the rim. The **pale turquoise glaze** that has trickled towards the edge is a common feature of Urbino *istoriato* wares. Pin holes show where air, which was trapped under the glaze, has burst through during firing.

Istoriato Maiolica & Prints

The growth of printing from the mid-15th century onwards greatly influenced Italian maiolica decorators of colourful *istoriato* (narrative) wares. Biblical, historical and mythological paintings by the Renaissance artist Raphael were reproduced by Italian engravers, while German woodcuts and French book illustrations were also popular sources.

◀ This detail of the Prodigal Son shows the artist's skill at painting in the confident, **bold style** found in the best 16th-century maiolica painting. Note the **subtle shading** of the figure's face and the tiny, precise brushstrokes used on his clothes.

Dish showing Hydra and Hercules, *c*.1530

Print by Gian Jacopo Caraglio (*c*.1526)

Cantagalli

In keeping with the 19th-century interest in Renaissance art, Italian pottery was dominated by copies of earlier models. The most famous maiolica potter at this time, Ulysse Cantagalli of Florence, produced copies of wares from Urbino and other Italian maiolica centres to meet the demand for high-quality reproductions. Much of his work fooled the experts.

Cantagalli's distinctive cockerel mark

▶ On 19th-century and later versions of maiolica, the **glaze** tended not to adhere well to the body and bubbled, or 'crawled', when it was fired, leaving a **pitted surface**. In contrast, the surface of early maiolica is very rarely pitted because of the high quality of production.

Late maiolica charger, c.1890
This large istoriato *charger (decorative plate) is illustrated with the biblical story of the Massacre of the Innocents. In contrast to the 16th-century dish, the painting is mechanical, the colours softer, and the composition not so well thought out.* [N]

▲ Although engaged in an act of violence, the sweet, almost childlike, expression on the soldier's face reflects the 19th-century taste for sugary, **sentimental depictions**. Look a little closer at the other parts of this figure and note the **clumsy execution** of such features as the banana-shaped fingers.

◀ On the back of the charger, the **scrubbed area** beneath the mock 16th-century inscription shows where a **later mark** has been **gouged out** in order to deceive potential buyers. This is a particularly common feature of Cantagalli wares.

◀ Another clue to the charger's later date is shown in the **lack of attention to detail** in the composition of the soldiers' legs and feet, which are crudely drawn. Maiolica figures on 19th-century *istoriato* also tend to be outlined with sharper, **blacker outlines** than 16th-century originals.

Story of Delft & Delftware

AFTER CHINESE PORCELAIN *was introduced to Europe in the early 17th century, blue-and-white wares became fashionable as enormous quantities were imported by the Dutch East India Company and other traders. When war interrupted trade with China in 1647, both Dutch and English manufacturers jumped at the opportunity to fill the gap in the market by making and selling copies of these sought-after products.*

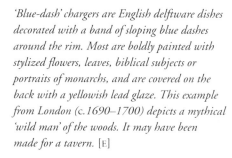

'Blue-dash' chargers are English delftware dishes decorated with a band of sloping blue dashes around the rim. Most are boldly painted with stylized flowers, leaves, biblical subjects or portraits of monarchs, and are covered on the back with a yellowish lead glaze. This example from London (c.1690–1700) depicts a mythical 'wild man' of the woods. It may have been made for a tavern. [E]

This view of a warehouse in China (left) illustrates the vast array of blue-and-white porcelain that captured the imagination of European traders in the 17th century.

When the popularity of blue-and-white wares began to wane at the beginning of the 18th century, Dutch Delft potters responded by introducing the bright colours used on Chinese porcelain for export to Europe. As a result, this mid-18th century Delft plate has multicoloured decoration. [J]

Tin-glazed earthenware was produced in the Low Countries from the late 15th century, initially by immigrant Italian potters who settled in Antwerp. The Dutch, however, developed their own decorative style that was more directly derived from Chinese porcelain, imported in bulk by the Dutch East India Company from the beginning of the 17th century.

Within 50 years, the city of Delft had become the main centre for tin-glazed earthenware production in the Netherlands, with other flourishing factories established in Rotterdam, Haarlem and Amsterdam. Since this growth coincided with the decline of the Dutch brewing industry, many potteries made use of abandoned breweries, producing a host of ornamental and domestic wares. Favouring blue and white, Delft potters reproduced Chinese designs from the late Ming period. Other forms of decoration, used on dishes, drug jars, flower vases, plaques, plates and tiles, ranged from Dutch landscapes and biblical stories to still-life flower paintings.

Chinese blue-and-white porcelain was also exported to England by the mid-17th

The long spindly trunks and sponged foliage of the trees help to identify this plate (left) as having been made in Bristol (c.1760). The smooth, bluish glaze on English delftware contrasts sharply with the whiter, 'peppered' surface of Dutch Delft. [M]

Among the popular styles of unusual English Delftware were puzzle jugs, bleeding bowls (used by surgeons), flower bricks and apothecaries' pill slabs. This puzzle jug from Liverpool, (c.1750), has a humorous verse written on the side to tease and challenge the drinker. [K]

century, but only the wealthy could afford this expensive luxury. Recognizing a market among the middle classes for an acceptable alternative, English potters produced 'delftware' in London, and at centres established in Bristol, Liverpool and Glasgow.

Unlike the wares made in the Netherlands, English delftware was coarse and hard, more thickly potted, and covered with a blue- or pink-tinged glaze that was easily chipped. Bearing a superficial resemblance to Chinese porcelain, the decoration tended to be clumsy and crude, lacking the fine, detailed brushwork typical of Dutch Delft. In addition to fashionable chinoiserie, regional decorative motifs began to emerge by the late 17th century. The English favoured designs that included bold flowers, oak leaves and portraits of monarchs, such as Charles II or William and

Mary. Although English delftware never achieved the artistic refinement of Dutch Delft, it had a distinctive charm. By the end of the 18th century, the growing popularity of English cream-coloured earthenware led to the decline of the tin-glazed earthenware industry in both Britain and the Netherlands.

Chinoiserie

The term 'chinoiserie' is used for European decoration inspired by oriental ornament, particularly Chinese designs. This style was extremely popular in the 17th and 18th centuries, largely owing to the expansion of trade between Europe and China. Chinoiseries take the form of pseudo-Chinese figures, flowers, pagodas, exotic birds, animals and landscapes that are imaginatively, rather than accurately interpreted. As well as earthenware and porcelain, chinoiserie decoration was also applied to European furniture (*see* p.62), silver and glass.

English delftware tea-caddy, *c.*1750 [J]

Dutch Delft punch-bowl, *c.*1710 [H]

A Closer Look *Delft & Delftware*

Both Dutch Delft and English delftware are made of soft earthenware covered with a lead glaze made white and opaque by the addition of tin oxide. Each type exhibits subtle differences between the body, glaze and palette. Dutch Delft is usually quite finely potted and has a thickish, white, often pitted, glaze painted blue or with bright colours. The body of English delftware is usually quite thick and is often more clumsily potted. It has a smoother glaze that tends to be tinged slightly blue or, rarely, pink. Both wares were inspired first by blue-and-white Chinese porcelain and then by brightly coloured Chinese and Japanese porcelain, which were imported into Europe from the 17th century by the Dutch East India Company.

▲ The Delft palette often uses a strong, **bright indigo blue** that is more intense than the blue used on English delftware. Look closely and you will see that the decoration has been outlined in **manganese purple**; this is known as 'trekking'.

Dutch Delft
punch-bowl, c.1730–40
In the early 18th century, the production of
blue-and-white Delft declined as the demand
for colourful wares decorated with Chinese
designs increased. [J]

◄ Look at the bottom of the foot and you can see the **body** where the glaze has chipped off. Chips are a useful aid to identification. The Dutch Delft body is usually a warm, **yellow-buff** colour, as shown here, and has a slightly **gritty texture** that resembles sand or brick.

Some Delft Marks

Most of the many factories in Delft did not mark their wares. However, during the second half of the 17th century, some potteries identified their products, but this practice was largely abandoned during the 18th century. English delftware very rarely bears any marks.

 Adriaenus Kocks who worked at the Greek A Factory (est. 1658)

 The Porcelain Claw Factory (est. 1662)

 The Three Bells Factory (est. 1671)

◄ If you look carefully at the surface of the glaze, you will see **discoloured spots** regularly **pitting** the surface. This is known as 'peppering', and has been caused by air bubbles trapped in the glaze exploding while the piece was being fired in the kiln. However, peppering is not ever found on English delftware.

IMPORTANT CENTRES OF ENGLISH DELFTWARE PRODUCTION	
(YEAR DELFTWARE FIRST PRODUCED)	
NORWICH	1560s
SOUTHWARK	c.1625
LAMBETH	1630s
BRISTOL	c.1650
LIVERPOOL	1700s
WINCANTON	1730s
GLASGOW	1748

▲ The colours used on English delftware are usually more muted than those on Dutch Delft. Not only is the **blue softer**, but delftware potters were fond of using a **soft, sage green** (*see* detail, right). Because the tin-glazed surface is absorbent, the colours, which are painted directly on the surface, sink into the glaze. **Red**, however, sits slightly proud and you may be able to feel this.

▲ Turn the dish over and you will see that the **foot-rim** on this delftware plate is **thinner**, and has a **slight flare** to it, unlike a Dutch Delft plate of the same period. The wear on the foot-rim will be uneven. Note also that the **glaze** on this delftware has a slightly more **pinkish tinge** than the much whiter Dutch Delft. If you see either Delft or delftware with a very smooth, unchipped surface, your suspicions should be immediately aroused. Perfect examples are extremely rare, since both types of ware were made to be used – you should expect to find chipping on the rim and foot-rim.

English delftware plate, c.1750–60
This brightly coloured English plate features a design similar to those that appeared on imported Chinese porcelain. Crude and rather sketchy, the patterns on this type of plate are rarely close copies of the original. [M]

Story of the Staffordshire Potteries

Staffordshire spaniel, *c.*1850 [Q]

In the 17th century, Staffordshire was just one of several rural districts that produced a lead-glazed earthenware – known as slipware – and salt-glazed stoneware, but within a hundred years it had become the centre of the British pottery industry. Thanks to plentiful local clay supplies and coal deposits, the factories developed some of Europe's finest pottery.

Slipware was the first true regional pottery produced in Britain. Made in Staffordshire from the early 17th century, an earthenware body was first covered with a white 'slip' – a creamy solution of clay and water – then coloured slip was trailed over to form patterns. The body was then coated with a thick lead glaze. From decorative display pieces to practical domestic vessels, these charming, rustic wares were produced throughout the 18th and 19th centuries.

The production of salt-glazed stoneware, an attractive alternative to porcelain, also thrived in Staffordshire. Originating in Germany, the technique came to England in the late 17th century, where it was patented by John Dwight of Fulham in London. Salt-glazed table and decorative wares were made by firing the stoneware in the kiln at a high temperature, then throwing in salt that melted to form a glassy, granular glaze Such wares were made in great quantities throughout the 18th century. Most were decorated with moulded designs and sometimes highlighted with coloured enamels.

Several families dominated Staffordshire ceramic production. One famous early potter was Thomas Whieldon, who developed a range of coloured lead glazes, which mingled together in firing to produce a mottled pattern. The Whieldon lead glazes were limited to brown, green, grey, yellow and blue, sometimes combined to create a 'tortoiseshell' effect.

In the 1740s, a type of cream-coloured earthenware covered with a transparent lead glaze was developed. Refined enough to be a substitute for porcelain (*see* pp.112–13), this 'creamware' featured moulded decoration, painted enamels or transfer prints.

Slipware's distinctive character was due to its slip-trailed decoration and stylized images, as seen on the charger (top) depicting Charles II's coronation. Made for display, this dish (c.1675) bears the typical trellis border and the signature of its maker, William Talor. [C]

Agateware is an unusual form of stoneware. Different-coloured clays were rolled together to create an attractive marbled effect as this teapot (c.1740–50) shows. Popular in the 18th century, agateware was often made in shapes similar to silver objects of the same period. [I]

Toby jugs are among the most amusing objects produced in Staffordshire from the mid-18th century. Many different forms of Toby jug, including this sailor (c.1775), were produced by the well-known maker Ralph Wood. [I]

One of the famous Staffordshire families, the Pratts, developed a lead-glazed earthenware decorated with bright enamel colours, as seen on this jug (c.1820). Produced by many factories, Prattware was painted in blue, green, yellow, orange, brown and purple. [K]

Produced in numerous centres, including Leeds, Bristol and Liverpool, the most successful maker of creamware was Josiah Wedgwood, who called it 'Queensware', after Queen Charlotte. In 1779, he developed a variation of creamware, known as pearlware, which remained popular until the middle of the 19th century.

In addition to slipware decoration, many other types of decorative techniques were used by the Staffordshire factories. From the 19th century, metallic decoration, or lustre, was popular for vessels such as teapots, mugs, jugs and chamber pots. Lustre, which originated in 9th-century Mesopotamia, was applied in bands or all over to create a splashed or mottled effect.

Underglaze blue printing, where a design was transfer-printed on the body before it was glazed, was a significant innovation, since it enabled engraved images to be reproduced on ceramic objects (*see* p.107). Introduced by Josiah Spode in 1781, many patterns using this technique were made in oriental style to meet the demand for inexpensive, earthenware domestic wares.

'Mason's Ironstone', patented by Charles James Mason in 1813, was another hardwearing earthenware, which was either decorated with hand-painted, oriental-style patterns, or transfer printed. Still produced today, ironstone was used for large dinner services, domestic vessels and ornamental wares.

Josiah Wedgwood

Josiah Wedgwood (1730–95) occupies an important place in the history of ceramics. He developed a range of high-quality pottery at his factories at Burslem and Etruria, which were the first to introduce mechanized production. Black basalt, *rosso antico*, caneware, jasper ware, agateware and creamware became highly fashionable and were widely imitated worldwide. Wedgwood was also the first British manufacturer to commission leading artists to create designs, including the sculptor John Flaxman, who was responsible for many of the jasper ware designs. By wedding art to industry and beauty to utility, Wedgwood achieved unparalleled success in supplying fine ceramic wares to all levels of society.

Josiah Wedgwood by George Stubbs

Well-modelled groups of figures painted with brilliant enamels, such as this one dating from c.1825–30, were produced by dozens of potteries in the North Staffordshire district from the early 19th century. Scenes from everyday life were the most popular subject. [N]

One of the best-known designs for blue-and-white, transfer-printed ware, is the 'Willow' pattern (right). Introduced in the early 19th century, the pattern was adapted from Chinese porcelain designs and featured an invented 'fable' of the lovers Koon-see and Chang fleeing from their oppressors and being changed into doves. [S]

A CLOSER LOOK *Staffordshire Figures*

Porcelain figures were extremely sought after in the 19th century, creating a huge demand for cheaper imitations, so dozens of small potteries in the North Staffordshire region produced decorative figures for the mass market. These earthenware replicas of expensive Chelsea and Derby porcelain proved so popular that they are still in production. The two figures shown here appear similar, but look closely and you will see some striking differences between the 1800 example and the 1920s reproduction. The original has been carefully modelled, painted in vibrant colours and feels quite heavy in the hand; later examples are harsher in colour, lighter in weight and the glaze may have been given an artificial crackled look (crazing). Look out also for scratches in places where you would not normally expect to find wear, this is another mark of a fake.

Figure of Peace, 1800
This figure from classical antiquity is actually made up of several parts, each one having been individually press-moulded and then fixed together with a thin, watery clay called slip. [O]

◀ Typical of the Neo-classical style prevalent at the end of the 18th century, this goddess has a refined face and **flat 'Roman' profile**, often found in figures of the period. Where the **glaze** has gathered in **crevices** (known as 'pooling') it is darker and slightly bluish in tone. The distinctive pinkish mark around the goddess's neck shows that she has been repaired at some time.

▶ Because the clay has been pressed by hand and with tools into a mould in an original Staffordshire figure, the **square base** should be quite substantial. Its thickness is irregular and dotted with **finger and tool marks**. The large vent hole allowed air to circulate during the firing process, preventing the figure from exploding.

Figure of a shepherd, 1920s
Unlike the earlier figure, this 20th-century
shepherd has been slip-cast in a two-piece
mould. A slip-cast figure is always much lighter
than a press-moulded figure. Note also
that the colours used
are harsher. The
'sticky' blueberry-
jam-coloured
jacket, the
acid-yellow
breeches and
the dull, greyish
green of the base
are nowhere
near as 'pure' as
the colours used to
paint the 19th-
century goddess. [S]

Staffordshire Flatbacks

From the 1840s, Staffordshire potters began making press-moulded 'flatback' figures for mantelpieces, that are decorated on one side only. Produced in huge numbers, flatbacks cover subjects ranging from royal, political, theatrical and circus personalities to animals and criminals. Colours are thickly applied, with little attention to detail. Raised titles may appear on the base.

Dick Turpin,
*c.*1850–60 [N]

D · TURPIN

◀ Look closely at a later reproduction and you will almost certainly be able to spot many **clumsily executed details**.
This figure has not only a gormless expression, but dotted 'piggy' eyes and simplified 'mitten' hands.

▶ Compared to the base from 1800, this 1920s example has a thinner, more **regular shape**. Such figures also have a **smooth interior**, because in the slip-casting process the excess creamy slip is poured off leaving an even 'skin' of clay in the mould.

A Closer Look *Mason's Ironstone*

In the early 19th century, hardwearing earthenware table services became a popular and cheaper alternative to the more fragile Chinese porcelain. Stone China was made by various companies from the early 19th century, but the most famous type was 'Mason's Patent Ironstone China', made from 1813, by Charles James Mason of Lane Delph, Staffordshire. Although produced to compete with porcelain, ironstone lacked porcelain's translucence. It was a dense,

heavy, greyish-white ware, which held heat well. Ironstone was, therefore, ideally suited for making dinner and dessert services for everyday use, as well as jugs, large ornamental vases and potpourri vases. Mason's Ironstone was extremely fashionable during the first quarter of the 19th century and was produced in vast quantities for both the home and export markets.

Mason's Ironstone vase, c.1820
This octagonal baluster vase has been brightly painted with a flamboyant, Imari-inspired peony pattern that covers the entire surface. Large ornamental vases were fashionable throughout the 19th century. [1]

◀ The **gilding** on Mason's Ironstone is usually lavish. It was honey-gilded (gold leaf was applied using honey as a fixative), which gives a warm, almost **pinkish glow**. Expect to see some **wear** on areas that have been regularly handled.

Marks

Early marks include a circular 'Patent Ironstone China' or 'Mason's Patent Ironstone China' pressed into the clay in a line. The black or blue mark printed over the glaze features 'Mason's Ironstone China' surmounted by a crown and was occasionally enamelled with pink or green (seen below) and was used from 1815. Marks after 1820 usually have the name 'MASON'S' printed over the crown.

Printed mark,
from 1815

Impressed mark,
1813–20

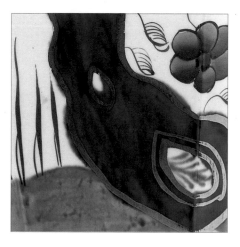

▲ The **underglaze cobalt blue** on Mason's Ironstone was thickly applied, to give a deep, rich blue, or thinly applied as a wash, which appears slightly blotchy. You should be able to feel the **iron-red enamelling**, which sits slightly proud of the glaze. Enamelling is vulnerable to wear and can be scratched.

◀ The standard pattern wares at Mason's were produced in great numbers and were probably decorated by child labour, hence the painting found on many of the wares is a little haphazard. Because the blue was applied too rapidly and freely it had a tendency to **dribble** and **blur**. Here you can also see where some water or oil was carelessly splashed on the thinly applied **salmon pink** background. These imperfections are all part of the charm of Mason's Ironstone.

Imari

The brightly coloured porcelain exported from the Japanese port of Imari from the mid-17th century was lavishly decorated in blue, iron-red and gold. Great quantities of 'Chinese Imari' also came to Europe in the 18th century, and the popular patterns were widely copied by European ceramics factories. In England during the Regency period (c.1811–20), these boldly decorated oriental wares were extremely fashionable. As the demand increased, Imari colours and designs were freely interpreted by various factories and were known as 'Japan' or 'Indian' patterns.

Imari baluster vase, 19th century [D]

▲ Since most Ironstone wares were intended for everyday use in the home, it is usual to find examples with a chip or two. Here you can see the **concrete-grey** colour, typical of these pieces, and also the unglazed body, which is **rough** and **grainy** to the touch.

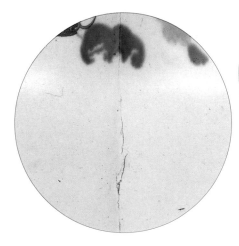

▲ Vases such as this were made in a two-piece mould, which created a visible **seam** that runs down the side. Because the body was heavy it had a tendency to **shrink** during firing, causing the seam to come apart. These firing faults do not greatly affect the value of a piece.

A Closer Look *Majolica*

laborately moulded earthenware, decorated with thick, vivid lead glazes and known as majolica, was developed from 1850 by the Staffordshire firm of Minton and first exhibited at the Great Exhibition of 1851 in London. The main sources of inspiration were Italian maiolica and the naturalistic pottery of the 16th-century French potter, Bernard Palissy. From the mid-19th century, majolica quickly became popular in Britain, Europe and

the USA. Wares made ranged from domestic vases, plates, dishes and jugs to enormous ornamental vases and seats for the conservatory, all heavily encrusted with lavish ornament in the exaggerated style favoured by the Victorians. American majolica tended to be less well modelled than the best British examples; the colours were also more muted and the modelling not as sharply defined.

▲ The best-quality British majolica has carefully applied coloured glazes that have not dribbled or blurred. Pieces that have a **cobalt-blue background** colour are highly valued, as are those that have a pink background, although this is rare. Good-quality majolica wares have extremely **hard, glossy glazes**. If you notice a patch of glaze on a piece that looks dull, it may have been restored.

English partridge tureen, c.1870
Some of the most popular majolica products were novelty tablewares. The most sought-after examples of this tureen made by George Jones & Sons (est. 1862) of Stoke-on-Trent have chicks nestled around the mother bird. [D]

▶ The detachable **white liner** inside this tureen was used for baking pies; the finished dish was then presented at the table inside the elaborate tureen. The most desirable majolica objects to collect are those with a pink or **turquoise interior**.

◀ George Jones & Sons excelled at making whimsical wares, which featured **crisp moulding**. As shown here, the edges of the design were well defined, because the moulds were regularly replaced by the factory before they became worn.

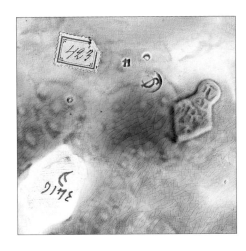

◀ A **mottled glaze**, which is known as 'snakeskin' often appeared on the base of pieces by George Jones & Sons. Other factories tried to copy it, but their colours were never as intense. An **unglazed 'thumb' mark** (*see* left) enclosed the pattern number.

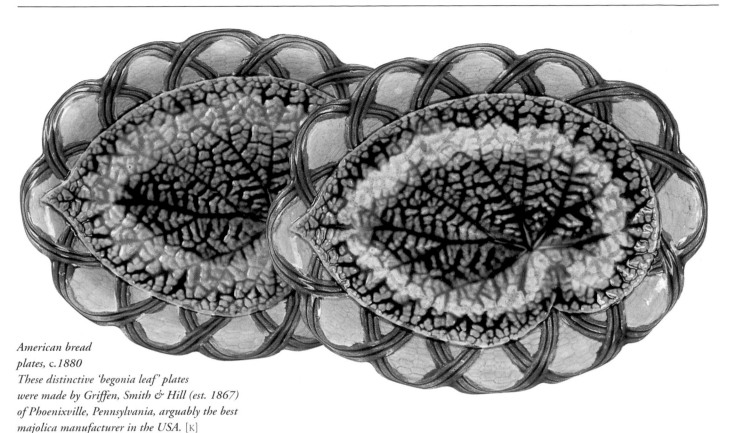

American bread plates, c.1880
These distinctive 'begonia leaf' plates were made by Griffen, Smith & Hill (est. 1867) of Phoenixville, Pennsylvania, arguably the best majolica manufacturer in the USA. [K]

▼ On the base of the American plates you can see the distinctive stamped **monogram** of Griffen, Smith & Hill. The name 'Etruscan' was the factory's trademark for its majolica wares. The printed number ('07') in the cream patch indicates the **pattern number**.

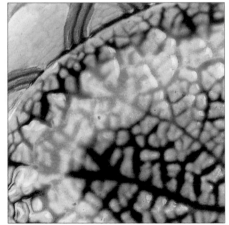

◀ Look carefully at the surface and you will see that the coloured lead glazes have not been as carefully applied as on the George Jones tureen. The **glazes** have run together, causing the **edges to blur**. The deeper pink stripe is more desirable than the lighter pink stripe on the other Griffin, Smith & Hill plate (*see* above left). Notice also how the **moulded decoration** is much **flatter** than the decoration on the game tureen; this is often a sign of lesser quality.

Other Majolica Manufacturers

The top British majolica manufacturers included Minton, Wedgwood and George Jones & Sons. Others included the firms of Brown-Westhead Moore & Co., Joseph Holdcroft and William Brownfield. In the USA, the best firms included the Bennett Pottery in Baltimore, Maryland and the Eureka Pottery, in New Jersey.

Stamped mark of Wedgwood

Types of Art Deco Ceramics

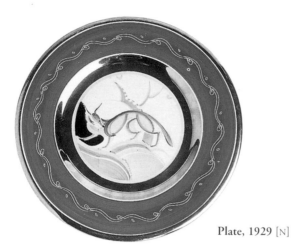

Plate, 1929 [N]

Plate, 1930s [Q]

Susie Cooper

An influential British ceramic designer, Susie Cooper set up a company (est. 1929) in Burslem, Staffordshire, producing a wide range of tablewares in hand-painted earthenware.

■ As well as designing ceramic shapes, she created many hand-painted and transfer-printed designs, all executed with great attention to detail and ranging from brightly coloured abstract designs to stylized animals and flowers.

■ From 1932, Susie Cooper wares used this printed mark.

Royal Winton

Royal Winton is the trade name for the moulded decorative wares and tablewares produced by Grimwades Ltd. (est. 1885) in Stoke-on-Trent.

■ As well as lustreware and cottage ware, this firm is famous for its colourful chintzware – tableware completely decorated with floral patterns – which was very fashionable in the 1930s.

■ Royal Winton also used chromolithography – an innovative type of surface printing – to great effect. Wares decorated in this way appear to have been hand-painted; but look closely, there are no brushstrokes.

Masked girl with monkey wall mask, 1930s [J]

Goldscheider

The Austrian firm of Goldscheider (est. 1885) was known for its earthenware and porcelain in the 1920s and 1930s.

■ Figures made by Goldscheider include dancing couples in contemporary dress, ballerinas and Pierrettes, and characters from the opera and ballet, decorated in vibrant, contrasting colours.

■ Terracotta wall masks painted in brick-red, green, yellow and black, were particularly popular.

■ Goldscheider also produced ceramic copies of the work of Viennese sculptor Bruno Zach, who specialized in stylized female dancers in acrobatic poses.

■ From 1918–46 the name was written above a stylized 'GVA' symbol.

Essevi

Artist Sandro Vacchetti, who at one time worked for the Lenci company (*see* opposite above), opened a factory in Turin called Essevi in 1933. While Lenci made expensive items, the Essevi factory concentrated on cheaper mass-produced pieces.

■ Essevi specialized in large masks and figures made of a fine earthenware body covered with a high gloss or matt glaze in Art Deco colours.

■ The firm's wares are marked 'Essevi, made in Italy, Torino' and sometimes include a painted date.

Butterfly girl by Goldscheider, *c.*1930 [H]

Lenci

The Italian firm Lenci (est. 1919) produced earthenware and porcelain figures of women, nude or in contemporary dress.

■ A pioneer of Italian Art Deco, this factory's large output included decorative tableware painted with Cubist designs. Until 1939, Lenci also specialized in religious figures, such as the Madonna and Child, as well as wall masks.

■ Lenci figures have elongated limbs, and are brightly decorated with a combination of matt and shiny glazes.

■ Factory marks are usually hand painted in black on the base, and are often dated.

Figure of an Indian girl, 1930s [J]

Clarice Cliff

Clarice Cliff was one of the most prolific and innovative British potters working in the 1920s and 1930s. She is best known for her brightly coloured wares in streamlined Art Deco shapes.

■ Her most successful designs include 'Bizarre' ware and the limited edition 'Age of Jazz' series, which featured cut-out silhouette figures painted on both sides.

■ Clarice Cliff fakes abound, so check for washed-out colour, poor-quality painting, and an uneven or murky glaze.

■ Early pieces are marked with the pattern name and Clarice Cliff's signature, as well as a stamped factory mark.

'Bizarre' floor vase, 1930s [D]

Rookwood

Rookwood (est. 1880) of Cincinnati, Ohio, created an extensive range of tablewares and vases. The firm is known for its glossy glazes called 'standard' and matt glaze called 'vellum'.

■ Most Rookwood is marked on the base with an 'RP'. A flame was added over the mark for each year after 1886, until 1900, when Roman numerals were added.

'Vellum' vase, 1924 [F]

Weller

The large commercial firm of Weller (est. 1872) in Zanesville, Ohio, first made a variety of hand-decorated slipwares called 'Lonhuda', which were inspired by the matt-glazed wares made at Rookwood. After World War I, Weller produced more standard, mass-produced items.

■ Later shapes are geometric and angular. They are decorated with simple low-relief designs.

■ Glazes on later wares tend to be matt in such Art Deco colours as sherbet pink and soft green and pick out the dominant motif.

■ Wares include every conceivable type of useful and decorative pieces such as vases, planters, tea services and bowls.

■ Marks on the base usually include the name 'Weller'.

Geometric vase, c.1930 [O]

Story of Stoneware

DATING BACK TO ANCIENT TIMES, *stoneware is a dense, hard and extremely robust material. Made from clays that produce a water-resistant body when fired to very high temperatures, stoneware has proved to be extremely useful for all kinds of domestic wares, including teawares, vases and drinking vessels. Furthermore, the durable clay could be thinly potted and elaborately decorated with moulded or applied ornament.*

German
Bartmannskrüg,
c.1615 [E]

The glaze covering this 17th-century German jug, which may have been made in Frechen, has a thin, pitted surface that resembles orange peel. Most stonewares are brown, owing to the iron impurities present in many of the clays used. Sometimes red lead was combined with salt to give the glaze a glassier appearance. This was later discovered to be highly dangerous. [K]

In this 17th-century Dutch still life (left), a Yixing metal-mounted teapot is surrounded by Chinese porcelain tea cups, saucers and bowls. Such teapots were imported to Europe in great quantities in chests of tea and copied by, among others, the Elers brothers of Staffordshire, Böttger at Meissen, and Delft potters such as Ary de Milde, who was known as 'Mr Teapot Maker'.

Each teapot made at Yixing, such as this example (c.1690), was renowned for its shape and unglazed red body. The plum blossom shown here has been applied, or sprigged, a type of decoration also seen on Chinese blanc-de-Chine. [K]

Stoneware was probably first produced from *c.*1200 BC in China. By the 8th century it had become a highly refined, pale grey ware decorated with a greenish grey glaze, made in the region of Yue on the east coast. By the early 12th century, the Yue kilns had been overtaken by those in Longquan, a town in the same province. There extremely fine wares known as celadons were produced and decorated with a thick green or bluish green glaze, made to resemble jade.

In medieval Europe, stoneware was made by potters in the Rhine valley. Towards the end of the 15th century, they discovered that by throwing common salt into the kiln once it reached its hottest point, the salt reacted with the silica present in the clay to form a thin, tight-fitting glaze.

Among the most distinctive medieval German stonewares are fine, greyish white wares made in the Siegburg area, the blue-and-purple glazed wares of the Westerwald region and the brown stonewares of Cologne and Frechen. Tankards, jars, bottles and pitchers, but not dishes or plates, were decorated with applied, stamped or incised (cut with a sharp tool) decoration.

Inspired by the hard-wearing German stonewares, which were imported in great quantities into England in the 17th century, English potters desperately tried to recreate them. One London potter, John Dwight, was eventually successful, obtaining his first patent in 1672 and thereafter copying German mugs and tavern wine bottles in a fine, off-white, stoneware. He had originally set out to make porcelain, but lacking the knowledge had to satisfy himself with making stoneware.

Dwight also succeeded in making a red stoneware, which he patented in 1684. Despite threatening litigation to anyone who tried to copy him, the Elers brothers of Staffordshire (*see* p.110) nevertheless produced a fine, red, slip-cast stoneware that was similar to Chinese Yixing wares. This was well suited for making teapots and

teawares. In Germany, too, efforts to discover the secret of making porcelain resulted in Johann Friedrich Böttger's production of red stoneware at Meissen. It was called '*Jaspisporzellan*' because of its resemblance to the semi-precious stone, jasper.

Around 1720 a fine, white, salt-glazed stoneware was developed in Staffordshire (*see* p.110). Since it was cheap to produce and stronger than any other ceramic body made in Britain at the time, this ware was produced in large quantities and exported to Europe and North America. Tablewares and teawares were decorated with scratched or moulded decoration, or brightly coloured enamels. Forty years later, Josiah Wedgwood introduced his elegant Neo-classical stoneware – black basalt and 'jasper' wares, caneware and *rosso antico*.

Stoneware continued to play an important role in British ceramics throughout the 19th century. White stonewares similar to those made a hundred years earlier were still being produced, usually as moulded jugs and teapots. Highly original plates and vases were created by the firm of Doulton (*see* p.111), which employed students from the Lambeth School of Art as decorators. In the 1920s, the studio movement, led by Bernard Leach (*see* p.111), drew inspiration from oriental and medieval stonewares.

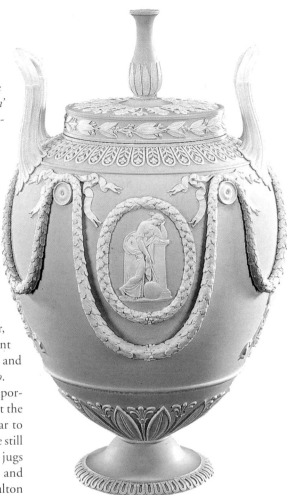

In the late 1770s, Josiah Wedgwood perfected a fine stoneware decorated with white classical figures and motifs, which he named 'jasper' ware. This vase and cover (c.1800) is an excellent example. [F]

Many stoneware pieces were based on contemporary gold and silver designs. As with this jaspisporzellan *tankard (c.1710–1715), by J. F. Böttger, they were mounted with precious metals. Böttger also employed decorative techniques usually used on semi-precious stones, including polishing and cutting.* [C]

Transfer Printing

This method of decorating ceramics was probably developed in Liverpool from 1756 by John Sadler. Transfer printing involves inking an engraved copper plate with ceramic colour, then taking a paper print from it. The the print is pressed onto the surface of the vessel, leaving a single colour impression. The transfer, which was usually in black or blue, could be applied before or after glazing, and the resulting decoration resembled an engraved print. Occasionally only an outline was printed, which was then coloured in by hand. Multicoloured transfer prints were introduced in the 1840s.

Salt-glazed stoneware plate, *c*.1760–70 [K]

A Closer Look *Siegburg Stoneware*

By the 15th century, Siegburg in the German Rhineland had become an important centre of stoneware production. From the 1550s, the town's fame increased thanks to the manufacture of *Schnellen* (tall, tapering tankards), *Sturzbecker* ('somersault' cups) and *Schnabelkanne* ('beak' jugs). Ornamentation included biblical, heraldic and allegorical scenes, as well as emblems of the Holy Roman Emperors. The refined, off-white body was well suited to the fine strapwork (intertwined bands) and foliate (stylized leaf) decoration inspired by the engravings of artists such as Virgil Solis, and carried out in Renaissance style. The production of Siegburg wares declined from *c.*1610, owing to competition from other Rhenish centres, but the wares were copied throughout the 19th century.

Siegburg Schnelle, late 16th century Schnellen made from the mid-16th century were usually fitted with pewter lids and handles. [H]

◀ The thin, salt glaze used at Siegburg showed the **off-white clay** to best advantage. Very **thin, rectangular panels** with **incised decoration** were cut to fit the tapered tankard, while flower sprigs, made in clay moulds were applied to the surface. As you can see here, the panel has been so carefully applied that it has not cracked during firing, as often happened with 19th-century copies.

▼ Decorative moulds frequently feature **marks** that incorporate the initials of the designer. On this *Schnelle* the initials 'HH' designate the workshop of the potter Hans Hilgers. Because moulds were used for several years before they were discarded and panels featuring different dates were sometimes applied to the same pot, a date (here it is 1591) does not always indicate the correct year of production.

◀ One reliable way to distinguish a 16th-century *Schnelle* from a later copy is to turn the vessel over and look at the **bottom**. The base of an original is **gently concave** and has an angular, **sharp edge**. It is never marked. On 19th-century and later versions. the base is usually quite flat with a more rounded edge. Such reproductions were often marked. In addition, the white or greyish stoneware in later reproductions tends to be less refined. Its off-white colour may have a 'dirtier' appearance, even a yellowish tinge.

A Closer Look *Westerwald Stoneware*

The Westerwald district in the Rhineland (especially the towns of Grenzhausen and Höhr) is well known for its grey, salt-glaze stoneware. Potters who travelled from Siegburg to Westerwald in the 1590s, produced hollow vessels such as the *Enghalskrug* (narrow-necked jug) and *Kugelbauchkrug* (bulbous tankard), the most common type of late 17th-century German stoneware. Along with applied and incised designs, Westerwald wares have a distinctive blue wash that is occasionally enhanced with discreet touches of manganese purple. A thriving export trade to England and the Low Countries developed in the late 17th century, and some vessels were even stamped with images and dates of English monarchs.

Genre Paintings

Early collectors referred to Westerwald pottery as *grès de Flandres* or 'Flemish' stoneware. No doubt this was largely because pots and jugs, which can be readily identified as Westerwald and Siegburg wares, appear with great frequency in still life and genre paintings of the Low Countries dating from the 16th and 17th centuries.

An anonymous 17th-century genre painting showing a Westerwald tankard

▶ The bottom of this *Kugelbauchkrug* reveals a gently **concave base** that is much the same shape as that of the Siegburg *Schnelle*. Modern versions of this type of ware have a more rounded edge than their 17th-century predecessors. The body is a definite **grey**, resembling fine concrete. Westerwald wares of this period are unmarked.

Westerwald Kugelbauchkrug, 1691 The technique used on the Siegburg Schnelle *has also been employed to ornament this fat-bellied* Kugelbauchkrug, *which is decorated with medallions and flower-heads. Note the blotchy, almost black-blue wash that was often found on this type of ware, as were occasional touches of manganese purple.* [J]

▲ The stoneware used by the Westerwald workshops was **less refined** than the variety used at Siegburg, so it was not possible to achieve the same degree of definition in the incised decoration. On later reproductions, the designs tend to be more complex, and generally look as though they have been produced by mechanical means.

Types of Stoneware

Staffordshire salt-glazed teapot, c.1750 [J]

Elers ware lidded water jug, c.1695 [I]

18th-century Staffordshire salt glaze

Early 18th-century Staffordshire potters created a more refined stoneware, which was often made into shells, houses and animals.
■ Made by pouring a creamy slip into a two-piece mould, the off-white, greyish body of this teapot has been covered with a very thin salt glaze that feels granular, like orange peel, if you touch it.
■ The majority of Staffordshire salt-glazed pieces were left undecorated, but some had details painted in enamel colours.

Elers ware

Dutch immigrants John and David Elers established a pottery at Bradwell Wood, Staffordshire, in the late 17th century. They produced a fine red stoneware, which was copied by other potters until *c.*1760.
■ Strongly influenced by south Chinese Yixing stonewares (*see* p.106), imported into Europe by the Dutch, the fine redware was used to make durable tea and coffee wares and other domestic tablewares.
■ Many pieces have imitation Chinese seal marks on the base.

Wedgwood black basalt vase, late 18th century [D]

Black basalt

Black basalt ranks among the most popular ornamental pieces made by Josiah Wedgwood.
■ The fine-grained stoneware body was coloured with cobalt and manganese oxides and left unglazed.
■ The sprigging (applied decoration) on basalt is of the finest quality. It was added with extreme care by skilled potters, so you will never see any toolmarks around the edges.
■ Items include large vases and a range of library busts.
■ Black basalt should have a soft surface sheen.
■ After 1768, such items were marked 'Wedgwood and Bentley'.

Bristol stoneware jug by J. & J. Bright, 1820 [K]

Bristol stoneware

From the early 19th century, brown, salt-glazed stoneware consisting mainly of vessels jugs, mugs and bottles for taverns, was produced in Bristol.
■ Decoration included sprigged panels of fruit, vines, and classical, hunting and rustic landscapes.
■ Although quite heavy and generally robust, these wares are now quite scarce, since many were broken over the years, probably in tavern brawls.
■ Some pieces are marked with the name of the potter, as well as a date.

Stoneware teapot,
c.1865 [R]

19th-century Staffordshire stoneware

Staffordshire factories continued to produce large quantities of hard, fine, white stoneware, including jug and teapots, during the 19th century.

■ The moulded decoration on 19th-century pieces is much less crisply detailed than on 18th-century wares (*see* opposite far left).

■ Pieces were left unglazed or had a thin 'smear' glaze, with a waxy or soapy appearance.

■ Vessels were often marked with a diamond-shaped registration mark.

Doulton

Established in 1815 in Lambeth, South London, Doulton was an innovative stoneware manufacturer.

■ Wares often have incised and applied decorative motifs and beaded borders in Victorian colours such as murky blue, dull green and dark brown.

■ The salt-glazed stoneware was made by students at the Lambeth School of Art from 1871. Artists included Hannah Barlow, George Tinworth, Emily Edwards and Frank Butler.

■ Doulton ware is marked with the stamped, printed or painted factory name, as well as the date and initials of the artist.

Doulton stoneware vase, *c*.1875 [L]

Mettlach

Jean François Boch founded the Mettlach factory in 1809 in the Rhineland. In 1836 it merged with various glass and ceramic factories owned by the Villeroy family.

■ Mettlach was famous for producing stonewares in the late 19th century in the *Historismus* style, which portrayed idyllic rural life in medieval and Renaissance Germany.

■ Wares were mostly copies of earlier tankards, plates and dishes.

■ Usually wares have incised and multicoloured decorations in the style of book illustrations.

■ One Mettlach mark, from 1842, features a castle. 'VB' stands for Villeroy & Boch.

Mettlach pewter-mounted stein, *c*.1890 [K]

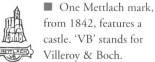

Bernard Leach slab bottle, *c*.1930 [H]

Bernard Leach

Together with a Japanese potter, Shoji Hamada, Bernard Leach established a pottery factory at St Ives, Cornwall, in 1920.

■ Drawing inspiration from oriental and medieval designs and traditional English pottery, his wares are, typically, decorated with contrasting areas of glazed and unglazed surfaces.

 ■ 'BL' was the most common mark used; it was either painted or stamped.

Story of Porcelain

THE FIRST PORCELAIN *was developed from the 7th century in China, where china stone and china clay were combined to produce a strong white, translucent material that could be moulded, painted or incised with decorative patterns. From the early 16th century, Jingdezhen in east China became the most important centre of production and large quantities of porcelain were exported from here.*

Ming basin, 15th century [A]

The formula for making porcelain remained undiscovered by European potters for a thousand years after its development in China. By the late 16th century, porcelain exported to Europe from China by Portuguese traders had created a demand that far exceeded the supply. Increased trade with China throughout the 17th century further increased the enthusiasm for the exotic porcelain among Europe's elite, a fashion echoed by the craze for drinking Chinese tea. At this time, ceramic experiments in Italy and France led to the development of fine cream-coloured soft-paste porcelain, but German Saxony was the first country in Europe to uncover the valuable secret of making hard-paste porcelain in 1710 (*see pp.124–25*).

This discovery was the accidental result of research conducted in the quest to create gold through alchemy. A brilliant alchemist, Johann Friedrich Böttger, stumbled upon the formula for fine,

Soft-paste porcelain was first produced in Europe at the Medici factory in Florence between 1575 and 1587. This Renaissance-shape flask is carefully decorated with a Chinese-inspired design in underglaze blue. [A]

The Meissen factory became celebrated for its refined decorative style and use of rich colours. Especially popular were items for the tea table, such as this tea-caddy c.1730, which is painted with charming chinoiserie (European imitations of Chinese art) scenes of elegant figures surrounded by lacy designs. [F]

The English firm of Worcester (est. 1751) was renowned for producing tea and coffee wares such as this mug (c.1751). Worcester wares contained soapstone, which enabled the soft-paste porcelain to hold hot liquids. [F]

The Union Porcelain Works of Brooklyn, New York, was the first American factory to produce hard-paste porcelain in the 19th century. This oyster plate dates from c.1880. [Q]

red stoneware and refined it with white Saxon clay. The first hard-paste porcelain factory in Europe was established at Meissen in 1710. It was to dominate European porcelain production for more than 50 years.

With good clay supplies and talented artists and modellers, the Meissen factory became the envy of European princes and aristocrats. Factories producing hard-paste porcelain sprang up in cities such as Vienna and Venice, as the secret of Böttger's recipe was spread, largely by disenchanted Meissen workers. A French factory at Vincennes, established in 1740, seriously challenged Meissen's superiority with quality wares decorated in dazzling colours and fine gilding, The acquisition of a hard-paste formula in 1768 assured the reputation of the factory (which had by this time moved to Sèvres, near Paris) as the European leader in porcelain.

By 1770 there were nearly 20 hard-paste factories in Europe making copies of Meissen and Sèvres porcelain. Throughout the 19th century, many factories continued to manufacture porcelain, generally in styles based on popular models from the past. After the end of World War I in 1918, porcelain continued to evolve, with factories throughout the world producing innovative and highly original designs.

Late Ming export porcelain, as seen in this 17th-century still life (above left), were known as kraak wares. This distinctive blue-and-white porcelain takes its name from the Dutch term for the Portuguese merchant ships, or carracks, which were used to transport the wares to Europe.

Parian (statuary porcelain) was a popular 19th-century material used to make inexpensive imitations of marble sculpture. Popular subjects included classical figures such as this nymph (1867). [K]

Shipwreck Cargoes

By the 17th century, many European nations had established trading companies with interests in India and the Far East. The Dutch East India Company played a leading role in the trade of oriental porcelains. However, many ships returning from China, sank en route. Some of these cargoes have since been discovered. In 1984 the cargo of blue-and-white porcelain from the Dutch ship *Geldermalsen*, which sank in 1752, was salvaged and is now known as the 'Nanking' cargo.

Dish from the 'Nanking' cargo, *c.*1750 [K]

A Closer Look *Hard & Soft Porcelain*

Porcelain is classified as hard paste or soft paste. Hard-paste, or 'true', porcelain is a mixture of china clay (kaolin), china stone (petuntse) and quartz. Hard paste is usually very white and translucent and has a smooth texture resembling icing on a cake. The glaze is typically glassy and thin. By contrast, soft-paste, or 'artificial', porcelain is a combination of china clay and crushed glass, quartz or white clay, and has a slightly more grainy texture. The colour of soft paste ranges from pure white to grey, and the glaze tends to be quite thick, softening details and gathering in pools in crevices, where it can be clearly seen. The term bone china refers to a particular type of soft-paste porcelain, developed in England, which included ground animal bones. As seen in these examples, the wares of each factory differ greatly.

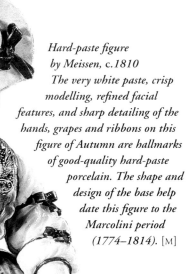

Hard-paste figure by Meissen, c.1810
The very white paste, crisp modelling, refined facial features, and sharp detailing of the hands, grapes and ribbons on this figure of Autumn are hallmarks of good-quality hard-paste porcelain. The shape and design of the base help date this figure to the Marcolini period (1774–1814). [M]

Soft-paste figure by Longton Hall, c.1750–60
Thickly potted, with a simple, quite crudely modelled face, fingers and base, this figure of Spring shows how details such as toes and fingers are obscured by the thick glaze used on soft-paste porcelain. [K]

▼ One of the best ways to identify the paste of a piece is to look for a part that is chipped. Here the large chip on the base of this **hard-paste** figure is very **shiny** and looks like **flint**; the edge will feel **sharp** to the touch.

▼ **Soft-paste** porcelain is much more porous than hard paste. On this unglazed base, notice how the soft paste has absorbed moisture and dirt, resulting in **spotty-brown staining** and **discoloration**. Cracks and chips on soft-paste porcelain can also stain or discolour.

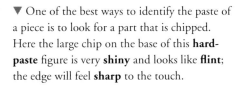

Soft-paste dish by Vauxhall, c.1760
Vauxhall soft-paste porcelain often has a pitted surface. [O]

Soft-paste group by Vincennes, c.1755
This French group of grape eaters was fired only once, producing what is called 'biscuit' porcelain. Because it was left unglazed, the details are crisply defined. Biscuit porcelain was fashionable during the Neo-classical period, since it resembled the marble used for classical sculptures. [F]

▶ If you turn the Vauxhall dish over, you will see that the glaze has a slight **iridescence**. This is known in the antiques trade as 'sticky blue'. The **bluish glaze** on Vauxhall tends to **pool** in crevices, around the foot-rim in this example. The **chip** on the foot-rim will feel **soft** and granular, unlike the Meissen example.

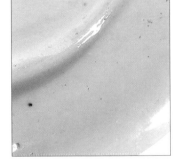

▼ After 1756, figures and wares made at the Derby factory were fired in the kiln, supported by three balls of clay. These left a triangular arrangement of **greyish 'patch' marks** on the unglazed base. Look out for these marks; they are one of the best ways of identifying **soft-paste** Derby porcelain made at this time.

Soft-paste group by Derby, c.1765
The modelling of soft paste at Derby was so good that many of the details were not obscured by the glaze. [J]

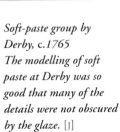

A CLOSER LOOK *Ming Porcelain*

For many people, the name Ming is synonymous with fine Chinese porcelain. From the late 14th century, Ming emperors encouraged the production of porcelain, often supervising designs and permitting vessels to be marked with the royal seal of approval, a reign mark. This Imperial interest encouraged the potters of Jingdezhen to refine materials and techniques and create stylized designs. Ming porcelain is particularly skilfully potted and each piece has an individual feel. Early Ming was usually very carefully painted with balanced and spacious flower designs; figures were more rarely used. From *c*.1520, standards declined, owing to the huge demands of the Ming court for porcelain and, later in the century, the vast quantities needed to satisfy the increased demands of the export trade.

▲ The custom of adding **reign marks** became a regular practice during the reign of Xuande in the 15th century. Ming marks of this period are always **blurred** because the glaze was very thick and filled with tiny air bubbles. These bubbles are visible under a magnifying glass.

Early Ming bowl, 1426–35 The strong brushwork and well-balanced, stylized lotus design is typical of the classic, early Ming period. [A]

▼ In order to create the typical blue colour, **cobalt** was ground into a powder. The cobalt used on Ming was quite uneven, causing **irregular, dark speckling** in the painting. On most early Ming, spots of cobalt have broken through the thick glaze during firing and oxidized black, creating an effect known as 'heaped and piled'.

▲ One good way to identify early Ming porcelain is to look at the inside of the base of the bowl. Here you should see a **greeny-blue ring** where the thick glaze has pooled. Keep an eye out also for a **ring of reddish brown** on the outer unglazed edge of the foot-rim, where iron in the clay has oxidized during the firing process.

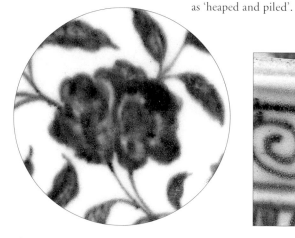

◀ The **edge** of the **foot-rim** is decorated with an **early Ming classic scroll**, which was one of the most popular early Ming border designs. Again, note the characteristic blackish flecks in the decoration caused by oxidation.

▲ The rim of the jar has **black flecks**, which were probably caused by dirt in the kiln during firing, or by impurities in the paste. This type of **flaw** is typical of the late Ming period, when standards of production had declined.

▲ If you look closely at the upturned jar, the **foot-rim** has been **crudely trimmed**, so that it has an angular rather than a rounded profile, as can be seen on early, top-quality Ming.

▲ Porcelain jars were frequently painted with **symbolic decorative motifs**, such as this stylized *shou* character that signifies good luck, long life, happiness and riches. Late Ming potters tended to use an undiluted, imported purplish cobalt that did not allow detailing, hence the **blotchy appearance** of the painting.

▲ Another late Ming feature is the **floating, painted reign mark**, which has not been enclosed within a double circle as was common on early examples. The mark is also much less well executed than an earlier reign mark, which was drawn by a skilled calligrapher.

Important Ming Reign Marks

德年製	大明宣	化年製	大明成
Xuande 1426–35		**Chenghua** 1465–87	
治年製	大明弘	德年製	大明正
Hongzhi 1488–1505		**Zhengde** 1506–21	
曆年製	大明萬	啓年製	大明天
Wanli 1573–1619		**Tianqi** 1621–7	

Late Ming jar, 1522–66
The main part of this ovoid jar, like most Ming hollow vessels, was made in two parts. If you run your hand down the side of such a jar you can feel the horizontal seam around the middle, where the two sections have been joined together. This seam will be also visible on the inside of the jar. [C]

Types of Chinese Ceramics

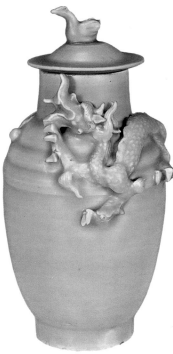

Longquan celadon funerary urn, 1127–1279 [C]

Celadon

The finest celadons were mainly made during the Song dynasty (1127–1279).

■ Wares include bowls and vases, which were based on ancient bronzes and jades.

■ The thick, light bluish-green glaze is almost luminous.

■ Note that the decoration is limited to simple moulded designs or relief patterns. Flower, bird and fish motifs were carved or incised with a knife and later examples were stamped.

■ Celadon stoneware produced in the Longquan kilns in eastern China was known for its fine, off-white, porcelain-like body.

■ The foot-rim is a strong reddish colour. If it is chipped, you will be able to see the slightly off-white body.

Qingbai ewer, 1127–1279 [C]

Qingbai

Qingbai ('blue-white') wares were produced during the Song dynasty in Jingdezhen, although the province of Jiangxi is best known for making this type of porcelain.

■ If you look at the base, you will notice that the body consists of a sugary white porcelain, covered with a glassy bluish, or greenish, glaze.

■ Wares often have simple incised or stamped decoration.

■ Qingbai wares feel very thin, since they are very finely potted. Shapes are refined and elegant.

■ This combination of very simple forms and delicate glazes gave way to increasingly ornate, cluttered designs during the Yuan dynasty (1279–1368).

Wucai **baluster jar, 16th century** [C]

Wucai

The *wucai* ('five colour') palette was developed during the reign of Jiajing (1522–66), and was an adaptation of the *doucai* palette (*see* opposite).

■ Decoration is in underglaze blue (as an outline or wash) and overglaze iron-red, green, brown, yellow and black.

■ *Wucai* decoration was used on large as well as small pieces, and is generally less refined than its *doucai* predecessor. Designs often seem as though they have been carelessly painted; if you compare *wucai* designs to those on *doucai,* they look much less precise.

***Blanc-de-Chine* figure of Guanyin, 18th century** [C]

Blanc-de-Chine

The term *blanc-de-Chine* takes its name from the French term for the white porcelain produced by the Dehua kilns in south-east China, from the late Ming dynasty to the present day.

■ Hold *blanc-de-Chine* up to the light and you will notice that the unpainted, highly translucent body is covered with a thick, transparent, rich creamy, or sometimes almost ivory, glaze.

■ *Blanc-de-Chine* was copied by such factories as Bow, Meissen and Saint-Cloud (*see* p.130).

■ Typical *blanc-de-Chine* wares include figures of Buddhist deities, such as Guanyin, the Goddess of Mercy, small cups and bottles. They are often decorated with reliefs of plum blossom, magnolia and pine.

Famille verte

The *famille verte* or 'green family' of enamel colours dominated by a brilliant apple green, was introduced during the Qing dynasty (1662–1722). This palette was the same as *wucai* (*see* opposite below left) except that a bright overglaze blue replaced the duller underglaze blue.

■ The palette includes yellow, aubergine, blue, iron-red, black and gilding.

■ Designs include rocky landscapes, flowers and the Eight Precious Things.

■ Look at the glaze close up – it should be quite thin and 'glassy'

Famille verte **baluster vase, 1723–35** [D]

Peachbloom brush pot, 18th century [A]

Peachbloom

Single-colour glazes derived from copper – of which 'peachbloom' is one – enjoyed a revival during the Qing Dynasty.

■ Difficult and expensive to produce, wares covered with a glaze of 'peachbloom' were largely reserved for small pieces for the scholar's desk, such as brush pots, small jars and vases.

■ If you look closely at a piece you will notice that the colour is deep and rich; 'peachbloom' is a soft, pinkish red, mottled with pale, cloudy brown patches and delicate, moss green flecks.

Doucai

Among the finest porcelains made during the Chenghua dynasty (1465–87) are wares in the highly refined decorative style known as *doucai*, or 'fitting' colours, so called because they fit together like the pieces of a jigsaw puzzle.

■ First outlined in underglaze blue, the design was painted with enamel colours, including iron-red, green, yellow and aubergine. If you look closely, the colours appear translucent.

■ Early *doucai* wares are generally small and fine and include bowls, small jars, stem and wine cups.

■ Decoration includes animals, dragons, plants and flowers, and figures, often set in a landscape.

Doucai **baluster vase, 18th century** [B]

Famille rose **dish, 18th century** [F]

Famille rose

In the early 18th century, the *famille rose*, or 'pink family' of enamel colours dominated by rose-pink, was developed.

■ Favourite decorative motifs included branches and rockwork, flowers, birds, landscapes and charming interior scenes.

■ *Famille rose* decoration appears on many Chinese wares, which were made in vast quantities for export to Europe during the 18th and 19th centuries. It occurs most commonly on large dinner services bearing the coats of arms of wealthy British families.

A Closer Look Arita Blue & White

Blue-and-white porcelain was the most popular ware produced at Arita, on the Japanese island of Kyushu from *c.*1615. Like its Chinese equivalent, Japanese blue-and-white porcelain was decorated with underglaze cobalt blue. The finished decoration ranged from a poor-quality, greyish or blackish blue to rich sapphire or bright, purplish blue depending on impurities present in the cobalt and how much colour was applied. By the mid-17th century, Japanese potters were producing a wide range of refined blue-and-white wares for the domestic market and the newly established western export trade. Popular Chinese patterns – with flowers and figures – from *kraak* wares made during the late Ming period for export were often freely adapted. Arita porcelain does not chip as much as Chinese wares, but it is more easily scratched.

◀ **Background designs** on Arita blue-and-white porcelain are usually **dense** and **complex**. The band of scrolled foliage, known as *karakusa*, or octopus scrollwork, was a favourite decorative pattern painted on late 17th- and 18th-century Arita blue-and-white wares.

▲ Inspect the shape of the **jar's neck** and you will see that it is **slightly splayed**, a characteristic of lidded jars made for the European market between *c.*1660–80.

▲ Between the fan-shaped panels, note the formalized **pendant decoration**, which looks like European late Baroque ornament, such as *Laub-und-Bandelwerk*.

Arita gallipot, c.1680
This jar is actually based on a European shape. The Dutch East India Company supplied the Japanese with wooden versions of European ceramics and Chinese kraak *porcelain jars and vases, asking them to copy the wares in porcelain.* [C]

Arita ovoid jar, c.1660–80
The panels decorating this large jar show how the Japanese were influenced by the decoration on Chinese kraak *porcelain. Each panel is shaped like a Chinese fan, filled with typical motifs of flowering shrubs divided by scrolling foliage and lotus flowers.* [D]

▼ In the centre of the neck of the jar, you can see an approximate copy of a Chinese **artemisia leaf** surrounded by ribbonwork. This was a popular decorative motif found on late Ming wares and one of the Eight Precious Things, the symbols of the Chinese scholar. Here the artemisia leaf has been so badly drawn by Japanese painters that it is almost unrecognizable as a piece of foliage, adding weight to the theory that Japanese decorators used Dutch models of Chinese wares.

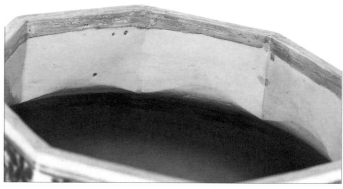

▲ One way to identify a piece of Arita is to look inside the **neck of the jar**; the body will be coarse and the glaze will be **crudely finished**. Run a finger along the top edge and the surface should feel quite coarse. This unglazed edge is also pinkish because impurities in the clay have oxidized to this colour.

▶ The base of Arita jars and other types of vessel is quite unlike Chinese wares. Usually Arita pieces have a **small ridge** or **bulge** at the **base**, a detail that was copied from European wares. In contrast, Chinese wares have a clean, unbroken line that goes right down to the foot-rim.

▶ Japanese porcelain was often fired on a bed of grit. Because the paste of Arita wares was quite clastic and heavy, there was a tendency for it to sag while being fired. As you see here, the base of the jar has picked up some **kiln grit** on its base.

Arita octagonal jar, c.1680
On first looking at this piece, you might think that the jar is Chinese because of the Chinese-style landscape, pagodas, bridges and figures. However, its sloping shoulders, with pendant petals and a band of fine parallel lines, are entirely Japanese. [C]

Types of Japanese Ceramics

Kakiemon bowl, late 17th century [C]

Kakiemon

Taking its name from the legendary 17th-century porcelain maker and painter Sakaida Kakiemon, who is said to have invented the enamelling process in Japan, Kakiemon porcelain reached its peak in the 1680s.

■ The milky white porcelain body, or *nigoshide,* made in the Arita kilns was usually sparingly painted in an asymmetrical style with overglaze enamels of iron-red, sky blue, turquoise, yellow, black and sometimes purple.

■ Small dishes, bowls, bottles and vases were painted with delicate patterns.

■ In 18th-century Europe, the Kakiemon style was widely copied by factories including Meissen, Chantilly (*see* p.130), Chelsea and Bow.

Imari

Named after the port of Imari, near the Arita district of Japan, this colourful porcelain was developed in the late 17th century.

■ The Imari palette includes dark underglaze blue with iron-red, gold, yellow, green, sometimes turquoise and purple.

■ Apart from red, all the colours sit quite high on the glaze's surface; you can usually feel them.

■ Large display pieces, tablewares and ornaments were decorated with patterns based on textile designs.

■ Later Imari wares were densely painted, primarily with red.

■ Imari wares were copied in China, Holland and England.

Imari jar and cover, c.1700–1725 [C]

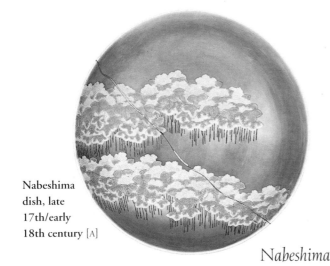

Nabeshima dish, late 17th/early 18th century [A]

Hirado figure, 1860–80 [J]

Nabeshima

The Nabeshima clan governed the region of Japan that included the district of Arita. Wares known as Nabeshima were made exclusively for family members, probably from the 1650s until *c.*1870.

■ Nabeshima wares are extremely rare and very desirable.

■ Pieces are of an off-white, flawless porcelain body, covered with a grey or blue-tinged glaze.

■ The potting was very regular and the wares were never marked.

■ The crisp painted decoration included stylized leaves and flowers.

Hirado

From the late 18th century, the kilns in the area around Hirado, near Arita, produced a fine-quality porcelain modelled into elegant shapes.

■ The pure white porcelain body resembling the texture of icing sugar was covered with a soft, bluish glaze.

■ Especially popular were white figures of children and animals, including fish, dragons and ducks, occasionally detailed with rust brown.

■ Blue-and-white wares may be decorated with children playing, pine-clad landscapes, stylized leaves and geometric patterns.

Satsuma

From the 16th century, Satsuma was an important centre of ceramic production, although it is best known today for its mass-produced wares made for the export market from the mid-19th century.

■ Cream-coloured earthenwares, with finely crackled glazes, were decorated with thickly applied enamels overlaid with gilding.

Satsuma octagonal vase, c.1900 [I]

■ Popular decorative motifs included landscapes, flowers, animals and genre scenes, as well as elaborate figures of geishas, warriors and holy men.

■ Wares ranged from high-quality to decidedly mediocre pieces.

■ The best-quality wares are signed or marked with the potter's name.

Kinkozan

Named after a Japanese family of potters working from the late 19th century near Satsuma. Kinkozan wares are very similar to those from Satsuma and it is easy to confuse the two.

■ Kinkozan wares are painted with detailed panels, often depicting miniature scenes of people carrying out everyday activities. Most wares were heavily embellished with gilding, which has a tendency to flake and rub.

■ Items produced include flower vases, incense burners and display ornaments.

Kinkozan earthenware vase, c.1900 [I]

■ Kinkozan wares range from cheaply made, harshly coloured porcelains to exquisitely crafted designs featuring pictures of warriors.

■ Pieces are usually signed by the artist.

Red Kutani

From around the 1880s, the potters of Kutani made vast quantities of this mainly porcelain body of eggshell thinness.

■ Red Kutani wares were decorated with overglaze colours dominated by iron-red (hence its name), heightened with lavish gilding and frequently having black or grisaille (black and grey) details.

■ Decoration tended to consist of figures in landscapes, geishas, flowers, trees and birds.

■ Huge quantities were exported to Europe and the USA; the quality is usually mediocre to poor.

Red kutani vase, late 19th century [Q]

Noritake tea service, 1930s [L]

Noritake

The Noritake factory was established in 1904 in Nagoya in central Japan and is best known for teawares exported to Europe and the USA.

■ The factory made hand-painted wares aimed at the European market, in an effort to compete with popular printed ceramics.

■ The hard-paste porcelain wares copied Victorian and Edwardian designs and were decorated with flowers, fruit and foliage, or landscapes painted in pale pastels highlighted with gold.

■ During the 1920s and 1930s Noritake commissioned designs from eminent designers, such as this tea service by Frank Lloyd Wright.

■ Wares are often marked with the name 'Nippon'.

Story of German Porcelain

Meissen teapot,
c.1730 [C]

IN THE EARLY 18TH CENTURY, *the central German state of Saxony was the first country in Europe to discover the formula for making hard-paste porcelain. Its factory at Meissen produced high-quality wares, which for around 50 years were regarded as the finest in Europe. Although other German states set up competing factories, none was ever as successful as Meissen.*

The search for a hard-paste porcelain recipe rivalling the much admired Chinese imports was not successful until the early 18th century, when the alchemist Johann Friedrich Böttger (*see* p.112) chanced upon the formula. By 1710 the first hard-paste ('true') porcelain had been made in Europe, and the Royal Saxon Porcelain Factory was established at Meissen, near Dresden, by Augustus the Strong, Elector of Saxony. With a smooth, white glaze that matched the purity of both Chinese porcelain and the renowned Japanese porcelain, Kakiemon (*see* p.122), the Meissen factory also developed a highly distinctive house style using chinoiseries (European imitations of Chinese art),

deutsche Blumen (German flowers), land, harbour scenes, hunting subjects, battle scenes and armorials (coats of arms).

Many skilled painters, designers and modellers contributed to Meissen's outstanding success. Advances in the development of porcelain at the factory were largely due to the arrival, in 1720, of the colour-chemist and painter Johann Gregorius Höroldt, who broadened the range of wares and expanded the colour palette. From the 1730s, vigorously modelled and exquisitely painted figures created by Johann Joachim Kändler further enhanced Meissen's reputation.

In addition to figures, Kändler and his team of designers and modellers created an extensive range of dinner services, tea and coffee services, and centrepieces. By the 1730s, Meissen porcelain had become extremely fashionable, although from the

Figure of an egg seller, c.1755. The finest of all products made at the Nymphenburg factory are figures by the Swiss modeller, Franz Anton Bustelli. A master of the German Rococo style, Bustelli created figures with expressive faces and gently twisting, slightly elongated bodies. [C]

1760s the factory started to lose its place as the dominant European porcelain maker to centres such as Sèvres in France.

By the mid-18th century, other German states had established porcelain factories, most significantly at Nymphenburg, Höchst, Frankenthal, Berlin, Ludwigsburg and Fürstenberg. While producing a similar range of wares and figures largely

Many of the finest German porcelain figures were produced at the Frankenthal factory. This commedia dell'arte *figure of Mezzetin (c.1760) is a good example of the Frankenthal style. It has a simple pad base, is stiffly modelled with a doll-like face and has highly detailed decoration.* [D]

Under the directorship of the Viennese painter J. J. Ringler, the small factory at Ludwigsburg produced beautifully modelled tablewares, such as this coffeepot (c.1760), with an ozier (basketwork) border and lid. Painted in soft pastel colours it is scattered with flowers undoubtedly inspired by the deutsche Blumen, *first introduced on Meissen porcelain.* [J]

based on those produced at Meissen, each factory developed their own characteristic style using distinctive hard pastes (the mixture from which porcelain is made).

German factories made porcelain in the fashionable styles inspired by Meissen and later the French factory of Sèvres. German porcelain makers mastered the early 18th-century Baroque and Rococo styles with panache, and after a less dramatic Neo-classical phase, the flamboyant Rococo Revival style dominated German porcelain from the mid-19th century.

Inevitably, the mass-production methods developed during the 19th century resulted in a vast output of inexpensive and often mediocre porcelain. Furthermore, in the late 19th and early 20th centuries, at least 40 porcelain workshops and decorators in and around Dresden copied Meissen-style wares. Best known among these was the factory of Carl Thieme at Potschappel, and the work of the decorator Helena Wolfsohn, who specialized in painting vases, tea and coffee wares.

Hausmaler

Some of the finest painting found on German porcelain was done by *Hausmaler* ('home painters') in Augsburg and Breslau. From the 1720s, these freelance artists bought blanks (undecorated tablewares) from the Meissen factory and decorated them with single- or multicoloured enamels and elaborate gilding in their studios and workshops. The most famous decorating workshops were owned by the Seuter and Auffenwerth families, who specialized in Meissen-style chinoiseries, town and landscapes, and mythological and genre (scenes from everyday life) subjects.

Teabowl and saucer decorated by a *Hausmaler* workshop, c.1730. [I]

Johann Peter Melchior, a master modeller at Höchst, made figures, such as this rustic group (c.1765), celebrated for their delicate detailed features. A hallmark of Melchior's figures is a base covered with grass and earth, or rockwork painted in green or brown. Höchst figures can often be distinguished by the dark brown spots used to depict their eyes. [F]

Early tablewares produced by the Fürstenberg factory often have specially moulded edges in order to disguise any impurities in the hard-paste porcelain. This part dinner service (c.1785), is an example of the factory's significant output of Neo-classical wares and shows the influence of the French factory of Sèvres in the border decoration. [F]

A Closer Look *Early & Late Meissen*

Figures were produced at Meissen from the early days of the factory, but the best pieces were made by, and during the time of, Johann Joachim Kändler, who was the factory's chief modeller from 1733 to 1775. When the Rococo Revival was at its height in the 1830s, the factory started to reproduce figures using the original moulds and some of the designs. Figures of 18th-century subjects, such as shepherds and shepherdesses, made up much of Meissen's huge output. Although the 19th-century copies may look superficially like the early originals, watch out for differences such as the style of the face and the colours used. Later copies often have sweet, rather sentimental, faces compared to the original figures; copies were also painted with harsher, 'chemical' colours and often stand on bulky Rococo-style bases.

▲ Note the **crisply defined modelling** of the tricorn hat and the captain's long hair. The painting is more careful and the details sharper than on the 19th-century figure (*see* opposite).

▲ If you examine the base you will notice how an early Meissen figure stands on a simple **mound base** with delicately applied flowers. In the late 1740s, this style of base was abandoned in favour of a taller, heavier style.

Early Meissen, c.1745
This captain is one of the traditional Italian commedia dell'arte *figures modelled by Peter Reinicke. Compare this confident and posed figure, which has a definite sense of lively and dramatic movement, with the more static stance of the 19th-century group of figures opposite. Early figures are usually also painted in strong colours.* [H]

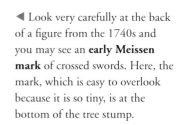

◀ Look very carefully at the back of a figure from the 1740s and you may see an **early Meissen mark** of crossed swords. Here, the mark, which is easy to overlook because it is so tiny, is at the bottom of the tree stump.

Important Modellers

The greatest modeller at Meissen, J. J. Kändler, shared the limelight with Peter Reinicke and J. F. Eberlein, among others. Talented modellers at other German factories included Franz Anton Bustelli at Nymphenburg, and J. P. Melchior at Höchst. Some modellers, such as Simon Feilner, moved between factories, taking their individual styles with them.

Meissen figure of Harlequin Alarmed, by J. J. Kändler, *c*.1740 [A]

▶ During the mid-1730s figure bases were often glazed, but by *c*.1740 bases were unglazed and had a small vent hole. This **unglazed, flat base** shows the **greyish clay** of Meissen porcelain dotted with black flecks. Run a finger across the base and feel the slight bumps where the tool marks have not been ground away.

▶ Although this **ponytail** has been modelled to show some movement, it still looks quite **stiff**. Unlike most 19th-century figures, which are heavily painted all over, the **jacket** of this figure has been left **uncoloured** to show off the white paste.

◀ Compared to the cleaner apple green of the leafy decoration on the pad base of the earlier figure, the **green** on this 19th-century example is much **harsher**. Colours were also applied in a haphazard way – look at the edge of the jacket (towards the top of the detail).

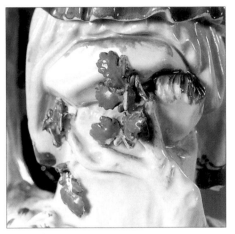

Late Meissen, c.1870
Popular 18th-century porcelain figures such as this pair of lovers were reissued by Meissen in the 19th century. Although pedestal bases had been used at Meissen from the 1750s, the scrolls and gilding were much more complex on later versions. [J]

Other Meissen Marks

Königliche Porzellan Manufaktur (Royal Porcelain Factory; used 1723–4)

'Dot' period (1763–74)   Used from 1924

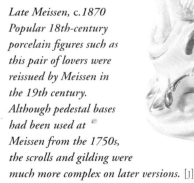

◀ Turn the 19th-century figure upside down and you will see a **series of marks** in addition to the Meissen crossed swords (this version was in use from 1818 until 1924). Figures made throughout the 19th century are marked on the base with large, incised numbers that may identify the model; the red '67' is the painter's number. Notice also how the **base** is **concave** and covered with a distinctive **hard, glassy glaze**.

A Closer Look Sèvres & Paris Porcelain

The two leading French centres of porcelain production in the late 18th century were Sèvres and Paris. In Paris at least 15 factories operated from the 1780s to the 1840s. The main difference between the wares made at each centre was the type of paste used. Until 1768, when china clay (kaolin) was discovered in the region of Limoges in central France, Sèvres made a creamy white, soft-paste porcelain, which was at first sparsely decorated, but was later covered in strong background colours. In contrast, only a pure white, hard-paste porcelain was used to make Paris wares. Following the revival of the Rococo style in the mid-19th century, many factories in Paris and Limoges copied 18th-century Sèvres wares. They made fair reproductions of the Sèvres originals, but if you compare pieces, you will notice some striking differences.

SOME IMPORTANT SEVRES COLOURS	
BLEU LAPIS (DARK BLUE)	FROM 1749
BLEU CELESTE (TURQUOISE)	FROM 1752
POMME VERTE (APPLE GREEN)	FROM 1756
ROSE POMADOUR (RICH PINK)	FROM 1758

Sèvres vase hollandais, 1758
This fine vase with a detachable base is decorated in **bleu camieu** *– cameo-like painting in a single colour – set within a fine raised gold cartouche (frame). This type of vase was used for planting bulbs – 'hollandais' refers to Holland where bulbs such as hyacinths and tulips came from.* [B]

▼ The decoration on early Sèvres porcelain is characterized by **fine painting** often, as in this detail, in the style of the French court painter François Boucher. Note the extremely **fine brushstrokes** in this detail. The colours also appear to sink into the satiny glaze.

▲ The **interlaced 'Ls'** on the base stand for Louis XV. Inside is a **date letter**, which was first introduced in 1753. Here, the letter 'F' signifies the year 1758.

◄ The gilding carried out at the Sèvres factory is considered to be the most sumptuous ever applied to porcelain, largely because the process was strictly controlled – if pieces were not considered good enough, they were simply thrown away. Notice how the **rich gilding** sits thickly on the surface and has a warm, **reddish glow**. Run a finger gently over the surface and feel the **raised surface**. Look closely – or use a magnifying glass – to see the very fine lines showing where the gilding, which was carefully built up in layers, has been carefully tooled to give it a three-dimensional appearance.

▶ Although **turquoise blue** (*bleu celeste*) was used as a background colour on Sèvres porcelain from 1752, it mostly decorated 19th-century copies made at the Paris factories. However, later turquoise tended to be a **greyer blue** and lacked the depth and richness seen on earlier Sèvres. The **gilding** seen here, although abundant, is much **flatter** than on the 18th-century Sèvres example.

Paris vase, c.1880
The Paris factories relied heavily on earlier designs from Sèvres, although they freely adapted shapes and patterns. The shape of this vase did not exist in the 18th century, and the panel of flowers inside a gilt border surrounded by scrollwork is a version of earlier styles. [J]

◀ The most popular decorations found on Paris porcelain include classical subjects and floral arrangements, many of which were copied from famous paintings. Since many Paris wares were painted by decorators working out of the factory, there was little quality control. Look carefully at this panel and you will notice that the **painting** is of a **lesser quality** than on the Sèvres vase. The **hard, glossy glaze** used on Paris porcelain was resistant to enamelling and gilding, so the decoration tends to sit on the surface.

▶ Many pieces from the Paris factories were left unmarked, although some, like this vase, have a **fake** underglaze blue **Sèvres mark** of interlaced 'Ls'. The lack of a date letter within the 'Ls' provides another clue to the piece's true origins. The Sèvres mark is the most commonly faked mark on porcelain.

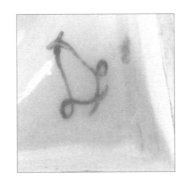

18th-century European Factories

Chantilly tea bowl and saucer, *c.*1725–50 [J]

Chantilly

The Chantilly factory (est. *c.*1725) had as its patron the Prince de Condé, an avid collector of Japanese Kakiemon porcelain.

■ This soft-paste porcelain has a distinctive, opaque creamy glaze that concealed the imperfections in this experimental porcelain.

■ The factory produced a wide range of useful and decorative wares, many of which copied the Kakiemon style (*see* p.122).

 ■ A small red hunting horn was used as a mark until *c.*1750, thereafter it appears in underglaze blue, red or purple.

Saint-Cloud

Saint-Cloud (est. *c.*1695) near Paris was the first French factory to produce porcelain commercially. It specialized in small wares, including snuff boxes and cutlery handles (*see* p.167).

■ The creamy soft paste is covered by an ivory glaze, with hints of olive green in the crevices.

■ The glaze can be marred by minute black flecks.

■ Early wares were painted in underglaze blue. After *c.*1730 Kakiemon-style enamelling and *blanc-de-Chine* wares were decorated with relief decoration of oriental designs.

■ Wares are sometimes marked with an incised or painted 'StC' over a 'T'.

Saint-Cloud cosmetic pot, *c.*1740 [K]

Mennecy

The factory opened in Paris in 1734 under the patronage of the Duke de Villeroy; it moved to nearby Mennecy in 1748.

■ The mellow, ivory-coloured soft paste was covered with a creamy white, glassy, translucent glaze.

■ Mennecy specialized in small decorative objects and small tablewares, decorated with a delicate palette of rose pink, sky blue, yellow, turquoise and green.

■ French control marks on the silver mounts may help dating.

D·V· ■ The letters DV, for the Duke de Villeroy, are usually incised, but sometimes may be painted.

Mennecy snuff box, *c.*1750 [J]

Capodimonte group of figures, *c.*1750 [B]

Capodimonte

Founded in 1743 in Naples, the factory produced fine porcelain until 1759, when the works were moved to Buen Retiro in Madrid.

■ The soft paste is translucent and creamy white with a brilliant glaze.

■ Giuseppe Gricci, the chief modeller, created animated figures with small heads, sparingly painted in muted pastel colours.

 ■ From 1745 the Capodimonte mark was an impressed fleur-de-lis painted in gold or underglaze blue.

Vienna pair of lovers, *c.*1760 [H]

Vienna

This hard-paste porcelain factory (est. 1718) was founded in Vienna with the assistance of workers from Meissen.

■ The body is greyish white; the thin glaze has a greenish tinge.

■ Figures are often stiffly posed and have simple gilded pad bases.

■ Colours used included a greyish green, lilac, puce and yellow.

■ After 1744 wares were marked with the Austrian shield. Figures also have numbers and letters for decorators and repairers.

Ludwigsburg

The factory changed from faience to porcelain production in 1758.

■ The greyish white, close-grained, hard-paste body is almost entirely obscured by the glaze, which is generally very smoky and greenish where it has pooled in the crevices.

■ Figures are crisply modelled and decorated in a range of colours – puce, green, yellow, cobalt and black.

■ Look under the figure bases and you will often find a crossed support (seen here).

■ The standard mark between 1758 and 1793 was a pair of interlaced 'C's, in underglaze blue but sometimes gilded.

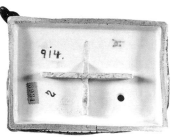

Ludwigsburg figure, *c.*1760 [H]

Tournai plate, *c.*1775–80 [K]

Tournai

Although this factory (est. 1751) was situated in Flanders (now Belgium), its porcelain was French in decoration and design.

■ At first the creamy soft paste was off-white. Later the paste was ivory with a soft, translucent and slightly glassy glaze.

■ Pieces are moulded with spiral panels and basketwork edges, and are sometimes painted with landscapes in single colours.

■ The early mark of a tower was painted in blue, crimson or gold; after *c.*1765 crossed swords with four small crosses.

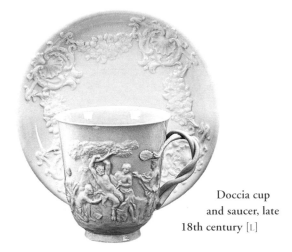

Doccia cup and saucer, late 18th century [L]

Doccia

The Doccia factory (est. 1735), near Florence, is still in operation today.

■ The greyish hard-paste porcelain has a thin, sticky-looking glaze.

■ Shallow relief moulding of classical subjects is a favourite ornamentation for teawares and small decorative objects. Doccia was one of the few continental factories of the time to use underglaze blue transfer printing.

■ The usual mark, stamped or painted red, blue or gold was a star. A Crowned 'N' was used for 19th-century copies of wares from Naples.

A Closer Look *Worcester Porcelain*

One of the most successful 18th-century English porcelain factories, Worcester (est. 1751) specialized in tea, coffee and decorative tablewares. Finely potted and with a thin, even glaze, Worcester porcelain contained soaprock, a type of granite that made it very hard-wearing. Moulded decoration included branch or twisted ropework handles and applied flowers, many examples of which copied or adapted designs from the Meissen factory. In the late 1760s, chinoiseries and flowers favoured on early wares gave way to a more opulent style inspired by the French factory of Sèvres (*see* p.128). Decorative wares were painted with background colours, panels of flowers and exotic birds surrounded by gilded frames. Among the most popular wares produced in Worcester during the 1770s were trelliswork baskets.

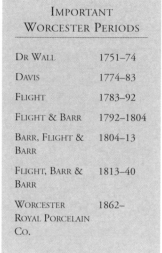

Worcester basket, c.1770
This trelliswork basket shows the influence of the two most important 18th-century European factories: Meissen in the shape and Sèvres in the applied flowers, warm honey gilding and coloured background. [H]

▶ Worcester trelliswork baskets had a tendency to **crack** at the intersections during firing, so small **flowers** were applied to strengthen them. As seen here, these flowers often split right through the centre when fired.

▼ Enamelled decoration at Worcester reached a high standard. In this detail you can see one of the famous Worcester **birds** known as 'fancy' or 'fabulous' birds. First introduced in the 1760s, this type of bird was a speciality of the painter George Davis.

▼ The **'scale-blue' background** seen in this detail was an important invention at Worcester in the mid-1760s. You can usually date the pieces on which it appears to the 1770s and 1780s. The very intense underglaze blue and feathery gilding is typical of the best Worcester porcelain.

▼ This **mark** was used at Worcester between *c.*1765 and 1790 on this type of heavily decorated wares. However, be extra careful of wares that bear this mark, since it was used on 19th-century copies of Worcester particularly by Paris firms such as Edmé Samson & Cie (*see* p.139).

Other Marks

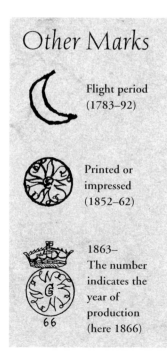

Flight period (1783–92)

Printed or impressed (1852–62)

1863– The number indicates the year of production (here 1866)

A CLOSER LOOK *Painted & Printed Wares*

Painting is one of the most popular techniques for decorating pottery and porcelain. The underglaze method of painting designs with cobalt blue before glazing, which originated in 13th-century Persia, was used by the Chinese for decorating porcelain and later adopted by factories throughout Europe. In addition to underglaze blue decoration, a range of colours was also developed for earthenware, stoneware and porcelain. These included a limited number of high-fired colours, and a larger range of low-fired colours, or delicate enamels, that were applied over the glaze. However, hand-painting was time-consuming and costly. With the invention of transfer printing in the mid-18th century (*see* p.107), wares with prints taken from engraved copper plates proved to be an inexpensive alternative.

Transfer-printed porcelain saucer, c.1780
The 'Fisherman' design seen on this dish was a popular transfer-printed pattern. Transfer printing was used on earthenware, stoneware and porcelain and a few early pieces were highlighted with hand-painted enamel colours. [P]

Hand-painted Worcester saucer, c.1770
Loosely hand-painted decorations often have a freedom and individuality, which is lacking in their transfer-printed counterparts. [N]

▶ The **free style** of this design indicates that it was **hand-painted,** as do the lack of any regular hatched lines that indicate transfer printing. Cobalt oxide (which is black) was painted on to the once-fired porcelain, allowed to sink into the body and then given a second firing. It was finally dipped into the glaze and given a third firing, when the blue colour emerges.

▲ In this detail you can see the **cross-hatching** created by the engraved lines on the copper plate. Although this design has been carefully applied, on mass-market wares breaks in the design may appear where the transfer has split, or where the ends of the print do not meet.

18th-century British Factories

Lund's Bristol sauceboat, *c.*1750 [I]

Chelsea pot and cover, *c.*1755 [H]

Lund's Bristol

Founded at Bristol by Benjamin Lund, this factory (est. *c.*1749) produced blue-and-white porcelain.

■ The hard-wearing soft-paste contained Cornish soapstone, a substitute for the china clay used to manufacture hard-paste porcelain.

■ The decoration frequently appears out of focus, since the heavy glaze used tended to blur the underglaze blue.

■ A restricted range of shapes included teapots, mugs, coffee cups, pickle dishes and shells, and patty pans.

■ Rarely marked, a few sauceboats and creamboats were embossed with 'Bristol' and the date, 1750.

Chelsea

Chelsea (est. 1744), was one of the earliest English factories to concentrate on the production of enamelled porcelain.

■ Wares made during the Triangle period (1744–9) copied Rococo silver shapes and were often left white. During the Raised Anchor period (1749–52), decoration emulated Japanese Kakiemon porcelain, Vincennes and Meissen.

■ The Red Anchor period (1752–6) is famous for animal and vegetable tureens, botanical plates, Meissen-style figures and flower decoration. The Gold Anchor period (1756–69), imitated the sumptuous colours and gilding fashionable at Sèvres.

Vauxhall

The Vauxhall China Works (est. 1751) was set up on the south bank of the river Thames.

■ The soft-paste porcelain contained soapstone, with a creamy glaze that sometimes looks 'peppered', or pitted.

■ Influenced by silver, delftware, Chinese porcelain and salt-glazed stoneware, Vauxhall produced a variety of wares including teawares, candlesticks, flowerpots, cream jugs and more than 20 types of sauceboat.

■ Decoration included inky underglaze blue, an Imari palette of red, blue and gold, and brightly coloured European flowers painted in the Meissen style.

Vauxhall vase, *c.*1755 [G]

Bow

The Bow factory (est. 1744), also known as 'New Canton', was less exclusive than Chelsea, producing wares and figures for a wider market.

■ The white and chalky granular soft-paste porcelain contains bone ash, which tends to stain. The glassy, blue tinged glaze is liable to crackle and pool around the base.

■ Some wares were decorated in vivid underglaze blue in Chinese and Japanese taste, including *blanc-de-Chine* plum blossoms, the 'quail' pattern and Meissen-style flowers.

■ The red anchor and dagger marks were used between 1762–76.

Bow dancer, *c.*1760–65 [J]

Lowestoft butter boat, *c.*1765 [J]

Liverpool – Chaffers teapot, 1770 [J]

Lowestoft

Founded in Suffolk, the Lowestoft factory (est. 1757) closed in 1802.

■ The firm's soft-paste recipe included bone ash, which tends to discolour; wares were often covered with a grey-green tinged glaze.

■ Early wares were simply painted in dark, inky underglaze blue with Chinese and delftware-style patterns, sometimes with moulded decoration, and often in salt-glaze stoneware shapes. Flowers and Chinese figure subjects dominated later multicoloured wares.

■ A speciality of the factory was inscribed and dated pieces made for the local market.

■ The mark was a version of the Worcester crescent.

Liverpool – Chaffers

Although at least four factories produced porcelain in Liverpool, the firm founded by Richard Chaffers in 1756 was one of the most successful.

■ The soft-paste porcelain body contained soapstone, covered by a greyish glaze tinged with blue or green that tended to 'pepper' or pit.

■ Most wares were decorated in bright underglaze blue, and also sometimes iron-red and gilding. The enamel colours used were based on a harsh *famille rose* palette.

■ The factory produced teawares, but few figures. Designs are heavily influenced by English delftware and Chinese blue-and-white patterns, and occasionally 'Japan' patterns borrowed from Worcester.

Plymouth

Plymouth (est. 1768) was the first English factory to produce hard-paste porcelain.

■ The greyish hard paste has a yellow-tinged glaze covered with black speckling.

■ Rococo vases and large figures on high scroll bases were among the factory's most successful products.

■ A range of wares was decorated with coloured enamels, or with a blackish, blurred, underglaze blue.

■ Motifs included oriental flowers, figures and landscapes that emulated Worcester wares.

■ Much Plymouth porcelain was marked with a combination of 2 and 4, which was the alchemist's sign for tin.

Plymouth baluster mug, *c.*1770 [J]

Derby tureen, *c.*1785–1800 [J]

Derby

The Derby factory (est. 1750) was taken over by two Chelsea decorators in 1770. The period until 1784 is known as the Chelsea-Derby period.

■ The early chalky white soft paste is covered with a glass-like, creamy glaze, inclined to dribble.

■ The factory specialized in crisply modelled figures and vases, tureens, leaf-moulded plates and baskets that were heavily influenced by Meissen.

■ Figures were fired on pads of clay, leaving a triangle of three greyish 'patch' marks on the base (*see* p.115).

■ Marks include this crowned 'D' used from 1770–82.

135

A CLOSER LOOK *Derby Porcelain*

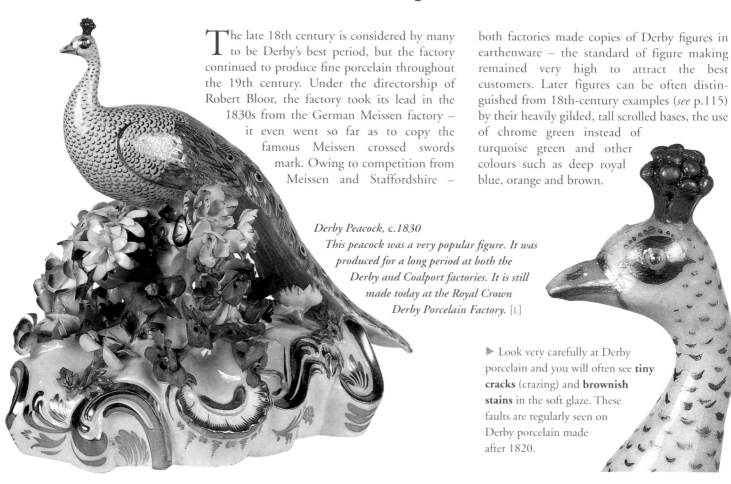

The late 18th century is considered by many to be Derby's best period, but the factory continued to produce fine porcelain throughout the 19th century. Under the directorship of Robert Bloor, the factory took its lead in the 1830s from the German Meissen factory – it even went so far as to copy the famous Meissen crossed swords mark. Owing to competition from Meissen and Staffordshire –

both factories made copies of Derby figures in earthenware – the standard of figure making remained very high to attract the best customers. Later figures can be often distinguished from 18th-century examples (*see* p.115) by their heavily gilded, tall scrolled bases, the use of chrome green instead of turquoise green and other colours such as deep royal blue, orange and brown.

Derby Peacock, c.1830
This peacock was a very popular figure. It was produced for a long period at both the Derby and Coalport factories. It is still made today at the Royal Crown Derby Porcelain Factory. [L]

▶ Look very carefully at Derby porcelain and you will often see **tiny cracks** (crazing) and **brownish stains** in the soft glaze. These faults are regularly seen on Derby porcelain made after 1820.

▲ Applied flowers and leaves on 19th-century figures were not modelled individually by hand, as in the 18th century, but **moulded** or **stamped**, which gave them a more regular shape. This cluster of dark purple flowers is a particular feature of 19th-century figures.

▲ Notice how the finely gilded feathers look **metallic** and **shiny**. This was because the expensive and time-consuming method of 'honey-gilding', which has a warm, pinkish glow, was abandoned in favour of inexpensive – and highly dangerous – mercury gilding.

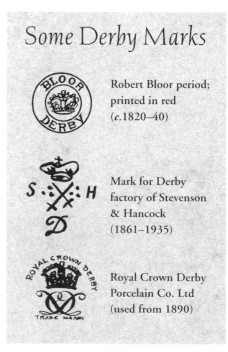

Some Derby Marks

Robert Bloor period; printed in red (*c.*1820–40)

Mark for Derby factory of Stevenson & Hancock (1861–1935)

Royal Crown Derby Porcelain Co. Ltd (used from 1890)

A CLOSER LOOK *Tucker Porcelain*

The first successful porcelain produced in the USA was made by the firm of William Ellis Tucker of Philadelphia, from the mid-1820s until 1838. Throughout its short life, this factory adopted various names, but was most commonly known as 'Tucker & Hemphill'. The hard-paste Tucker porcelain was most frequently painted with flowers, portraits or narrative scenes. Early wares from the factory were painted with landscapes or figures in a limited palette of sepia and dark brown, copying the designs on blue-and-white Staffordshire pottery. The colours and designs later became richer and more varied. Popular, vividly painted floral designs, highlighted with gilding, were copied from the French factory of Sèvres. The shapes of Tucker ornamental porcelain closely resemble the Neo-classical wares of the Paris factories.

Tucker pitcher, 1828–38
Pitchers of all sizes and types were a speciality of the Tucker factory. This vase-shaped pitcher with an arched handle is a shape unique to Tucker. [H]

▶ The **moulded leaf** shape, seen here under the handle, is a common feature of a Tucker pitcher. The thick glaze has a **greenish tint** that has a tendency to pool. When held up to the light, early examples have a greenish cast – later pieces appear orange or straw coloured.

▼ This charcoal-grey (known as 'grisaille') hand-painted landscape with a cottage and flanking tree is a **typical Tucker decoration**. It is thought to have been taken from English printed wares of the same period.

◀ If you look at the base of this pitcher you can see the **rough, pitted** hard paste visible on the thick, **unglazed foot-rim**. Most Tucker porcelain pieces, such as this, are **unmarked**, and are very hard to distinguish from the French porcelain on which many of the examples were based. Some pieces, however, are marked in red enamel with 'Tucker & Hulme' or 'Tucker & Hemphill'.

19th-century European Factories

**Vienna tray by
Joseph Nigg, 1807** [C]

Vienna

In the 19th century, the Vienna factory (est. 1718) made Neo-classical wares, with rich backgrounds highlighted by sumptuous gilt scrollwork.
■ The factory was well known for its fine tea and coffee services and decorative wares painted with classical scenes, topographic views and flowers framed with heavy raised gilding, and copies of Meissen figures.
■ The paste used at Vienna was a hard paste. On 18th-century pieces the paste is greyish with a glassy glaze, while on 19th-century wares the paste is very hard and glassy looking.

Berlin

The first, short-lived Berlin factory (est. 1751) was followed by a second one (est. 1761).
■ The body is a hard paste, greyish in tone and covered with a slightly bluish glaze.
■ The factory is probably best known for its 19th-century porcelain plaques decorated with copies of well-known paintings. If you look carefully at some of the cheaper examples, you can see printed outlines, which have been filled in with enamel colours.
■ Early pieces are marked with a sceptre. From 1832, the mark was an orb with the letters 'KPM' (Königliche Porzellan-Manufaktur) in
KPM underglaze blue.

Berlin vase, *c*.1860 [D]

**Jacob Petit teapot,
c.1840** [L]

Jacob Petit

One of the leading porcelain manufacturers in Paris from the 1830s was Jacob Petit; the factory produced hard-paste ornamental wares.
■ Wares were mainly made in Rococo and Gothic Revival styles with moulded or painted flowers, coloured backgrounds and metallic gilding.
■ Typical wares include tea services and clockcases, elaborately painted
jP. and encrusted with flowers and rockwork, as well as novelty scent bottles and inkwells.
■ Wares were marked with the letters 'JP' in underglaze blue.

Meissen ewer, *c*.1870 [H]

Meissen

In the 1830s, Meissen adopted a Rococo Revival style that survived until the 1920s. Complex pieces were encrusted with ornaments and covered with harsh enamel colours and glossy gilding.
■ It can be very difficult to identify 19th-century Meissen wares, since many other factories, particularly those in and around Dresden and in Thuringia and Silesia, were making exact copies.
■ The body of 19th-centuy Meissen is hard and pure white; it is covered with a hard glaze.
■ The famous Meissen crossed swords mark tended to be larger and longer in the 19th century than the mark used in the 18th century.

Carl Thieme

Carl Thieme's enterprise (est. 1872) at Potschappel, near Dresden, was one of many 19th-century factories copying Meissen Rococo Revival wares.

■ The hard-paste porcelain is almost as refined as at Meissen.

■ Wares include huge vases, candelabra and mirror frames, encrusted with scrolls, shells or garlands of fruit and flowers and painted in bright enamel colours.

■ Wares made in the 19th century were marked with a painted cross and the letter 'T'. From 1900, wares were printed with the 'SP' cypher and 'Dresden' to indicate the factory's new name, Sachsische Porzellanfabrik.

Carl Thieme vase, c.1880 [H]

Vienna-style plate, c.1870 [N]

Vienna-style wares

After the Vienna factory closed in 1864, a large stock of undecorated porcelain was sold off to factories who reproduced Vienna-style wares.

■ Look carefully at the heavy, flat gilded borders and the crude painting on a Vienna-style piece and compare it to a Vienna original – you will find that it falls short of the refined quality of the original.

■ Beware of wares marked with the underglaze blue shield of the Vienna factory, since many of the blanks sold were already marked.

Edmé Samson & Cie

The most prolific imitator of early ceramics was Edmé Samson & Cie (est. 1845) of Paris.

■ Samson reproduced a huge variety of oriental and European porcelain, as well as faience, Delft and English porcelain.

■ When copying soft-paste wares, chemicals were added to give the hard paste a creamy appearance.

■ Many Samson copies adhere closely to the forms and colours of the originals.

■ Most Samson wares bear the company's entwined double 'S' mark, as well as good imitations 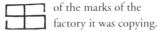 of the marks of the factory it was copying.

Samson armorial vase, c.1890 [J]

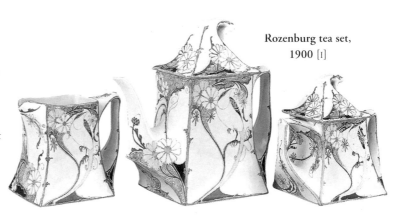

Rozenburg tea set, 1900 [I]

Rozenburg

In the late 19th century, Juriaan Kok took over a small pottery at Rozenburg near The Hague in the Netherlands.

■ The factory is most famous for a fine eggshell porcelain that is extremely thin and light, made from 1899–1913.

 ■ Many wares are imaginatively decorated and hand-painted with flowers, leaves, birds, insects and spider webs.

■ Wares are marked with the name of Rozenburg above a stork, which symbolizes The Hague (Den Haag).

A Closer Look *Belleek Porcelain*

The Belleek factory was established in 1857 in County Fermanagh, Ireland. At first the factory made earthenwares, but from 1863 specialized in the production of an extremely fine, translucent porcelain. Still in operation today, Belleek is particularly known for its thick, iridescent glaze that resembles mother-of-pearl. Wares made include extravagantly modelled vases, figures and busts, mirrors and tea services, often in the form of shells, with names such as 'Neptune'. Elaborate, openwork baskets, made of intricately handwoven strands of clay, with applied flowers, leaves and shamrocks, are among the factory's finest products. In the USA, firms such as Knowles Taylor & Knowles (est. 1872) and the Lenox Co. (est. 1889) produced good-quality porcelain called 'American Belleek' (*see* p.143). However, their wares bear little resemblance to Irish Belleek.

Irish Belleek basket, 1863–90 Covered baskets are very difficult to produce, since the base and cover were made to fit each other exactly. If one piece failed to turn out perfectly after firing, both sections had to be discarded. [H]

▲ An **intricate top handle,** made to resemble tangled twigs, was used on Belleek basket lids until *c.*1935, and can provide a valuable clue to dating. Each flower, leaf and twig on an early basket was **carefully modelled** by hand. An abundance of flowers and leaves usually indicates an early period of production, and baskets of this kind are very collectable.

◄ Baskets plaited from two strands of clay were first made *c.*1865, and are now very rare. The **three-strand** basket was made until *c.*1900. Beware, however, as the factory has since reissued both two- and three-strand baskets.

▼ The **glaze** of early Belleek is a **rich ivory** colour and is very smooth. The clay used to make earlier wares also has a slightly greyer tinge than later examples.

▼ One of the most outstanding aspects of Belleek porcelain is the wonderful **iridescent glaze** used on many wares. In this detail you can see the sparkling lustrous glaze that resembles mother-of-pearl covering the beautiful handmade details.

◄ Most 19th-century baskets had side handles that emerged from under a rosebud. Because of the fragility of porcelain, the handles often broke. Would-be buyers should look out for baskets with **no handles** whatsoever, since when one handle fell off, sometimes the other was removed too. This can affect the value of a piece.

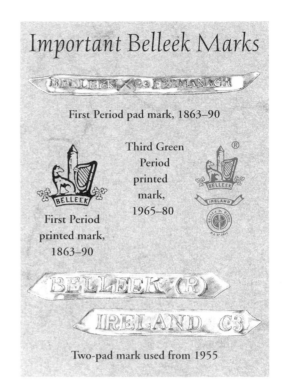

▲ Compared to the earlier basket, the **top handle** on this 20th-century piece is **less intricate**. In order to give it the look and texture of coral, each section has been rolled in tiny scraps of clay. This type of handle was introduced after 1940.

▲ The **fancy, plaited strands** seen around the edge of the basket suggest that it was made at a later date. Earlier baskets usually have only one simple twisted strand around the edge.

Important Belleek Marks

First Period pad mark, 1863–90

First Period printed mark, 1863–90

Third Green Period printed mark, 1965–80

Two-pad mark used from 1955

Irish Belleek basket, c.1980
After c.1940, baskets tended to be decorated with a few multicoloured flowers that lacked the exquisite details of those applied to earlier baskets. [J]

▲ Note how the thick, **'wet-look' glaze** has collected and 'pooled' in the **crevices**, which you should expect to find on all Belleek baskets of this type whatever their age. The **four-strand** woven centre is a sign, however, that the basket is a 20th-century product.

BELLEEK PERIODS	
1ST PERIOD	1863–90
2ND PERIOD	1891–1926
3RD PERIOD	1926–46
1ST GREEN OR 4TH PERIOD	1946–55
2ND GREEN OR 5TH PERIOD	1955–65
3RD GREEN OR 6TH PERIOD	1965–80
1ST GOLD OR 7TH PERIOD	1980–92
BLUE MARK OR 8TH PERIOD	1993–

▶ Delicate pinks, greens, blues and yellows were sometimes applied. In general, **multicoloured painting** indicates that the basket was made in the 20th century.

▶ If you look carefully at modern Belleek wares, you will notice that the **glaze** has a **gritty** finish; if you run your finger over the porcelain, it will feel like there are grains of sand embedded it.

141

19th-century British & American Factories

Davenport

Davenport dinner service, *c*.1815 [G]

The factory of Davenport (est. 1794) in Longport, Staffordshire, produced a wide range of quality earthenware, creamware, bone china and even glass throughout the 19th century.

■ Wares tend to have detailed decoration in bright colours and gilding. Decorators often copied Derby patterns, but also created imaginative designs of their own, some in the style of Japanese Imari (*see* p.101).

■ The firm produced porcelain dinner services in many different styles, and is particularly known for its blue-and-white tableware.

■ Pieces are usually marked with the Davenport name and a pattern number. Between 1870 and 1886, a crown mark was also used.

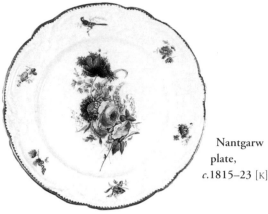

Nantgarw plate, *c*.1815–23 [K]

Nantgarw

The factory of Nantgarw (est. 1813) in South Wales aimed to make porcelain that was as good as the high-quality wares from Paris.

■ Hold a piece of genuine Nantgarw up to the light and you will see that the body is a pure white, translucent soft-paste porcelain, covered with a thick glaze.

■ Wares made included plates, cups, saucers and decorative ornaments.

■ A good way to identify Nantgarw is to look for the triangle of three small circles on the base left by the supports used during firing.

NANT-GARW C.W. ■ Wares were marked with the factory name. The initials 'C.W.' stand for China Works.

Spode

Spode chocolate cup and saucer, *c*.1820 [K]

Established at Stoke-on-Trent in 1776, Spode achieved fame with a range of wares decorated with botanical, topographical or Imari patterns.

■ The pure white body was covered with a thin glaze.

■ Credited with the invention or improvement of bone china from *c*.1796, Spode produced well-modelled, thinly potted shapes with gilding and coloured backgrounds.

Spode ■ Before 1830, the factory name was painted on porcelain; sometimes a pattern number was included.

Rockingham tea service, *c*.1830–35 [H]

Rockingham

The short-lived Rockingham Works (1826–42) was based in Yorkshire, taking its name from the Marquess of Rockingham.

■ The high-quality, warm, ivory-toned hard-paste porcelain had a glaze that was often blemished by fine crazing (cracking).

■ A pioneer of the Rococo Revival, Rockingham specialized in fancy-shaped wares, richly coloured with scroll decoration and encrusted flowers. Wares included pot-pourris, vases, tea and dessert services.

  ■ The factory trademark of an heraldic griffin, was initially printed in red, then changed to puce after 1830, when 'Manufacturer to the King' was added.

Ridgway dessert dish, c.1830 [P]

Ridgway

Fine-quality bone china, earthenwares and porcelain were first produced by Ridgway in Hanley, Staffordshire, from the late 18th century.
■ On close inspection you will see that the body is compact and quite white; the glaze is good and clear.
■ Ornamental wares, tea, dessert and dinner services were decorated with formal flower or landscapes on a deep blue or white background, highlighted with bright gilding.
■ Most wares made before 1840 were unmarked. The letters 'J. W. R.' or 'J. & W. R.', painted or stamped, were sometimes applied to wares made between 1814 and 1830.

Ott & Brewer

Established in Trenton, New Jersey, USA, in the mid-1860s, this firm produced ivory-coloured porcelain.
■ Wares often copied English Royal Worcester porcelain of the same period.
■ Ott & Brewer was known for its eggshell thin, intricately formed porcelain, which rather misleadingly was called American Belleek after the Irish porcelain firm (*see* pp.140–41).

Ott & Brewer pitcher, c.1890 [N]

Minton vase, c.1895 [H]

Minton

Minton (est. 1793) in Stoke-on-Trent is famous for its high-quality, innovative porcelain.
■ The early soft paste was thinly potted with a grey-tinged glaze, in which you can sometimes see fine black specks. After 1821, Minton made a flawless hard paste, covered with a thin, glassy glaze.
■ The first soft-paste wares were painted or printed with Neo-classical designs. Decorative wares include flower-encrusted ornaments, Sèvres-style vases and jars with biscuit porcelain figures and coloured backgrounds.
■ By the mid-19th century, wares were stamped with the Minton name, and pattern numbers were also used.

Royal Worcester

The Royal Worcester Porcelain Co. (est. 1862) produced both domestic wares and fine ornamental pieces.
■ The factory excelled at wares inspired by Japanese porcelain, Indian ivories and oriental metalwork.
■ Royal Worcester's fame was enhanced by a group of talented craftsmen, among them George Owen, whose 'reticulated' porcelain imitated pierced ivory.
■ Royal Worcester had a complex system of marking. The two digits beneath the mark indicate the year of manufacture. From 1867 these were replaced by a letter.

Royal Worcester vase and cover, c.1915 [D]

Silver

ALL SILVERWARE HAS AN INTRINSIC WORTH based on the current market price of the precious metal from which it is made. Consequently, ownership of useful and decorative silver items, like those made of gold, has been seen as an indicator of affluence for centuries. Furthermore, since pieces can be sold by weight for melting down into bullion, silver is also an investment against hard times. From the collector's point of view, however, other qualities are much more significant when determining the collectability and value of specific pieces. The standards of design and craftsmanship are very important, as is the shape and decoration – albeit the assessment of the latter is subject to changing tastes in fashion and personal preference. Good patination of the metal is also desirable, while date and maker can be crucial. Above all, the ability to recognize the presence or lack of these features is the key to successful silver collecting.

English snuff box, *c.*1840 [J]

How to Look at Silver

Some of the finest English silver was made during the Regency period (1811–30). This teapot (1816) by Paul Storr is a good example. [I]

All detachable parts – branch, sconce and nozzle – on this candelabrum (1844–48) should have matching hallmarks. [H]

Certain pieces are always sought after. Any items made by the Danish silversmith Georg Jensen, such as this bowl (1919), are very collectable. [G]

JUST AS THE OLD SAYING *'all that glisters is not gold' warns the prospective buyer of this precious metal to exercise caution, so too do the hallmarks found on silver, since some of them can cause confusion. A lady once asked me to identify a silver biscuit barrel, hallmarked EPNS. 'Is it English Pure Natural Silver, and worth a great deal?' she said. Sadly I had to tell her the truth. The biscuit barrel was Electroplated Nickel Silver and worth far less than a solid silver one.*

The collector's dream – a piece of antique silver in perfect original condition – is rarely found. For most of us, looking at silver is about making sense of a less than perfect piece. This means checking for appropriate wear, trying to match the surface, style and decoration with the information provided by any hallmarks, and deciding whether any discrepancies are due to alterations and repairs, or fakes and forgeries.

Alterations and repairs are legitimate, but invariably reduce value. Look out for christening mugs and tankards that have been 'converted' into jugs by adding a spout, and surfaces embellished with decoration added at a later date, especially during the Victorian period. Engravings of coats of arms and initials were often buffed out and replaced as silver changed hands, frequently resulting in the silver becoming so thin that it 'gives' when gently pressed. These thin spots have sometimes been replaced, either with an applied patch, or – and this is more difficult to detect – the worn area has been cut out and replaced, and the repair lines concealed by engraving.

Colour is particularly important. I always take a soft cloth to rub away tarnish so that I can check it carefully. Over time, antique silver acquires a highly desirable 'blue hue', while modern silver has a bright mirror-like surface. Beware of a glittery, bright surface on an antique piece, it may well be a layer of silver plate used to conceal lead solder repairs. One way of detecting hidden repairs concealed by a highly polished surface is to breathe gently on the suspect area, which will highlight any irregularities present in the piece.

Weight affects value, so invest in some pocket spring-balance scales. Other useful tools include a pocket magnet, which will help identify silver-plated iron or steel pieces, and a pocket magnifying glass for checking hallmarks.

A good book of hallmarks will help to make the identification of English silver relatively simple – it is not worth trying to learn all the date letters and makers' marks, there are far too many. England has a detailed system of hallmarking, but most countries have some identifying marks, for example, makers' marks in the USA, and town and makers' marks in Spain.

Once you have closely inspected the piece for marks, you need to check their authenticity. Although it is a criminal offence to tamper with a hallmark, it is far easier to fake a mark than a whole piece. Forged marks made by soft metal punches have softer outlines than genuine marks, which are made with steel punches.

Another clue to a potential fake is the position of marks on pieces, which varies according to the year of manufacture. The correct positions will be detailed in a good reference book. One well-known trick is to take a set of genuine marks from a small piece, such as a spoon, and solder them onto a larger piece. Tell-tale signs include the marks appearing in a straight line over the base, rather than being clustered, and solder lines around the mark's edge.

STYLE

One of the first tests for evaluating a piece is to look at the overall appearance to see if it corresponds to the known style of the period. This salver has a shell-and-moulded border that was the height of fashion in the 1730s.

DECORATION

This salver has been engraved with a band of scrolls, foliage and latticework and a coat of arms. With a coat of arms, always make sure that the style corresponds broadly to the date letter of the hallmarks on the base.

Although the decoration on this George II salver (1739) is of the right period, many plain 18th-century salvers were decorated in the 19th century. [C]

HALLMARKS

Always check for hallmarks, which may be tucked away discreetly. Any irregularity should be treated as suspect and remember – worn marks are usually a good indication that the piece has been much used.

BORDERS

The borders of all silver items should always be thoroughly examined for splitting and repairs. Check the borders of salvers and other silver dishes carefully for distortion and replacement, which can be difficult and expensive to fix.

Hallmarks

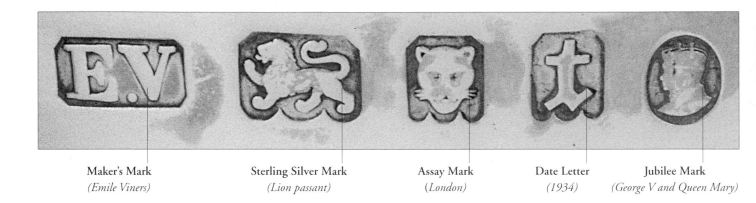

Maker's Mark
(Emile Viners)

Sterling Silver Mark
(Lion passant)

Assay Mark
(London)

Date Letter
(1934)

Jubilee Mark
(George V and Queen Mary)

Silver is a soft metal, and has to be alloyed (combined) with copper in order to make it durable. However, the amount of pure silver used varied until 1300, when Edward I established a system of marking English silver to set a common standard. The standard decreed that silver must contain 92.5 per cent silver to 7.5 per cent copper to be legally called 'sterling silver' and that it would be stamped with a leopard's head to show that it had been tested. A maker's mark was introduced in 1363 to discourage unscrupulous silversmiths from forging the leopard's head. A date letter (indicating the year the silver was tested) was added in 1478 and finally, in 1544, the lion passant (passing from right to left) was included to show royal control of the assay office. These four marks are known as the Established System; other marks have been added from time to time.

Assay Mark

The assay mark indicates the town where the silver was assayed (tested) for purity. From 1478, the 'touch wardens' (who examined and marked the silver) were required to test the silver in the Goldsmith's Hall (hence the term hallmark) to prevent the unlawful marking of substandard wares. London became the first hallmarking centre in Britain, and originally had no designated town mark. In 1544, the leopard's head (originally the

mark for sterling silver) was used as the London Assay Office mark. From the late 17th century, other assay offices were set up. Each centre had its own mark: Chester (1686–1962) had a sword and three wheat sheaves; Exeter (1701–1883), a castle with three towers; Newcastle (est. 1702), three castles; Birmingham (est. 1773), an anchor and Sheffield (est. 1773), a crown.

Maker's Mark

From 1363, the maker's mark was a 'device' (sign or symbol), since not many people could read at that time. This practice continued until the late 17th century, when combined initials and symbols were adopted. During the following century, symbols became obsolete and the mark comprised the initials of the maker's Christian name and surname. During the Britannia Standard period, from 1697 to 1720, silversmiths had to register a new punch, or tool, consisting of the first two letters of their surname.

Date Letter

The date letter, first used on London silver in 1478 and still used today, indicates the year when the item was tested at the assay office. This mark changes annually because a new assay master was at first appointed each year. The letters, which usually follow an alphabetical sequence, are different at each assay office. Each letter is enclosed by a shield, which can vary in shape from year to year.

Sterling Silver Mark

In England, silver made to the required sterling standard was initially marked with the leopard's head. Since this originated from the royal coat of arms, it was known as the 'King's Mark'. When the lion passant was adopted as the standard hallmark for silver in 1544, the leopard's head became the mark for the London Assay Office. The Britannia Standard mark replaced the lion passant from 1697 to 1720.

Britannia Standard

During the English Civil War, which began in 1649 and lasted for 11 years, enormous quantities of sterling silver were melted down and converted into coin in order to pay the troops. Following the Restoration of the monarchy in 1660, when Charles II ascended the throne, the demand for domestic silver rose so greatly that coins were melted down, or the edges clipped off, to create much-needed household objects. This practice was illegal and to counteract it the Britannia Standard was introduced in 1697, forcing silversmiths to adopt the new standard of 95.8 per cent pure silver. New hallmarks were initiated so that the system could be carefully regulated. The figure of Britannia replaced the lion passant, and the lion's head 'erased' (torn off at the neck) replaced the crowned leopard's head (at that time the assay mark for London). Sterling silver was once more adopted as the legal standard in 1720.

Duty Mark
Duty was first imposed on British silver in 1720. The costs of the American War of Independence (1775–83) increased the need for more revenue in Britain and duty was raised on silver calculated by weight. In 1784, a mark featuring the monarch's head in profile was adopted to prove that this duty had been paid to the government at the time of assay. The heads of successive reigning sovereigns appeared on English silver until 1890, when silversmiths successfully petitioned Parliament to abolish the tax.

 Commemorative Marks
At the maker's request, the assay office may authorize marks on silverware for a specific period of time to commemorate an important public event or anniversary. These marks are optional and are not strictly hallmarks. In Britain, commemorative hallmarks have included the Golden Jubilee of George V and Queen Mary in 1935, as well as the coronation mark for Queen Elizabeth II in 1953 and her 1977 Silver Jubilee mark.

 Scottish and Irish Marks
Marking systems for Scotland and Ireland are similar to those for England, although different standards were used, and sterling became the universally accepted standard. Marks on Scottish silver were introduced in the mid-15th century. The town mark of Edinburgh, initiated in 1485, is a castle with a central turret. From 1759 until 1975, a thistle replaced the assay master's mark (or date letter) in Edinburgh. Glasgow, meanwhile, adopted the lion rampant of Scotland and the sovereign's head in 1819, adding them to the town mark. From 1914, the thistle standard mark was used.

Ireland adopted hallmarking in the 17th century. Under British rule, a crowned harp, representing the sterling standard, was used. The crowned harp was Dublin's town mark from 1637, and the figure of Hibernia was added in 1731. But the marking system tended to be arbitrary and Irish silver does not always bear complete marks. This is especially true of 18th-century silver, where many variations will be seen.

European Hallmarks

France

 From the 16th century, French silver was stamped with a crowned letter by the silversmith's guild, *La Maison Commune*. Control of assaying and marking silver in France passed from the guilds to the state following the Revolution of 1789. In 1797, two standards of silver were established – 95 per cent and 80 per cent pure silver – denoted by the mark of a cockerel within a shield and the numerals 1 or 2 for the higher and lower standards respectively. From 1833, a mark featuring Minerva (above) was used for large items.

Russia

 Assay offices were set up in Moscow and St Petersburg in the 17th century and silver was marked with the city mark, assay mark and the maker's mark. The imperial double-headed eagle was originally the mark for Moscow. It was replaced in 1741 by a mark showing St George slaying the dragon (above). A standardized system of marking was introduced in Russia in 1896.

Germany

 Before Germany became a state at the end of the 19th century, the guilds (often groups of merchants) controlled the silver standard, and items were struck with both a town and maker's mark. Towns such as Dresden and Nuremberg also had a date letter system. In 1888, a crown and crescent mark (above) was introduced to signify a purity of at least 80 per cent. The exact purity of silver is signified by a number – in the detail above it is 800 parts of pure silver per thousand.

Spain

 In Spain, silver was marked with the maker's mark and the town mark from the 16th century. The mark for Madrid is a tower and the number beneath signifies the year of testing (above left it is 1852). The assay master also added his mark (above right).

American Hallmarks

A comprehensive marking system was never established in the USA. However, many American makers did mark their work with the initials of their first name and full surname, rather than using just initials like English silversmiths. Most makers stamped their silver with maker or company names, abbreviated or in full. This can help determine where or when an item was made, since shapes varied according to place and period of production. Some firms also used their own date marking system. For example, Gorham of Providence, Rhode Island, used a different symbol for each year.

S. Kirk & Sons, Baltimore

E. F. Caldwell & Co., New York

Silver Styles Time Line

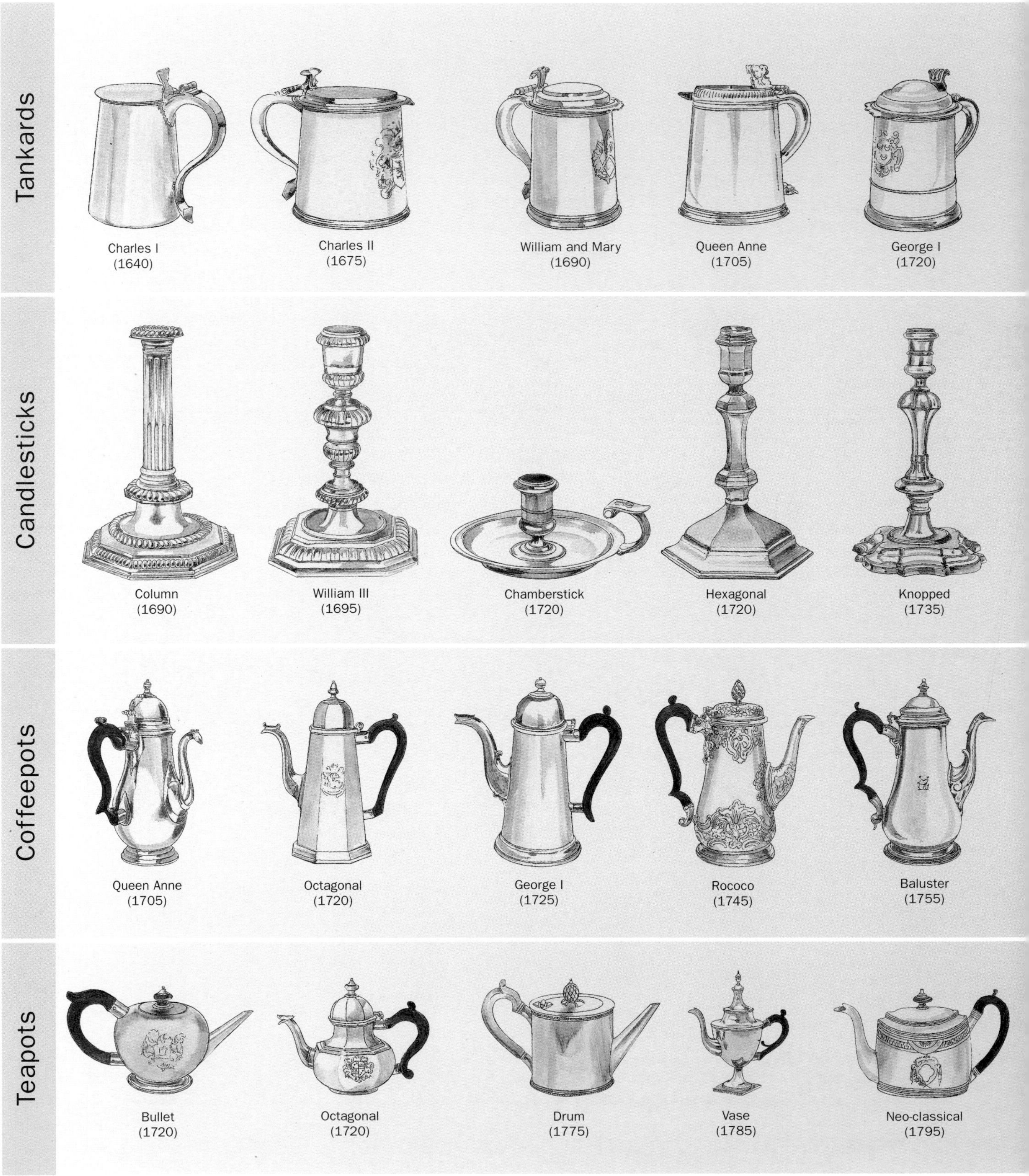

Tankards

Charles I
(1640)

Charles II
(1675)

William and Mary
(1690)

Queen Anne
(1705)

George I
(1720)

Candlesticks

Column
(1690)

William III
(1695)

Chamberstick
(1720)

Hexagonal
(1720)

Knopped
(1735)

Coffeepots

Queen Anne
(1705)

Octagonal
(1720)

George I
(1725)

Rococo
(1745)

Baluster
(1755)

Teapots

Bullet
(1720)

Octagonal
(1720)

Drum
(1775)

Vase
(1785)

Neo-classical
(1795)

George I
(1725)

Baluster
(1750)

Barrel
(1795)

Victorian
(1860)

Peg
(1880)

Rococo
(1750)

Neo-classical
(1775)

Neo-classical
(1780)

Regency
(1810)

Victorian
(1870)

Regency
(1815)

Empire
(1825)

Fluted pear
(1830)

Aesthetic
(1875)

Victorian
(1875)

Federal
(1796)

Regency
(1815)

Rococo Revival
(1835)

Arts & Crafts
(1880)

Art Deco
(1930)

Story of Lighting

Wall sconce,
London, 1692 [E]

ALTHOUGH CANDLES PROVIDED LIGHT *from medieval times, candlesticks were at first used only by the Church and the wealthy. Produced in great numbers from the 18th century, they became increasingly ornate in the 19th. To the present day candlesticks are among the most collected of all silver items.*

Oil lamps provided lighting until the advent of candles in the Middle Ages. Few early candlesticks survive since, during the English Civil War (1642–51), they were often melted down for coin. After the Restoration of the monarchy in 1660, candlesticks were 'raised', or hammered, from thin sheet metal.

By the late 17th century, highly skilled Huguenot craftsmen – who had fled from France as a result of religious persecution – had introduced the technique of casting candlesticks in solid silver. The base, stem and sconce, or candleholder, were cast separately then soldered together. Cast candlesticks were heavier and more durable than raised examples and often carried complex decorations.

The fashion in the early 1700s for simple, minimally decorated candlesticks gave way to more richly ornamented styles by the 1730s. A number of highly talented silversmiths adopted the flamboyant French Rococo style. Some of the finest candlesticks of this period are made with elaborately cast stems of female figures holding the candle socket above their heads.

By the 1780s, the fashion for lavish ornament had waned, to be replaced by the restrained designs of the Neo-classical period. At the same time, the growth of the industrial centres of Birmingham and Sheffield meant that candlesticks could be mass produced. They were now stamped from rolled sheet silver, and 'loaded', or weighted, with pitch, wood, or sometimes metal for stability. Mechanical die-stamping, where a sheet of silver is pressed between two patterned dies, was also used from the 1760s to produce less expensive candlesticks in Birmingham and Sheffield.

Like candlesticks, candelabra were often made in pairs. They were available from the mid-17th century, but most examples found today date from the 18th and 19th centuries. At first, candelabra were produced with just two simple branches. More branches were added progressively from the late 18th century, when the hour for dining was changed from mid-afternoon to evening, and more light was consequently needed.

Many useful lighting implements were also made in silver, including snuffers and tapersticks. Snuffers,

The simple octagonal base, faceted stem and vase-shaped capital (top section) on this candlestick (1709) illustrate the relatively plain style of silver made in the early 18th century, during the reigns of Queen Anne and George I. The base should be hallmarked underneath. The capital should be marked with the lion's head erased, and usually a maker's mark as well. [D]

Chambersticks were used to light the way to bed at night. This Neo-classical example (1780) is quite unusual since it still includes both its original scissor snuffer-cum-wick trimmer, and a detachable conical snuffer, which slots into the handle. [K]

An innovative feature of silver candlesticks made from the 1740s – such as this highly decorated example (1749) – was the detachable nozzle. This made it easier to clean off any unsightly wax residue. [FOR A PAIR G]

This three-light candelabrum (1794) is typical of the late Neo-classical period, with lightly constructed branches, bands of laurel leaves and slender, restrained proportions. The top of the stem forms a third candleholder, which in this example is covered with a detachable urn finial. [I]

This American candlestick (one of a pair) was made in Baltimore in 1795. With a fluted stem and sloping, square base, it reflects the popular Federal style of the period. [E]

An abundance of silver was needed to create the heavy ornamentation of this massive candelabrum (1817) by Paul Storr. The finely detailed eagle, leafy detachable branches and use of such motifs as bulrushes, shells, flowers, scrolls and dolphins anticipate the later Victorian fashion for naturalistic ornament. Such a large, richly decorated item would be cast in solid silver and consequently probably be made for a very wealthy client. [C]

scissor-like instruments with a small box attached, were used to trim the charred wicks (snuffs) of burning candles before the invention of the self-consuming candle wick in the 1820s. Taper-sticks were smaller versions of candlesticks that could hold tapers (thin candles), which were used to light pipes, illuminate a writing desk or melt sealing wax for securing letters.

In the 19th century, styles became increasingly ornate, in keeping with Victorian tastes. By the late years of the century, few candlesticks or candelabra were cast, since this method of production had become prohibitively expensive and mechanized manufacture meant that large sets, rather than pairs, of candlesticks were more affordable.

The late 19th and early 20th centuries saw many silversmiths resisting mass production. Instead, they concentrated on fine craftmanship, using quality materials and simple designs inspired by Japanese art. From the Arts & Crafts and Art Nouveau styles to Art Deco, 20th-century candlestick designers managed to embrace both historical revivals and minimalist modern design.

Important Candlestick Makers

By the mid-18th century, a number of London-based silversmiths specialized in the production of cast candlesticks and snuffer trays. These included the brothers John and William Cafe, James Gould I and his son James Gould II and Ebenezer Coker. Their candlesticks can look very similar; most were based on similar models, with square or hexagonal bases, and shell-and-gadrooned decoration on the bases and knops (decorative swellings in the stems).

Candlesticks by the Cafe brothers: top candlestick (1744) by John [FOR A PAIR F]; **bottom (1757) by William.** [FOR A PAIR G]

A CLOSER LOOK *Candlesticks*

Casting was used to make candlesticks from the late 17th century. This was an expensive method, however, and in the 1770s, mechanization enabled candlesticks to be stamped out from sheets of silver, then 'loaded' or weighted internally to give additional support. With the expansion of industry in Birmingham and Sheffield from the mid-18th century, candlestick manufacture became a specialized trade. New techniques of rolling (flattening) silver into sheets and die-stamping, where silver is pressed between two patterned dies to shape and decorate it, gradually replaced expensive, laborious casting methods. If you pick up a cast, and a loaded, candlestick, both will feel heavy. When you invert them, however, cast examples are hollow underneath while loaded ones have a metal plate or an inset wooden base to contain the filling.

▲ On a cast candlestick, the base is cast separately from the stem and all three pieces are then soldered together. The **capital** should bear the **lion passant mark**, sometimes the maker's mark as well.

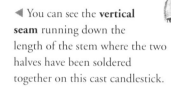

◄ You can see the **vertical seam** running down the length of the stem where the two halves have been soldered together on this cast candlestick.

▼ This engraved **coat of arms** in the well of the candlestick is original. It is in the right style and shows an appropriate amount of wear.

▲ Unlike loaded candlesticks, cast examples are usually **fully marked** under the **base**. Reading this mark from left to right shows that this candlestick was made in 1770, in London, of sterling silver, by John Carter.

▶ Candlesticks cast in solid silver are more durable than those that have been loaded. If you look at the **base** of a cast candlestick, it is **hollow** and quite **roughly finished** underneath.

Cast candlestick, 1770
Made by London silversmith John Carter, this example shows the beginnings of the Neo-classical style found in Europe and the USA during the late 18th century.
[FOR A PAIR **H**]

Wax pan, or nozzle

Capital

Shoulder

Column, or stem

Knop

Well

Base

▶ This loaded candlestick has been stamped from a thin-gauge sheet of silver that was shaped into a **hollow column**, which was then loaded with pitch, or filling, to provide support and stability. Like the cast candlestick, you may be able to see the **join** running down the column where the ends of the sheet have been soldered together.

◀ Remove the **nozzle** from this candlestick, turn it upside down, and you will see how thin the gauge of silver used is. The nozzle should be hallmarked, since it is a detachable piece. Unmarked nozzles are often replacements, or may have suffered repairs.

▶ The **decoration** on the loaded candlestick has been hammered out from the inside so that the swags of flowers and gadrooning stand out **in relief**. Look out for small holes – on the base and in the column – where the silver has been stretched very thinly. Repairs to such pieces are expensive as the entire candlestick must be partly dismantled and emptied of filling.

◀ On loaded candlesticks, the **hallmarks** are usually positioned in a straight line on the outer **edge of the base**, where the metal tends to be strongest. Reading the mark from left to right reveals that this candlestick was made by John Smith, in sterling silver, in London, in 1771.

▶ The **base** of a loaded candlestick is usually covered with an inset panel of wood or iron to contain the loading or filling. It is often covered with a piece of green baize to prevent it scratching tables or other wooden surfaces.

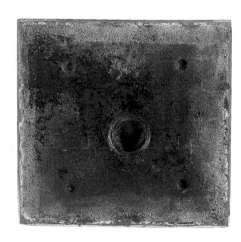

Loaded candlestick, 1771
Known as a cluster-column and made for table use, the shape resembles fasces (a bound bundle of rods), a symbol of the authority of ancient Roman magistrates. It was a popular Neo-classical motif.
[FOR A PAIR]

A Closer Look *Candelabra*

These two candelabra may both appear to be made of silver – but if you look closely, you can see that they have been created by two very different processes. The 19th-century example is made of Sheffield plate. This technique involved fusing silver and copper together, and then rolling it out into a usable sheet of metal. Developed in Sheffield by Thomas Boulsover in 1742, the process was widely used from the 1750s. By the 1840s, commercial electroplating, introduced by Elkington & Co., had largely replaced it. Electroplating, which was used to make the 20th-century example, involved depositing a layer of pure silver on an object, usually made of base metal, such a nickel or brass. This was done by electrolysis.

◀ If you look at the underside of the socket, you can see the **double sunburst mark** of the renowned Sheffield plate manufacturer Matthew Boulton. At the very edge, note where the border has been **rolled over** to hide the copper edge, which would otherwise be exposed.

Sheffield plate candelabrum, c.1810 Because Sheffield plate is not always hallmarked, you will need to look at the basic construction of a piece in order to identify it. [K]

▲ One of the ways to identify Sheffield plate is to look for **patches** where the silver has been worn away. Here the two rows of beading on the stem of the candlestick are showing signs of wear, revealing the dull **lead solder** beneath.

▲ Such decorative details as this neat gadrooned **border** were stamped out of very thin sheets of sterling silver. This 'foil' border was filled with lead solder to provide strength and then soldered on to the edge of the nozzle. Finally, the border was rolled under to conceal any exposed copper in the Sheffield plate. If you look closely at the border, you should be able to see small patches where the silver is wearing thin. This is usually a result of overcleaning.

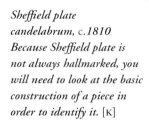

▲ Because Sheffield plate is made from a sheet of metal, you should be able to see the **joins** where the sheet has been soldered together. They are often difficult to find, but here the seam can just be seen.

*French
electroplated
candelabrum,
early 20th century
Electroplating is a cheaper and
easier way of mass-producing
'silver-looking' objects. Generally, electroplated
articles are brighter in colour than Sheffield-
plated pieces, since they are covered with a
layer of pure silver and not the lower
standard sterling silver.* [N]

◄ Some candelabra
are extremely
adaptable. For
example, this
base can be used as
a single candlestick
once the branches have
been detached.

▼ The top section slots neatly
into the central column. Always
check the **socket** carefully for
damage, as it is the weakest point
on the candelabrum.

▲ A piece of electroplated silver such as this is
first made in an inexpensive base metal (usually
copper or nickel) and covered with a thin
coating of pure silver only when the shape is
complete. One of the main differences between
Sheffield and electroplated wares is that there
are **no visible joins** on electroplated pieces
as the plating masks everything.

▼ On the base of the candelabrum
you can see the **mark** of the
French firm of Christofle, and
the **plater's symbol**.

Story of Drinking Wares

George II coffeepot, 1730 [G]

BEAKERS, TANKARDS AND MUGS *have been made in much the same shape since they were first used. From the early 18th century, when tea, coffee, and chocolate replaced beer as the most popular drink, tankards and mugs were made mainly as christening presents. People also needed vessels in which to serve these then exotic drinks, and silver pots, kettles and urns were made to meet the demand.*

Until the 19th century, vessels made of porcelain, glass and silver remained largely the privilege of the wealthy upper classes. The grandest houses used silver for most of their drinking vessels. Wares for serving punch, wine and spirits were also made in silver, and the extensive range of shapes available mirrored ceramic or pewter forms.

The simple cylindrical beaker, sparsely decorated with engraving, was one of the earliest forms of silver drinking vessel, with examples surviving from the 15th century. Robust tankards with hinged covers

The finial (top ornament) on the hinged cover of this French chocolate pot (c.1740), can be lifted off and a molinet (stirring stick), inserted to break up the sediment. This pot is known in France as a pot chocolatier. [E]

evolved from wooden versions and by the late 16th century were made in solid silver.

Alongside these popular vessels stood mugs, cups and goblets. For communal drinking at celebratory occasions, there were peg tankards and quaiches (a shallow, uncovered vessel popular in Scotland). Jugs for serving drinks ranging from water

This George III coffeepot (1760) is lavishly ornamented with flowers and foliage typical of the late Rococo period. Made by a famous London silversmith William Gould, the decoration has been hammered out from within the pot. [F]

A Family at Tea (c.1745) by Richard Collins details all the equipment needed to brew a pot of tea in the 18th century. Note the tiny pear-shaped teapot, which is kept warm by a matching burner.

to beer were also made in silver. By the mid-18th century, the demand for suitable containers for serving the new and exotic imports of coffee, tea and chocolate created a wealth of opportunities for silversmiths. Teapots, coffeepots and chocolate pots formed the cornerstone of a new industry devoted to this pastime.

Silversmiths also produced a huge variety of useful accessories during the 18th century, including sugar bowls and baskets, cream jugs and tea-caddies, as well as molinets and caddy spoons (for measuring dry tea). Large silver tea-kettles and urns, with matching stands and burners to keep the contents hot, provided a supply of hot water to refill tea- and coffeepots.

This Norwegian peg tankard (c.1700) is so called because it has a vertical row of pegs inside to aid drinking games. This type of communal tankard was also made in wood. [E]

earliest examples. The development of mechanization in the 19th century, and the increased use of rolled sheet silver, enabled the production of drum and oval-shaped tea and coffee wares. Later, Victorian items were bulbous in shape.

From the late 19th century, drinking wares were produced in many revival styles. In the 20th century, innovative ideas resulted in the production of a host of designs incorporating Art Nouveau, Art Deco and Modernist styles. Some British silversmiths, such as Omar Ramsden and Alwyn Carr (*see* p.168), reacted against mechanized production and stuck to hand-crafted methods, drawing their inspiration from the distant past.

The oval-shaped teapot (1795) was popular on the east coast of the USA from the late 18th century. Cheaply made from sheet silver, this pot, by Virginian silversmith Asa Blansett, has a pineapple finial, the symbol of hope. [G]

The growing popularity of wine drinking led to the development of the wine cooler. Since medieval times, ice had been kept in portable vessels designed for cooling flagons, bottle and glasses. Silver cisterns (bowls for washing glasses), wine coolers, Monteiths (bowls with notched rims for holding the feet of wine glasses while the bowls were chilled in iced water) and punchbowls took their place on the sideboard, testifying to the wealth and importance of the owner.

Other important wine-drinking vessels include goblets, which were made from the 16th century, and items such as bottle tickets (small plaques hung round a bottle labelling its contents), funnels, coasters, decanters and jugs. Lemon and orange juice strainers and nutmeg-graters were used for preparing punch.

Until the late 18th century, most vessels remained much the same shape as the

Wine coolers such as this massive, silver-gilt example (1822) were used for cooling bottles. They usually had a detachable collar and liner, behind which ice could be tightly packed. [FOR A PAIR A]

Charles Kändler

The renowned London silversmith Charles Kändler (active 1727–73) made numerous silver objects, which were all of high quality. Kändler probably came to London from Germany in 1726, and formed a partnership with the silversmith James Murray. Later established on his own in St James's, Kändler produced silverwares of extraordinary imagination, mainly extravagantly decorated in the high Rococo style. This tea-kettle testifies to Kändler's skill as a silversmith. Here he has created a lavish ornament by using embossing and finely cast and modelled mythological figures to maximum effect.

Tea-kettle with stand and burner (c.1735) by Charles Kändler. [D]

A CLOSER LOOK *Coffeepot*

The earliest coffeepots date from before 1700, by which time drinking coffee was an extremely popular pastime. Examples from this period have straight or octagonal sides, a domed or cone-shaped lid and a straight or faceted spout. You can identify them by their sparse decoration: such pots sometimes have a simple engraved coat of arms or applied decoration around the spout or base. By the 1750s, this style had developed into baluster- or pear-shaped pots on a raised foot. Coffeepots from this time tend to have curving spouts and embossed and chased (tooled) decoration. By the Neo-classical period, urn shapes were preferred. Handles are often curved and made of a fruitwood or ivory. Many 18th-century styles were copied in the 19th and 20th centuries, so hallmarks are valuable clues for dating.

English coffeepot, 1767
Made by the London silversmith Francis Crump, this pot is in the typical pear shape popular from the 1760s. [H]

▲ Inside the pot's cover, you can see the indentations where various tools have been used to **emboss** the decoration so that it appears in relief on the surface. In this detail you can just make out the individual **tool marks**.

▲ All separately made parts of a pot should be hallmarked. Inside the rim of this cover is the **lion passant** mark (*see* p.148). Unmarked covers are likely to have been damaged or replaced.

▲ This coffeepot originally had a fruitwood handle, but a silver one with **ivory insulators** replaced it during the Victorian period. Hallmarks on this handle will show the date it was changed.

▲ Several different methods were used to decorate this George II coffeepot. **Embossing** pushed the decoration from the inside, while the outside was **chased** to give definition to the design.

◀ **Hallmarks** under the foot of the pot should be clear and crisp. Beware of any worn or distorted marks, which could indicate that the piece has been damaged or possibly repaired.

A CLOSER LOOK *Teapot*

Expanding trade with China in the 17th century enabled merchants to import tea into Europe. At first only the wealthy enjoyed this novelty beverage, since it was an expensive commodity. The earliest teapots were quite small because they were not used for brewing tea, but for pouring hot water over tea leaves in cups. They were either globular or pear-shaped, or sometimes octagonal, echoing the shape of coffeepots. The spherical, bullet-shaped teapot came into fashion in the 1720s, and was especially popular in Scotland for about the next 40 years. Other teapot shapes include the urn, vase and drum shapes, which were widely used throughout the Neo-classical period in Europe and the USA, and the boat shape popular during Regency times. The Victorian era saw the revival of many of the most popular designs.

▲ This finely detailed flower-bud **finial** has been cast separately and bolted to the cover of the teapot. Always check details such as this since they have a tendency to break.

American teapot by S. Kirk & Sons, c.1880
Teapots with a curved shape, leaf-wrapped spout, C-scroll handle and flower finial were particularly popular in the USA during the 1880s and 1890s. [N]

▲ The firm of S. Kirk & Sons was celebrated for its skillful chased work. Look very closely at this **matted** (punched) surface and note how realistic this flower appears, having been worked from the front.

▲ The numbers 925/1000 denote the **sterling standard**. Marks of this type have been used on American silver since the 1880s. Earlier American silver may not be of the sterling standard and usually bears only a maker's mark.

IMPORTANT AMERICAN SILVER MANUFACTURERS	
GORHAM MANUFACTURING CO.	EST. 1831
REED & BARTON	EST. 1833
TIFFANY & CO.	EST. 1837
ONEIDA SILVERSMITHS	EST. 1848
REDFIELD & RICE MANUFACTURING CO.	EST. 1854
MIDDLETOWN PLATE CO.	EST. 1864
WILCOX	EST. 1865
WHITING MANUFACTURING CO.	EST. 1866
PAIRPOINT & CO.	EST. 1880
HOLMES & EDWARDS	EST. 1882

A Closer Look *Tankards*

From the late 17th century, tankards were the most common drinking vessels used in Britain. The earliest examples usually consisted of a simple cylindrical shape, with a flat, stepped lid of one or more graduated tiers and a sparsely decorated scroll handle. When wine-drinking became fashionable towards the end of the 18th century, people used tankards much less. From then on, they were designed mainly as gifts and tended to be larger, heavier and more highly decorated than early tankards. Domed covers replaced the flat lids, and many of these later examples were also gilded. In the 19th century, silversmiths often took plain, late 17th-century and Georgian tankards and decorated them, using embossing and chasing, in keeping with elaborate Victorian tastes; some even converted them into jugs by adding a spout.

▲ Tankards from the late 17th century should be **fully marked** below the rim and on the cover with the lion passant, date letter and the leopard's head for London. Marks should be as clear as these ones are.

▲ Tankards are prone to wear. If you look inside, you can see **two splits** under the hinge where the handle has broken and a rough repair above the hinge.

Charles II tankard, 1671
This tankard features a cylindrical body, stepped cover, and scroll handle often found on late 17th-century examples. Made by London silversmith Francis Leake, the style was also popular in the American colonies. [F]

▲ Make sure that the marks on the cover match those on the body. If they don't, the cover may have been replaced at some time. The **thumbpiece** on the double-scroll handle – popular at this time – allowed the heavy cover to be flipped open easily.

▲ Here there has been a clumsy attempt to **repair** the handle with lead solder. This method is a cheap, but amateurish, alternative to the professional job done by a silversmith, who would use silver solder. Lead repairs are unsightly and can be difficult to rectify.

◀ Early tankards were usually decorated very simply with modest bands of incised reeding (a border of narrow reeds), or an **engraved coat of arms**. The simplicity of this coat of arms suggests an early date.

◀ Beneath Francis Leake's initials is a **bird between two pellets** (dots). This combination distinguished his work from other makers with the same initials.

◄ If you lift the cover of a 19th-century tankard, it will probably be only **partially marked** inside. Here only the maker's mark, lion passant and date letter are present, in a small cluster inside the cover.

► The mark to the far right of this hallmark is the **duty mark**, used between 1784 and 1890, which shows that duty has been paid on this piece. Since duty was calculated by weight, sometimes unscrupulous silversmiths dodged this tax by submitting small items for assaying. After the piece had been hallmarked, they cut out the patch bearing the marks and soldered it on to a heavier piece. Such wares are called 'duty dodgers'. One way to spot such a piece is to look for solder around the edge where the mark has been 'sweated in'.

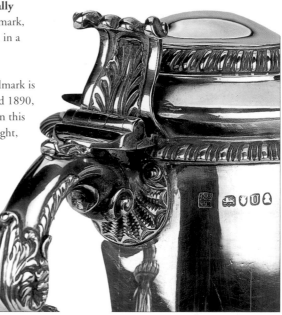

George III tankard, 1815
A tankard from this period is usually taller and narrower than earlier examples. [1]

▼ A **full set of marks** has been cleanly struck in a regular, straight line. The maker's mark of Alice & George Burrows is not as clear as the hallmarks. Poorly struck maker's marks are not uncommon.

▼ This elaborate **cast handle**, decorated with foliage and shell ornament, is in complete contrast to earlier examples, which were hollow, plain and made from a flat sheet of silver. Such handles were usually not marked.

◄ Look at the base of the 19th-century tankard and you will see small **blobs of solder** spaced at regular intervals around the edge of the base. These flat 'solder chips' were cut, heated and left to harden after melting, when the base was separately applied to the tankard. Silversmiths rarely cleaned off the under surfaces of handmade wares before the mid-19th century. The **scrape marks** show where the assay office has taken a sample scraping of silver for testing to ensure it conformed to the set standard.

Story of Flatware

FLATWARE, OR CUTLERY, *is among the most collected of all silver items. Spoons, used since pre-Roman times, were given as presents from the Middle Ages onwards, while forks were not much used until the 16th century. The practice of setting a table with cutlery for a meal was introduced in the 17th century. Later, sets of silver flatware came to reflect the wealth and status of a host.*

Lace-back 'dog-nose' spoons, *c.*1700 [L]

American parcel-gilt services – such as this one made in a stylized 'Queen's' pattern (c.1895) – often had many serving utensils. Fish 'slices', or servers, were included as the flavour tended to taint other foodstuffs. [FOR A SERVICE G]

The 'Hanoverian' pattern comes with two- or three-pronged forks. This knife (c.1715) has a 'pistol' handle and a 'scimitar' blade. [R]

M ost food was eaten with fingers or a spoon until the 16th century, when the Continent adopted the fork – until then used only for consuming desserts and sweetmeats – as the favourite utensil. Charles II's court adopted the practice of eating with forks while in exile in France, and brought it to England after the Restoration in 1660.

After Charles II's return, French silver styles became popular in fashionable English circles. New forms included the 'trefid' design, a development from an earlier, plainer English pattern, which had a stem with a splayed, notched end.

One popular variant, the lace-back tre-fid spoon, had decorative scrollwork on the back of the bowl. By the late 17th century, the trefid had developed into a simpler 'wavy-end' pattern – and the end of the forks and spoons lost their notches.

Dining forks followed the trefid style and usually had two or three 'tines', or prongs. Early forks tended to be quite small. At the time, tables were laid in accordance with the French fashion, with the reverse side of the spoon and fork handles turned upwards to display the crests and armorials of their owners.

Influenced by the growing fashion for matching dinner services, sets of 18th-century flatware were extensively produced. Few of these, however, exist intact today. The first pattern for matching flatware was called 'Hanoverian'. It had a flat, rounded end turned upwards, with a ridge running along the front of the handle.

From the 1760s, the Hanoverian pattern evolved into the 'Old English'. This had a plain, rounded end turned downwards instead of upwards, in line with the new fashion of placing cutlery face up on the

Flatware Patterns

The fashion for matching dinner services encouraged the trend for matching sets of cutlery in the early 18th century. In England, many flatware-makers produced the same patterns. However, in the USA patterns were patented and were the property of a single manufacturer; often the date when the pattern was patented can be found on the back of the stem. It is rare to find a complete, original set of flatware these days, since pieces were often replaced with new ones made in the same pattern when they became worn through heavy use or lost.

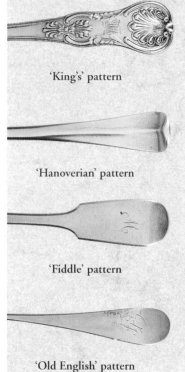

'King's' pattern

The Regency 'King's' pattern has a scrolled edge and shell-and-anthemion (stylized honeysuckle) design.

'Hanoverian' pattern

In the 'Hanoverian' pattern, which was made *c.*1710–70 during the reigns of the two Hanoverian kings (George I and George II), the stem has a central rib.

'Fiddle' pattern

So called because it looks like the back of a violin, the 'Fiddle' pattern was first introduced into England *c.*1775.

'Old English' pattern

In contrast to the 'Hanoverian' pattern, the 'Old English' pattern stem turns downwards at the end and has no rib. It has been fashionable from *c.*1760.

centuries included the 'Fiddle', as well as the 'King's' and 'Queen's' patterns (made from the early 19th century), with shaped stems decorated with shells and scrolling foliage. Services from this time are far more valuable if they are sold in their original fitted canteen boxes.

American 19th-century flatware was also elaborate. While European services included tablespoons and forks, in the USA dessert utensils had their own patterns. Often, parcel gilt (partial gilding) or frosted finishes were used to enhance them. Silver was also combined with metals such as copper and bronze, creating beautiful designs in the Aesthetic style of the 1870s.

The 'Fiddle' pattern, which had violin-shaped handles, was favoured in France from the early 18th century. Popular from the first quarter of the 19th century, the 'Fiddle, thread and shell' pattern as seen in this example (c.1830s) remains a particularly sought-after design today. [FOR A SERVICE E]

table. Around the same time, flatware-makers began to design forks with four tines instead of three. As dining habits grew more elaborate, silver-gilt (silver covered with a thin layer of gold) services specially made for desserts became popular.

From the late 18th century, the development of mechanized manufacture in Sheffield enabled flatware to be produced in a wide variety of patterns. The most popular styles in the late 18th and 19th

Extensive silver-gilt dessert services, such as this made in the 'Pierced Vine' pattern (1919), were popular in the 19th century. They often included items such as grape scissors, ice cream spoons, cream ladles and butter-knives. [FOR A SERVICE D]

A Closer Look *Flatware*

When examining flatware from different periods, several factors can help you ascertain date and condition. Apart from very decorative presentation pieces, flatware is meant to be used, and so it is important to check whether the items you are looking at will withstand constant use. For example, the tines of a fork should be straight and strong; beware of those that are of uneven length and worn. On all pieces, look out for sharp edges; these usually indicate that the silver has become thin, which may also mean that the shape of the piece has been distorted. If a piece gives under gentle pressure, this means that the silver is too thin. Decoration on flatware should be well defined, crisp, and not show signs of excessive wear. Finally, hallmarks should be clearly legible; they are often found on the back of the stem.

Dessert fork, 1875
The 'Albert' pattern, of which this fork is a good example, was popular during the reign of Queen Victoria. [R]

▼ If you look at the back, you can see that this fork has been **'single struck'**. This means that it has been decorated on one side only, in order to reduce the amount of silver used. If you pick up a single struck piece, it will feel thin and light. Considerably cheaper to produce than flatware decorated on both sides, they were often made in Exeter and Scotland.

'Sugar-sifter' spoon, c.1850
Beware of sauce ladles that have been converted into sugar-sifter spoons, such as this example, by being pierced with a pattern at a later date. The bowl of this French spoon is flatter and shallower than the bowl of a typical sauce ladle. [R]

▼ The **hollow handle** of this ladle has been filled with resin to provide strength. This detail shows a **gap** where the handle has begun to separate from the stem due to exposure to heat and hot water.

Mote spoon, c.1760
With its pierced decoration, this type of spoon was used to skim floating tea leaves from a cup of tea. [O]

Dessert spoon, c.1940
This spoon by the Danish designer Georg Jensen is made in the popular pattern known as 'Bittersweet'. Although relatively plain and simple, it is extremely stylish and of very high quality. [Q]

▼ On the back of the spoon, at the base of the bowl, you can see a common **Jensen mark**, which was used from 1945. Other marks include the initials 'G' and 'J'.

Marrow scoop, 1765
Roasted marrow bones were a popular delicacy in the 18th century. Long spoons with two long bowls, known as marrow scoops, were devised to help remove the nutritious jelly. [Q]

▲ This marrow scoop has been **marked** on the back of the stem between the two bowls, with a typically squashed and distorted date letter for 1765.

Berry spoon, 1740
A berry spoon was often simply a plain 18th-century tablespoon, later decorated in the 19th century. Note the tell-tale Hanoverian rib running down the front of the stem. [S]

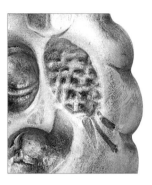

▲ The Victorian fondness for covering plain silver with **chased** and **embossed** decoration can be seen here. The back of the bowl has been elaborately detailed with fruits and vines to enliven the original very plain bowl.

▶ In this early apostle spoon, you can see how the **features** and details have **worn** over the years. Apostle spoons were not produced much after the 1650s. Fakes are often created by adding new figure terminals to 18th-century spoons.

Apostle spoon, 1615
Produced from the early 15th century, these spoons were made from wrought silver, with cast terminals modelled as apostles soldered on to slender stems. This example features St Thomas holding a spear, the symbol of his martyrdom. Apostle spoons were popular christening or wedding gifts. [G]

Caddy spoon, c.1785
Caddy spoons for measuring tea were first made in the 1770s. Usually stamped out of a thin sheet of silver, they tend to be light and damage easily. Caddy spoons are very collectable. [R]

Fruit knife, early 20th century
Mother-of-pearl was often used to create attractive handles for dessert knives and forks, as well as fish services. Look out for signs of discoloration, where rust may have set in on the iron tang – the prong that joins the silver blade to the handle – and for damage caused by immersion in hot water. [S]

Knife, c.1735
French porcelain was used for handles in the 18th century. This handle was made at the Saint-Cloud factory (see p.130). The steel blade is now rusty, a common problem with early knives. [R]

Types of 20th-century Silver

Russian teaspoon, *c.*1900 [R]

Cloisonné enamelling

Cloisonné enamelling was a particular speciality of Russian craftsmen from the end of the 19th century. The technique combines silver with coloured enamels to achieve a rich, textured effect.

■ A design is outlined by soldering filigree, wire, or metal strips into a metal base, creating a series of cells, or '*cloisons*'. Coloured enamels are poured into the cells, and the item is then fired in a kiln to produce the finished design.

■ The surface will feel bumpy and uneven where the metal wire outlines the smooth, coloured enamels.

Arts & Crafts pot and cover

From the early 20th century, Omar Ramsden and his partner Alwyn Carr specialized in designing handmade objects, occasionally set with semi-precious stones or enamel inspired by medieval designs. Rejecting mechanization, they drew inspiration from the past.

■ In keeping with the Arts & Crafts tradition of handmade wares, the hammered marks on the surface were not polished smooth after the piece was finished, but were left as a decorative effect.

■ Cabochon-set semi-precious stones add value to the piece.

■ A Latin inscription reads 'Omar Ramsden and Alwyn Carr made me'.

Pot and cover, 1913 [I]

Karl Fabergé photo album

The jewellery and silver firm of Fabergé was founded in St Petersburg in 1842. Karl Fabergé – son of the founder – worked for the Imperial family from 1881 and is celebrated for his ingenious Easter eggs.

■ The range of items made was vast and included dinner and tea services, cigarette cases, and highly decorative wares, such as tiny rock crystal vases with enamelled flowers on gold stalks.

■ Pieces were marked 'KF' or 'K Fabergé', or 'Fabergé' in Cyrillic (Russian) letters.

Fabergé photo album, *c.*1900 [J]

Tiffany & Co. cake fork, *c.*1900 [R]

Tiffany cake fork

The American firm of Tiffany & Co. (est. 1837) is famous for its mass-produced silverwares of superb quality.

■ The opulent decoration on this 'Olympian' cake fork has been stamped in a die. Its well-defined details are of a high quality, as might be expected from a high-quality company such as Tiffany & Co.

■ This Tiffany mark includes a pattern number and the initial M, which stands for Edward C. Moore, the president of the company at that time.

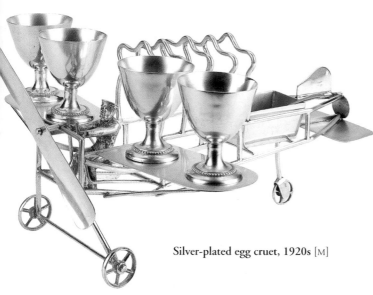

Silver-plated egg cruet, 1920s [M]

Silver-plated egg cruet

Mechanized production made available a great variety of affordable decorative and dining items in silver plate.

■ Novelty table items, such as this egg cruet in the shape of an aeroplane, were particularly popular in the 1920s and 1930s.

■ Egg cruet frames were fitted with detachable cups and spoons, which were parcel-gilded (partially gilded) to protect the silver from being stained by the sulphur in the eggs.

■ Over-zealous cleaning may damage the very thin layer of silver. You can often see the base-metal core of copper or nickel underneath.

Art Deco teapot

The Sheffield firm of Emile Viners (est. 1927) was known for its stylish, high-quality wares made in the geometric Art Deco style.

■ Ivory was a particularly popular material during the 1920s and 1930s and was often used for handles on Art Deco teapots. It was also used to insulate silver handles and finials on tea and coffee wares.

■ Since ivory has a tendency to crack as a result of constant exposure to temperature changes, some pieces may have badly damaged handles, which will affect the value of the item, since they are expensive to repair or replace.

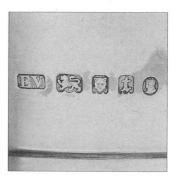

Emile Viners teapot, 1934 [O]

Arts & Crafts candlestick

One of the largest silver firms in Sheffield, Yorkshire, James Dixon & Sons (est. 1835) defied the modern trend towards mass production and concentrated on making beautifully designed wares with minimal decoration.

■ Although this candlestick looks heavy enough to have been cast, it has actually been stamped out of very thin silver, then loaded to make it feel more substantial.

■ The intriguing decorative detail on the base of this candlestick, resembling fish scales and rivets, was produced simply and cheaply with the help of a press.

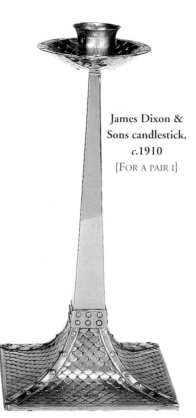

James Dixon & Sons candlestick, c.1910

[FOR A PAIR I]

Modern goblet

London silversmiths Aurum Designs (est. c.1970) produced goblets throughout the 1970s and 1980s.

■ Silver drinking vessels are frequently gilded inside to protect the metal from corrosion caused by the acid present in wine.

■ Textured surfaces, such as tree bark or lunar-surface finishes, are common features of the style.

■ Goblets, such as this one made to commemorate the anniversary of a cathedral, are solidly made, using a great deal of silver.

■ Pieces by Aurum Designs are made in limited editions and sold in fitted cases with certificates.

■ Other noted silversmiths working in a similar style include Christopher N. Lawrence and Stuart Devlin.

Aurum Designs goblet, c.1980 [Q]

Glass

USEFUL AND DECORATIVE GLASS has been made in numerous shapes and styles over the last 5,000 years, especially since the 18th century. Despite its inherent susceptibility to breakage, much old glass has survived, some dating back to ancient Roman times. Like ceramics, collectors of glass consequently have much to chose from. Types of glass include soda (of which *cristallo* is a fine example), potash and lead (also known as crystal). Manufacturing techniques range from crude core-forming to highly sophisticated mass production methods, such as pressing. Forms of decoration include colouring, engraving (by a variety of available methods), acid etching, cutting and gilding. Because relatively little glass made before the late 19th century bears marks of origin or date of manufacture, collectors must learn to recognize the visual characteristics of types, techniques, shapes and styles in order to be able to identify specific pieces correctly.

English bowl by Stuart & Sons, 1930s [O]

How to Look at Glass

The distinctive 'oily' grey colour of this mid-18th century English wine glass is typical of early lead glass. [K]

The engraving on stained glass, such as this German example (c.1860), is generally quite shallow, but can be felt if you run a finger down the side. [H]

Early opaline glass, as seen on this French breakfast set (c.1820), is usually milky white. Later examples are often coloured. [H]

GLASS COMES IN MANY SHAPES AND STYLES *and its methods of production are just as numerous. A collector friend who happens to be a doctor once aptly said that looking at glass was rather like diagnosing a patient. Only when you have detected all the 'symptoms', in the case of glass – the type, how it was made, its decoration (if any) and the overall condition – can you hope to make a sound judgement.*

The three main types of glass – soda, potash and lead (or crystal) – can be identified by colour, weight and the sound or 'ping' they make if you flick a finger against their sides. Soda glass has a yellowish/brownish tinge, is often full of small bubbles, and is lighter than potash or lead glass. It gives a dull ring when tapped, as does potash glass, which usually has a greenish/brown tinge. Early lead glass has an almost 'oily' grey colour and is full of blemishes, air bubbles and striations (ripples and irregularities). From *c.*1740, its colour became brighter, but nothing like as bright and shiny as modern lead glass. Lead glass is heavier than soda or potash glass and the 'ping' test gives a clear ring.

How a piece was made will also help with dating. The earliest glass was core formed, followed by free blowing, mould blowing and mould pressing. Early undecorated blown glass usually has a pontil mark (left by a glass-blowing tool) on the underside, but an early piece decorated by cutting or engraving may well have had the pontil mark polished off, leaving a smooth lens on the bottom. By the 19th century, however, most pontil marks were polished off. Pressed glass can be identified by its mould seams, which can be seen and felt.

Decoration can provide another clue to dating. Always feel the glass surface to determine whether the decoration is cut, engraved, etched or enamelled. On early cut glass, for example, the cuts are broad and shallow but, on pieces dating from the early 19th century, they will be deeper and more

'showy', thanks to the introduction of mechanized cutting wheels. Similarly, early engraved glass has a more granular look, while the finer abrading powders used for polishing after *c.*1860 gave a 'silkier' finish.

Check enamelled glass for wear. If the enamelling is badly worn it will greatly reduce the piece's value, and the same applies to gilding. Enamelled glass is rarely restored, but the gilding on a glass that has been regilded will look much harsher than the mellow tones of the original.

Always keep an eye out for alterations to the condition of pieces. For instance, small chips on the feet of wine glasses may have been polished out. It's also quite common to trim the feet to remove chips. If you suspect this, check the proportions. The foot should usually be wider than the bowl, not the same size or narrower.

Bowls with scalloped edges have often been restored, so look for discrepancies in the pattern. Few bowls have original trimmed edges, but a magnifying glass will show the flat edge resulting from trimming.

Certain types of glass attract particular types of 'restoration'. Wine glasses may be 'marriages' of different parts; check carefully for 'joins' where the stem meets the bowl. Be wary of a decanter that has 'just been rinsed' or filled with coloured methylated spirits – less than scrupulous vendors use liquid to hide limescale, which shows up as a cloudy surface on dry glass.

Most vital of all, make sure that you examine glass in natural light. I've bought 1930s reproduction Bristol blue glass instead of the real thing, largely because I bought it in the evening – and couldn't see that the colour wasn't quite right.

An English decanter, with three neck rings (c.1820–30). Three-ringed decanters were popular from the late 18th century. The shoulders and base are slice cut and the star-cut diamond pattern is also typical of the period. It retains its original mushroom-shaped stopper. [Q]

MATCHING PARTS
Always check that any covers and stoppers are correct. In the case of a decanter, the stopper should fit snugly and any decoration on the body should be repeated on the stopper.

PROPORTIONS
It is important to evaluate the overall proportions of a piece, since this can reveal much about its date. Late Regency decanters, such as this one, had a relatively large body and short neck.

CUT DECORATION
Deep cutting, fashionable from the beginning of the 19th century, requires high-quality glass with a bright reflective surface. English and Irish lead glass were particularly suitable.

COLOUR
If clear lead glass has a grey tone, it probably dates from the mid-18th to early 19th century. Later glass has a much brighter, whiter appearance, because of fewer impurities in the glass.

BASE
In glass of this age expect to find evidence of natural wear on the base. Fine scratches, also known as 'mossing', are perfectly acceptable.

DECORATION
This 'lacy' glass comport is a good example of quality American pressed glass designed to resemble embroidery. The background is always stippled, tending to look and feel like small beads. It served to conceal flaws and shear marks. The sharp rough edges around the rim of this comport are also typical.

METHOD OF PRODUCTION
Pressed glass was made in a one- two- or three-piece mould and raised seam marks are usually clearly visible. Because of the production process, such pieces have a smooth interior and patterned exterior. Pressed glass also often has a dull appearance with slight pitting.

This pressed glass comport was made by the Boston & Sandwich Glass Co., Cape Cod, Massachusetts, c.1840. It was the most prolific producer of 'lacy' glass in the USA, a fair proportion of which was exported. [L]

Story of Glass

A Roman blown-glass flask, *c*.**3rd century** AD [O]

THE FRAGILE BEAUTY OF GLASS *has guaranteed its popularity through the ages. Glassmaking, which began around 2000* BC *in the Middle East, became one of the most demanding of crafts and a complex mixture of science and artistry. New technologies have been constantly explored, but many ancient techniques have been retained or reinterpreted for 20th-century use.*

Although Venetian in influence, this goblet is one of the many façon de Venise *pieces made in the Low Countries. The diamond-point engraving on the bowl appears to record the birth of Francis Withens (10 May 1590); the form (shape) is typical of the second half of the 17th century.* [C]

In this mid-19th century print of the Falcon Glassworks, London (left), you can see glassmakers gathered around a glass furnace, where the molten glass was kept in a crucible. The standing figure to the right is blowing a gather *(bubble) of glass with a hollow blowing iron.*

Glass is basically made of sand (silica) and a flux (either sodium or potassium), which fuse together when melted at a very high temperature. The earliest glass was made *c*.2000–*c*.1500 BC in both Egypt and Mesopotamia. There glassmakers made small, hollow, rather crudely shaped flasks and bottles by forming a core of mud, straw and clay around a metal rod, then dipping the core into molten glass and winding hot, glass threads around it. When the Romans conquered Egypt, they adopted the Egyptian glassmaking

techniques and, around the 1st century BC, introduced glassblowing – a major innovation that is still used today. This technique involves gathering a lump of molten glass – a mixture known as the metal – on the end of a long tube called a blowing iron and inflating it. The soft glass can then be manipulated into various shapes or blown into a pre-formed mould.

As a result, glassmakers were able to make finer, larger vessels; flasks and bottles became virtually disposable items and were made in huge quantities throughout

the Roman Empire. As the Empire grew, glassmakers moved to northern Europe and traditions developed, influenced by the ingredients available. Egyptian, Roman and Venetian glassmakers made 'soda' glass, so called because it contained sodium carbonate (ashes of burnt seaweed), which was light and malleable. French and German glassmakers created potash glass, known as *verre de fougère* ('fern' glass), or *Waldglas* ('forest' glass), made by adding the ashes of wood or bracken. Both were stronger than soda glass and had a greenish

Bohemian glassmakers met the mid-19th century enthusiasm for extravagant decoration with pieces such as this magnificent stained, lidded goblet, c.1850, attributed to August Böhm. He was the master of the engraved historical scene, which combined colour, engraving, cutting and an elaborate form in one lavish piece. [C]

George Ravenscroft

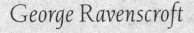

A London merchant turned glassmaker, George Ravenscroft (1632–83) developed a type of glass that was to add a new dimension to glassmaking. In 1676, in an attempt to prevent crizzling (a fine network of cracks) in the 'crystalline' glass that he had patented two years earlier, he added lead oxide to the batch. The result was a much heavier, shinier glass called lead glass or lead crystal. The formula, which guaranteed against crizzling, was perfected in 1681. By 1700, some 100 glasshouses were producing lead glass, ensuring the success of the English glass industry.

Ravenscroft lead-glass bowl c.1676. [A]

tinge. The Middle East was the major centre of production until the Venetian glassmaking industry, based on the island of Murano, received an influx of glassworkers following the sacking of Damascus at the beginning of the 15th century. Venetian glassmakers experimented with new and revived techniques and, in the mid-15th century, developed *cristallo* – a fine, colourless type of soda glass suitable for making elaborate shapes.

Many Venetian glassmakers travelled far and wide, and in the 16th and 17th centuries, *façon de Venise* (Venetian-style) glass was made throughout Europe. Venetian supremacy was challenged by the development in England of lead crystal in 1676. This was a bright, heavy glass with a highly refractive surface that was ideally suited to cutting. By the 1830s, the fashion for cut glass was overtaken in popularity by coloured glass developed by Bohemian glassmakers.

As the 19th century progressed, so too did glassmaking methods and the use of mechanization. American glass manufacturers pioneered new types of coloured glass and developed press-moulding – the technique that was to bring glass within the reach of every household.

The accelerating pace of change in styles and technology was reflected in glassmaking. From the 1890s, Art Nouveau glass was largely the preserve of French, German and Austrian makers in Europe, and Tiffany & Co. in the USA; Scandinavian glass came to the fore in the 1920s and 1930s, and by the mid-20th century, Italian glass was a leader again. Since the 1960s, commercial and art glass production have run parallel in an increasingly international glassmaking arena.

This 'Burmese' glass bowl (c.1890) shows the typical gradation of colour from yellow to pale pink, a combination favoured by Queen Victoria, for whom Thomas Webb & Sons named a range of glass, patented in 1886, 'Queen's Burmese'. [N]

A CLOSER LOOK *Wine Glasses*

Although at a first glance these two English lead-crystal wine glasses appear very similar, if you examine them closely you will notice several subtle differences that distinguish the early 18th-century original from the 1930s reproduction. The early glass is much sturdier, more compact, and made from a softer, slightly grey metal with an almost 'oily' feel. The rim of the bowl and the knop are slightly irregular and the glass contains imperfections. In contrast, the 1930s glass has a more elongated, elegant and regular form, as well as a bright, whitish, shiny, almost brittle, metal. When handled, the 18th-century glass feels heavy and solid, while the reproduction one is much lighter and more fragile. As a general rule, early glasses vary more in colour when they are grouped together, while later ones tend to be more uniform.

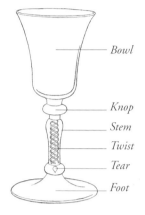

Bowl
Knop
Stem
Twist
Tear
Foot

Parts of a wine glass

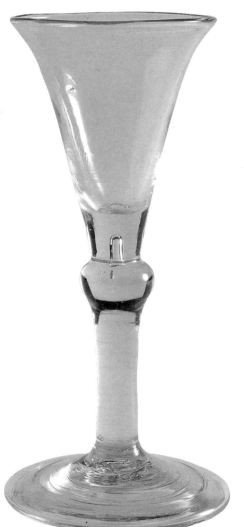

English wine glass, c.1720–30
This hand-blown, balustroid glass has a flaring trumpet bowl mounted on an inverted 'teared' baluster knop. It also has a folded conical foot. [N]

▼ If you hold this 18th-century glass up to the light, you can see how the bowl and stem seem to melt into each other. The solid glass surrounding the **'tear'** has the characteristic **ripples** and **striations** (caused by the glass being manipulated into shape with various tools) commonly found in early lead glass.

▲ During glassmaking, the gather of glass is blown and the stem drawn (pulled) out. Another bubble of glass is applied to the end of the stem, which is shaped to form the foot. A pontil iron is then attached to the bottom of the foot and this holds the glass while the bowl is shaped. On early glasses you can feel the rough, circular **'pontil mark'**, left after the finished glass is snapped off the iron.

◄ The **conical foot** (shaped like a low cone with a hollow interior) has a gradual, smooth slope that culminates in a **rounded edge** that tucks under to make the folded foot.

▶ Unlike earlier glasses, where the bowl and stem were drawn from a single gather of glass and the foot added last, this 1930s wine glass was made from three separate gathers of glass. When you hold it up to the light you will see that it displays a much more obvious, **abrupt join** where the two gathers of glass were united to make the bowl and stem. This is in marked contrast to the 18th-century example. A bright, white, almost **triangular reflection** can also be seen in the slight thickening at the sides of the base of the bowl.

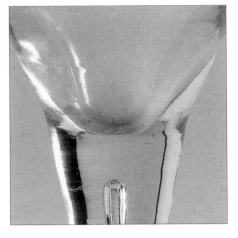

▲ The mechanical process used to finish the foot of the reproduction glass has produced much softer striations on the underside than those found on the 18th-century glass. Here the **pontil mark** has also been clearly polished out. Be warned, however, some reproductions do have pontil marks.

▼ Reproduction wine glasses with folded feet that were made from the beginning of the 20th century have very **regular** and **narrow folds**. On earlier glasses, the fold is usually less regular and may be either narrow or wide.

▲ The sharp angle seen in the trumpet bowl of the 1930s glass is echoed here in its **conical foot,** which has a far steeper and much more **irregular profile** than the 18th-century example. Just before the edge, the foot dips down then rises in a slight lip to form the fold.

English wine glass, 1930s
On this hand-blown reproduction, the inverted 'teared' baluster knop, plain stem and conical foot are topped by an angular trumpet bowl. [S]

Unfolded Feet

The folded foot, with its sloping, rounded edge, was a strong construction and, as a result, early glasses still in existence rarely have damaged feet. After *c.*1740, the folded foot was seldom used on stemware. It was eventually replaced by the unfolded foot that had a sharp edge that was more vulnerable and chipped easily (these chips have often been polished off). A reproduction unfolded foot will usually have a flatter profile and a more rounded edge.

Early unfolded foot with sharp edge

Reproduction unfolded foot with rounded edge

Types of 18th-century Wine Glasses

Bell-bowl baluster

This fine example of a baluster glass features a bell bowl over a ball knop and 'teared' inverted baluster, with base knops and a folded foot. Heavier versions, with larger proportions, had been introduced *c*.1700.

■ The metal should be a grey or oily-grey colour. Like all the glasses shown on these pages, it should ring like crystal when the rim is struck gently.

■ Balusters commonly have a folded foot, as shown here, but domed feet are also known.

■ Genuine glasses will have striations caused by tool marks and imperfections on the rim of the bowl. The pontil mark on the base should be rough and round.

English baluster, *c*.1720 [K]

Ogee-bowl balustroid

Ogee-bowl balustroid wine glasses, such as the one shown here, were introduced *c*.1720. This example features a central knopped drawn stem with a folded foot and has a rustic engraving of flowers around the top section of the bowl.

■ Balustroid glasses are less well made than balusters and have fewer, more rudimentary, knops.

■ About 50 per cent of such glasses are plain. Where present, engraving will be 'rustic' and feel rough and granular. High-quality engraving is usually found on examples from the second half of the 18th century, when engraving became more detailed, (*see* the facet-stemmed glass, below right).

English balustroid, *c*.1720–30 [O]

Newcastle light baluster

Made from *c*.1735–45, this typical example has a round funnel bowl over a teared annular (ring-shaped) and balled knop, with an air-beaded inverted baluster. It has a base knop and stands on a plain foot.

■ The Newcastle light baluster is always taller, more finely blown and more elegant than other baluster and balustroid glasses.

■ On good examples, the metal is brighter than earlier, greyer examples.

■ Many examples of light balusters are finely engraved, often by Dutch engravers, including Jacob Sang.

English light baluster, *c*.1740 [K]

Double-knopped air-twist wine glass

Here a round funnel bowl is combined with a multi-spiral air-twist stem with centre knops and a folded foot. Air-twist stems (with one or more twisted columns of air embedded) were introduced *c*.1740.

■ A folded foot is very rare in an air-twist stem glass; most examples have a conical foot.

■ The metal should be mid-grey, as was typical in the 18th century.

■ Avoid very bright examples – they are most probably later reproductions.

English wine glass, *c*.1740–50 [M]

Double-series ale glass

This example has an elongated ogee bowl engraved with a hops-and-barley motif, a double-series opaque-twist stem and a conical foot. Ale glasses held *c.*125 ml (5 fl oz) of a barley-wine-type ale.

■ Opaque white canes (rods) were used to decorate stems from the 1750s until *c.*1775.

■ Unengraved examples were used for both ale and champagne.

■ Note that the diameter of the foot should be considerably wider than the width of the bowl. A small foot may well have been trimmed to remove chips, reducing the value of the glass substantially.

English ale glass,
*c.*1755–75 [O]

Dome-footed mixed-twist wine glass

A waisted bowl and mixed-twist stem are combined with a domed foot in this glass. Mixed-twist stems, with one or more twisted columns of air combined with one or more opaque white twists, were introduced in the 1750s.

■ Domed feet are unusual on twist-stem glasses; they are more commonly found on balusters and balustroids.

■ Look for examples where there is a clearly defined space between the air twist and the opaque twist.

English wine glass, *c.*1765 [L]

Facet-stemmed wine glass

Facet stems were actually introduced in the 1750s, but were most commonly used between 1770 and 1790. The lipped ogee bowl of this wine glass sits on a six-sided diamond-cut facet stem with a central knop and plain foot. Its bowl is finely engraved with a decoration of baskets, flowers and fruit, which is typical of the period.

■ Diamond- and hexagonal-faceting on the stem is most common. Rarely found are 4-, 5-, 7- and 8-sided facets, as is shield and rectangular cutting. The edge of the cutting will feel sharp.

■ Many facet-stemmed glasses have polished-out pontil marks.

English wine glass, *c.*1775 [M]

Facet-stemmed goblet

Decorated with cut stars and engraved swags, the bowl of this goblet is mounted on a diamond-cut facet stem with a plain foot.

■ The cut and engraved decoration is similar to that found on some decanters of the period.

■ The distinctive, very short stem paved the way for the development of larger Regency wine glasses.

■ The quality of the bright metal reflects the technical advances in glassmaking.

■ Striations and tool marks are common features and are a good indication of authenticity.

English goblet, *c.*1790 [O]

Story of Cut & Pressed Glass

Illustration of a glass-cutter at work, *c.*1860

THE EARLIEST FORM *of glass decoration was cutting. Egyptian glassmakers hand cut glass into shape from the 8th century* BC, *and Roman glassmakers adapted gem-cutting techniques, holding the glass up to a rotating, foot-powered, stone or iron wheel to cut grooves and facets. Modern variants of this technique are still used today, alongside mechanically produced 'pressed' glass that was developed in the 19th century.*

American Cut Glass

Towards the end of the 19th century, the American glass-cutting industry was expanding to meet the needs of the burgeoning middle-class market. A number of companies were set up, such as T. G. Hawkes & Co., established in 1880 by Thomas G. Hawkes, an immigrant Irish glassmaker, and Hoare & Co., founded by another immigrant Irish glassworker, John Hoare. Hoare later founded the Corning Glass Works to make deep-cut, decorative, brightly polished pieces, after which the 'Brilliant' period of 1876–1914 was named.

One of the major constraints on cut decoration was the type of glass used. Most Roman soda glass was thin-walled and slightly brittle, so early cutting was, in the main, shallow with simple designs.

Not until the 17th century did a whole new range of cut decoration became possible, following the development of different types of glass. In Bohemia, experiments to improve the quality of glass used for cut and engraved decoration resulted, *c.*1675, in a new type of hard, brilliant potash glass that was suited to deep *Hochschnitt* (high-relief) engraving. In this type of cutting, the design was cut to stand proud of the surface. The technique had up to then been used on rock crystal.

The richly carved stem, elaborate knops and Hochschnitt *decoration on this standing cup and cover, made c.1700–1705, were inspired by rock crystal carving. It is typical of the work of Friedrich Winter, a distinguished Silesian glass cutter and engraver, who was one of the first to have a workshop with a water-powered mill.* [A]

Cut-glass plate by T. G. Hawkes & Co., *c.*1910 [M]

This cut-glass footed bowl (c.1800) demonstrates several of the distinctive features associated with Irish glass from the period. It has a shallow-cut, canoe-shaped bowl with a scalloped edge and a distinctive heavy 'lemon squeezer' foot with a typical square base. [J]

By the time of London's Great Exhibition of 1851, the excesses of decoration on cut lead glass, seen here on a jug by a Stourbridge company, Richardsons, were under attack. Art critic John Ruskin called such wares 'prickly monstrosities'. [M]

In England, the development of lead glass in 1676 by George Ravenscroft heralded a whole new range of cut decoration and started the fashion for cut glass. The thick, heavy, soft-bodied, brilliant lead glass was perfectly suited to deeper, more elaborate cutting. Heavier wheels were used to make deeper, sharper cuts, creating a sparkling, prismatic glass that proved to be excellent for reflecting all available light.

In 1777 the English Parliament levied a tax on glass, based on weight and size, and, as a consequence, shapes became lighter and patterns shallower. Deep cutting was now reserved for stems and bases. Glassworkers from Stourbridge and Bristol emigrated to Ireland and set up factories to avoid English taxation. From *c.*1780 to *c.*1825, luxury deep-cut pieces with elaborate designs were made in distinctive Irish styles until the Glass Excise Act of 1825 also taxed Irish glass by weight.

By the mid-19th century, Bohemian glassmakers were combining colour and cutting in their cased-glass pieces, which were made of two or more layers of glass. They used heavy cutting to show off

The Boston & Sandwich Glass Co. based on Cape Cod, Massachusetts, was one of the first and most prolific manufacturers of American pressed glass. This electric-blue compote, made c.1840, with its elaborate pressed pattern and stippled background is typical of the fancy 'lacy' glass made by the company. [L]

colour and relief patterns, rather than to reflect light and glitter, as clear glass did. However, the fashion for clear cut glass lasted late into the 19th century, since steam-powered cutting machines enabled even deeper and more elaborate designs to be cut in Europe and the USA. Cut glass continued to be an expensive luxury.

In the 1820s, a machine was invented at an American glassworks for producing 'pressed' glass, which made cut-glass forms and patterns at a fraction of the cost. Molten glass was poured into a full-size patterned mould, then 'pressed' into shape by a plunger that was pushed down into the glass to create a smooth interior and a patterned exterior. The result was a lighter, mass-produced glass.

By 1830 pressed 'lacy' glass, with a stippled background that concealed flaws and shear marks, was also being produced, and by the mid-1880s thousands of affordable household items were flooding the American market. The technology had also swiftly crossed the Atlantic, and by the 1830s clear and coloured pressed glass, including popular souvenirs, was being made in England, often in the north-east.

Most English pressed glass was made in the north-east of England, where companies such as George Davidson & Co. of Gateshead produced quantities of pressed household wares that looked like cut glass, such as the bowl shown here. The registration no. 96945 dates it to 31 March 1888. [S]

Tradesman John Blades's highly successful London business is commemorated in this print, dated 1823, of 'Mr Blades' Upper Show Room'. He supplied a variety of cut glass – from hookah bases to chandeliers – to such distinguished customers as George IV, the East India Company and the Shah of Persia.

A CLOSER LOOK *Cut & Pressed Glass*

Cut and pressed glass can look extremely similar, since some pressed glass was specifically designed as an affordable alternative to the more highly priced cut-glass pieces. Many typical cut-glass styles and patterns, including hobnails, strawberry diamonds, prisms, splits and fans, were copied. Because pressed glass was mechanically made, pieces generally have a more regular form than hand-cut glass. The most obvious difference, however, is in the quality of the glass itself. Glass cutting demands a thick, heavy, good-quality glass with a high lead content that has a shiny, even and bright reflective surface. Pressed-glass pieces are made of inferior glass that lacks this uniform surface and often has a dull, slightly pitted, 'orange peel' appearance. Weight is another useful clue: cut glass is generally much heavier than pressed glass.

IMPORTANT BRITISH CUT GLASS MANUFACTURERS	
DUDLEY FLINT GLASSWORKS	EST. 1770s
F. & C. OSLER GLASSHOUSE	EST. 1807
W. H., B. & J. RICHARDSON	EST. *c.*1836
THOMAS WEBB & SONS	EST. 1837
GEORGE BACCHUS & SONS	EST. 1840
STEVENS & WILLIAMS	EST. 1846
STUART & SONS	EST. 1881

English water jug, c.1825–35
This straight-sided jug combines several types of cut decoration: a scalloped rim, flat-cut flutes on the shoulder over simple diamonds, sliced thumb-cut flutes to the base, and a thumb-cut section on the handle. [P]

▼ The thickness and comparative softness of lead glass allows for **deep-relief decoration,** such as the **diamond cuts** shown here. The precise, angled edges should feel sharp to the touch and sparkle in the light. This style of cutting is typical of the Regency period.

▼ Cutting leaves a matt surface, which when polished with a variety of substances creates a smooth, reflective surface. Although not easy to spot, if you inspect the **flat-cut thumb section** on the handle closely, you will also notice the typical striations, or tool marks.

▼ Intaglio, or **incised cutting**, as seen here on the stylized leaf motifs on the neck of the water jug, will have the same sharpness and precise edges as the relief cutting. In this detail the striations in the surrounding glass are also clearly visible to the naked eye.

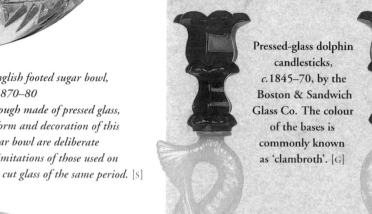

English footed sugar bowl,
c.1870–80
Although made of pressed glass,
the form and decoration of this
sugar bowl are deliberate
imitations of those used on
cut glass of the same period. [S]

American Pressed Glass

The first pressed glass was made in the USA in 1827 at the New England Glass Co., near Boston, Massachusetts. The technique was swiftly copied by its rival, the Boston & Sandwich Glass Co., on Cape Cod. So prolific was this company's production of pressed glass that 'Sandwich' became the generic term for American pressed glass. By the 1830s, pressed glass was being manufactured by many different companies, and by the late 1850s the majority of American glassware was pressed.

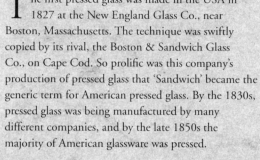

Pressed-glass dolphin candlesticks, *c.*1845–70, by the Boston & Sandwich Glass Co. The colour of the bases is commonly known as 'clambroth'. [G]

▲ The pressed edges of this standard **moulded pattern** lack the sharpness and precision of those found on cut glass. They feel slightly 'soft' to the touch, and the pitted surface does not allow the light to be reflected as brilliantly as with cut glass.

▲ Pressed glass was made in a one-, two- or three-piece mould, and **mould seams** are usually clearly visible, as seen here and in the stem of the sugar bowl in the main picture (above).

▲ Many pieces have a diamond-shaped **registration mark** with numbers and letters to identify the year of registration of the design, pattern and maker. The code III (top) designates glass.

Types of Cut Glass

Shallow diamond

The rare, shallow, diamond-cut decoration on this English cruet bottle is more often found on decanters. Decanters were produced in different sizes – a full-size decanter held an old Imperial quart (1.14 litres), 1 pint (568ml) was the usual size for spirits and smaller sizes were used for cruets. The shallow diamond cut style was introduced c.1750, when it was used on facet-stemmed wine glasses, and was most frequently used between 1770 and 1790 on Georgian glass.

■ The size of the cut decoration is often graduated, as seen here.

■ On decanters and cruets, the pontil mark is usually polished out to prevent the table surface being scratched.

English cruet bottle, c.1780 [Q]

Slice and flute

The combination of horizontal slice-cutting to form neck-grip rings, and shallow vertical flute cutting on the base of this ship's decanter was first introduced at the end of the 18th century. It is typically associated with one particular English glasshouse, which made decanters using a very grey and thick glass, which does not clean easily.

■ Sliced cutting, in which the glass is cut away to form grip rings, was also found on faceted stemware, c.1790–1810.

English ship's decanter, c.1790–1800 [L]

Irish saltcellar, c.1800 [S]

'Scallop' and 'fan'

Typically found on Irish glass from c.1790, particularly on canoe bowls (see p.180), 'scallop' cutting created a drape-like effect, while 'fan' cutting (as seen just below the scalloped edge of the saltcellar above) spreads out like a hand-held fan.

■ Fakes tend to be cut in an exaggerated, crude fashion.

Strawberry diamond

Seen here on the circular motifs, this type of diamond cutting is characterized by tiny hobnail diamonds with a criss-cross surface resembling strawberries. It was introduced c.1820–30, following the development of smaller cutting wheels.

■ The strawberry diamond pattern was used on most types of tableware, including glasses, decanters and bowls.

■ Many lidded bowls from this period had a spoon hole added later so they could be used for jam and honey.

English compote and cover, c.1825 [P]

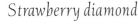

Step and slice

Introduced *c.*1820, step cutting
was a difficult technique to perfect;
any flaw in the very thick glass used
could result in the piece shattering.
■ Decanters with step-cut necks are
rare, since they are uncomfortable
to hold, but step cutting was also used
on bowls and other vessels.
■ The vertical slice cutting seen
on the base was a cleaner, slicker
technique used especially on
glass with a brighter metal
made from *c.*1820.
■ If you hold a step-cut
piece up to the light, it
should sparkle.

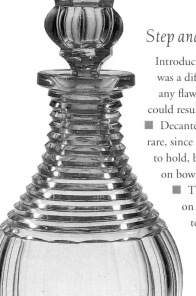

English decanter, *c.*1830 [Q]

Flute and lens

This English celery glass – a
generic term now used for any
19th-century footed vase – is
decorated with the flute-and-lens
cut decoration that was used
frequently throughout the 19th
century. It was a useful technique
that produced a stylish effect for
relatively little work.
■ Concave lens cuts (sometimes
also known as 'printies' or thumb
cuts) produced interesting optical
effects and were used often on
decanters, jugs and other large
ornamental pieces (*see* p.138).

English celery glass, *c.*1830 [R]

Pillar

The pillar cutting on the body
and stopper of this flagon was a
rare and difficult technique,
introduced *c.*1820s.
■ Most pillar cutting is
vertical; however, the
unusual pillar cuts seen
here have been made at a
angle of 45 degrees to
create the optical effect
of a diamond design and
are very rare.
■ The upstick handle
seen here was applied to
the body and pulled up.
Always check for hairline
cracks in the glass where
the handle joins, which
will weaken the piece.

**English spirit flagon,
*c.*1870–80** [R]

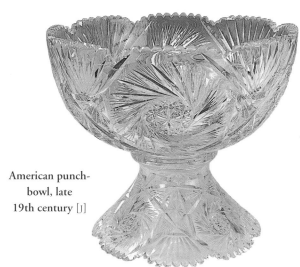

**American punch-
bowl, late
19th century** [J]

Brilliant

The complex, deep and highly polished decoration seen on this
American punch bowl epitomizes the 'Brilliant' style of cutting.
Introduced by American glass companies, principally in the Midwestern
states including Ohio and Pennsylvania; it was popular from 1876–1914.
■ This style was mainly used on large, impressive pieces of tableware.

Story of Coloured Glass

THE TWO MAIN WAYS *of making coloured glass – by adding coloured oxides to the batch or by exploiting the natural colouration caused by impurities in the glass – were used by glassmakers from the earliest times. Constant experimentation from the 15th century produced a variety of different colours, culminating in the iridescent and multicoloured glass of the late 19th century.*

Alabastron (*c.*600–500 BC) from the Eastern Mediterranean [O]

Opaque-white glass was used with great skill by Venetian glassmakers. They embedded threads of white glass in clear glass to form elegant lacy patterns, known as latticinio glass. This goblet and cover (c.1590–1610) is made in the façon de Venise *style, which was popular in Europe durng the 17th century.* [D]

Ancient Egyptian and Roman glass-makers added different metallic oxides to the batch (the ingredients used to make glass) to create the desired colour. Blue glass was the easiest to make, consequently many Egyptian pieces were a vivid turquoise blue, often decorated with opaque white and yellow glass threads that were 'combed' to produce a variety of patterns. Dark cobalt blue was a popular base colour for Roman cameo glass (*see* pp.200–201).

Coloured glass was also used to imitate highly prized gemstones such as agate, lapis lazuli, jasper, turquoise, chalcedony and porphyry. French and German glassmakers made the most of the natural colours produced when they added a flux (to reduce the melting point of the silica) of potash to the batch. This resulted in the distinctive greenish, yellowish or brownish colouration of the French *verre de fougère* and German *Waldglas*.

In the 15th century, Venetian glass-makers revived the art of 'chalcedony' glass and experimented with opaline glass. They developed a type of opaque white glass, known as *lattimo,* that was designed to imitate the newly fashionable and highly prized Chinese porcelain being imported into Europe at this time. *Lattimo* was then incorporated in the form of canes or rods to make the wonderful intricate patterns found in *latticino* glass.

At the end of the 17th century, Johann Kunckel, a German glassmaker, invented a new type of red glass – always one of the most difficult colours to produce – adding gold to create a deep ruby-coloured glass,

The distinctive greenish colour of Waldglas *can be seen to advantage in this Dutch* Römer *(c.1670). This popular drinking glass was decorated with blobs of glass called 'prunts' that were applied to the stem to make it easier to grasp. Here the prunts are in the shape of raspberries.* [L]

known as *Goldrubinglas* or *Rubinglas.* Another German glassmaker, Caspar Wistar, emigrated to the USA in the early 18th century. In 1739, Wistar established the first American glass factory, the Wistarburgh Glassworks in New Jersey, where he and his son produced clear and coloured glass. In England, large quantities of cobalt imported via Bristol gave rise to the name 'Bristol glass' for the blue (green and amethyst were also made) decanters, bowls and wine glasses that were produced in Bristol and elsewhere in Britain during the 18th century (*see* p.193).

By the mid-19th century, the European passion for clear cut glass had run its course. Inventive Bohemian glassmakers, such as Count von Buquoy, Friedrich Egermann and the German glassmaker Josef Riedel, successfully applied chemistry to glassmaking to produce new colours.

In 1817 von Buquoy produced an opaque black glass that resembled Josiah Wedgwood's black basalt stoneware. 'Hyalith' glass, a dense opaque sealing-wax red or black glass, often combined with gilded decoration, followed in 1819. Riedel's experiments with adding uranium to the batch resulted in the production of the startlingly bright *Annagrün* and *Annagelb* glass (*see* p.190).

These experiments inspired British glassmakers, who, in the 1870s, added small quantities of uranium to the batch and produced 'Vaseline' glass, with its characteristic yellow, blue and green tinge.

The deep ruby colour of this German wheel-engraved beaker and cover (c.1700) was created by adding gold to the batch, which accounts for its name – Goldrubinglas (gold-ruby glass). The expensive technique was used only for exclusive pieces, many of which also had luxurious silver-gilt mounts. [C]

Towards the end of the 1870s, the English firm of Thomas Webb & Sons patented a technique for making glass with an iridescent finish that resembled the shimmering colours found on excavated ancient Roman glass. As a result, a number of British and American patents were registered for creating an artificial iridescent finish by exposing pieces to the fumes of heated metallic compounds.

In the USA, Louis Comfort Tiffany developed the iridescent range of 'Favrile' glass (registered in 1894), and Frederick Carder developed 'Gold Aurene' at the Steuben Glassworks in Corning, New York. By the early 20th century, a spray-on iridescent coating was ready for use on an inexpensive pressed glass, known from the 1950s as Carnival glass because mass-produced examples were given as prizes at funfairs.

In the early 19th century, French glassmakers perfected a slightly translucent, whitish glass known as opaline, which was then further developed in a range of subtle pastel colours.

By the 1880s, American glass factories had developed a whole new range of parti-coloured art glass that included 'Burmese', shading from yellow to pink, 'Amberina', graduating from light amber to dark ruby, and 'Peach Blow', from cream to rose, or from pale blue to rose pink. Like the Venetian *lattimo* glass, opaline glass was first developed in order to imitate elegant Chinese porcelain.

Colouring Glass

The following metallic oxides have been traditionally used to make some of the most commonly found coloured glass:

- Copper – sky blue and turquoise
- Cobalt – dark blue
- Iron, chromium – green
- Uranium – yellow, greenish yellow
- Silver (small quantities) – golden yellow
- Cadmium sulphide with selenium – orange
- Copper, gold (small quantities), cadmium sulphide (with added selenium) – red
- Manganese – purple

Engraved covered goblet, made in Potsdam, *c.*1700 [G]

This pitcher (c.1815) with a 'lily-pad' decoration, is an early piece of American coloured glass. It was probably made in the state of New York. Similar wares were made at the Wistarburgh Glassworks, New Jersey, which was established by the glassmaker Caspar Wistar. [E]

In the early 19th-century, Bohemian glassmakers experimented with new types of coloured glass, including 'Lithyalin', invented by Friedrich Egermann. He made this hexagonal beaker (c.1830–40), with its lobed foot-rim. Its marbled colours combined with gilded decoration were intended to look like semi-precious stones. [I]

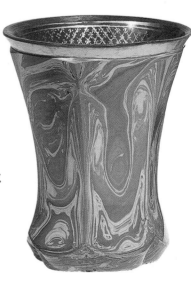

A Closer Look *Cased & Stained Glass*

Casing and staining are both ways of adding a layer of colour to glass. Casing is a more technically demanding and expensive technique in which clear blown glass is covered in a relatively thick layer of glass of a different colour. The two layers are fused together during the firing process. A design is then cut through the top layer, either by hand or with a cutting-wheel. With staining, a very thin layer of translucent enamel is applied to the surface of the glass, either with a brush or by dipping the clear glass into a coloured solution, which is then fixed to the surface by firing. You can easily distinguish between the two types of glass by comparing weights and thickness. Cased glass is heavier and thicker, with a greater depth and quality of colour and decoration. It is also shinier than stained glass, which has a duller finish.

IMPORTANT BOHEMIAN GLASS FActories	
HARRACH GLASSHOUSE, NOVY SVET	EST. 1712
GLASSHOUSE AT NOVY BOR	EST. 1760
JIRIKOVO UDOLO GLASSWORKS, NOVY HRADY	EST. 1817
BOHEMIAN GLASSWORKS, KARLOVY VARY	EST. 1857

Bohemian cased goblet, c.1850
This goblet is covered in a layer of deep blue glass, which has been carefully cut away on the stem to reveal the clear glass beneath. The fine wheel-engraved panel around the bowl shows a rocky landscape with a stag – typical of Bohemian decoration at this time. [G]

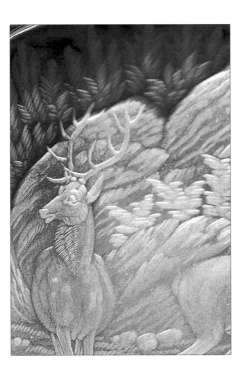

◀ If you look closely you will see the high quality of the **wheel-engraved** decoration. In order to create the detailed landscape, the glass has been pressed against the cutting wheel using different degrees of pressure to create deep or shallow engraving. Where the engraving is at its shallowest (see the bracken in the top left-hand corner of the detail), the glass remains pale blue, since the clear glass beneath has not been reached by the cutting-wheel. You can also feel the varying degrees of relief in the engraved surface. At the edge of the engraved decoration, where the engraving graduates from deep to very shallow, notice the soft **edge**, that looks almost **smudged.**

▶ One of the ways to distinguish cased from stained glass is to examine the depth and angle of the cuts. Run your finger down the back of the bowl and feel the gently **bevelled edges** on the circular concave cuts – known as **lens cuts** – in the cased glass. The characteristic gradual shading of colour from blue through to clear glass on the cut edges is also visible on close inspection.

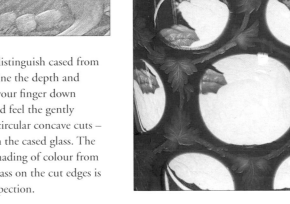

Friederich Egermann

Friedrich Egermann (1777–1864) was born in Blottendorf, Bohemia, and began his career as an enameller before concentrating on experiments with new types of coloured glass at his factory in Blottendorf. In 1828, he invented and patented Lithyalin – a multilayered, dense, opaque glass – in great secrecy. The technique involved applying metallic oxides to the glass so that when it was cut, usually with broad, concave facets, it resembled a semi-precious stone or an exotic wood grain. Egermann also experimented with staining, creating a distinctive yellow stain using silver chloride (*c.*1820), and a ruby red using gold (*c.*1830).

Lithyalin spa glass (1836) by the workshop of Egermann [I]

Stained tumbler and carafe, c.1860 Tumblers and water carafes were just two of the many popular spa souvenirs made throughout Europe during the 19th century. Made in Germany, this example is a rare example of a tumbler and carafe set – solo tumblers are much more frequently found. [M]

▶ Although the engraving on this stained-glass carafe is of exceptionally fine quality, it lacks the depth and range of engraving present in the cased-glass example. The very **shallow engraving** is almost imperceptible to the touch. Unlike cased glass, stained glass was not generally given an all-over colour; many pieces were only partially stained, presumably to make them cheaper and quicker to produce.

◀ The stained colour on this glass beaker has been applied using a paint brush, which has resulted in a **blotchy**, rather uneven covering. Usually a stained-glass object was blown first, then cut, stained and finally engraved. As you can see here the **stained colour** extends beyond the engraved border, which suggests that the engraving was carried out extremely quickly. Because there is no depth to the stain (unlike the cased-glass example opposite) the edge of the stained colour is very sharply defined.

Types of Coloured Glass

Bristol blue glass

The distinctive blue of this spirit decanter, came from cobalt imported via Bristol, gave rise to the generic name 'Bristol blue' for a type of English glass that was made from *c*.1760 until *c*.1825. Reproduction Bristol glass was made from *c*.1930 onwards. The shape of reproduction glass usually looks clumsy when compared with an original.

■ Bristol decanters often have gilt decoration in the form of a simulated label for the contents.

■ Bristol glass was also made in dark green and amethyst. Blue wine and spirit decanters and finger bowls are readily found, as are green wine glasses. Blue and amethyst wine glasses are rare.

Bristol blue decanter, *c*.1785 [R]

Opaline glass

Opaline glass was developed in France *c*.1825, where some of the finest pieces, including this two-tone opaline scent bottle, were made from *c*.1840–*c*.1870. Produced in Britain from *c*.1840, opaline glass was subsequently made throughout Europe.

■ All kinds of decorative pieces were made in free- and mould-blown shapes

■ A wide range of colours was used. Most popular was turquoise blue (seen here), rarest was a soft pink known as '*gorge de pigeon*'.

■ Gilding was often used as decoration, sometimes it was two tone (silver and gold).

French opaline scent bottle, *c*.1845 [H]

Annagrün glass

The greenish yellow colour of this goblet and cover was known as *Annagrün* (Anna-green), and, like the yellowish-green glass known as *Annagelb* (Anna-yellow), was named after the wife of the Bohemian glassmaker, Josef Riedel, who first made this type of glass in the 1830s.

■ The solid colour was produced by adding uranium to the batch, a technique that was used on decorative glass from 1830–48, when uranium was discontinued because of fears about safety.

■ True *Annagrün* and *Annagelb* glass has a harsh colour, unlike other 19th-century uranium-coloured glass, such as 'Vaseline' glass (*see* opposite above right).

Bohemian *Annagrün* goblet, *c*.1840 [F]

English green 'mercury' glass saltcellar, *c*.1850 [R]

'Mercury' glass

All 'mercury' glass, including this green saltcellar, was made by James Powell at Whitefriars for manufacturers.

■ Patented in 1849, the technique involved depositing a layer of silver nitrate on the inside of a hollow vessel. It was highly dangerous and only used for a few years before being abandoned, only to be revived by French and Bohemian glassmakers at the end of the century.

■ Clear glass with silver is the most common combination, but green (shown here), ruby, blue or purple casing is also found.

'Vaseline' glass

This straw opal perfume bottle is an example of 'Vaseline' glass, so-called because of its 'greasy' appearance. Inspired by 17th-century Venetian examples and introduced into England by James Powell at Whitefriars in 1877, it went out of fashion in the 1930s. Many British and continental makers made opalescent glass.

■ Minute quantities of uranium and metal oxides were used to produce the characteristic shades of yellow, blue, green and red (very rare) that varied between factories.

■ Whitefriars' straw opal and blue opal were used on tablewares, and especially for Venetian-influenced shapes such as this perfume bottle.

Whitefriars straw opal perfume bottle, *c.*1880 [M]

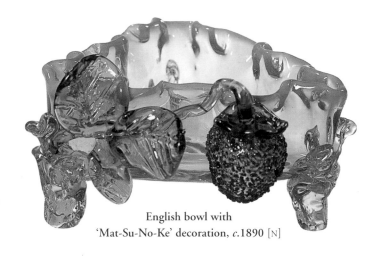

English bowl with 'Mat-Su-No-Ke' decoration, *c.*1890 [N]

'Mat-Su-No-Ke' glass

This crimped-edge, coloured glass bowl, with applied high-relief decoration, was influenced by Japanese decorative styles. It was made using the 'Mat-Su-No-Ke' technique, which means 'The Spirit of the Pine Trees'. Registered in 1884 by the British company Stevens & Williams, the skilled and expensive process – the decoration is first made separately, then applied to a blown body – was used from *c.*1885–*c.*1900.

■ 'Mat-Su-No-Ke' pieces should be checked very carefully for damage.

■ Many other English glassmakers imitated the technique, including Thomas Webb & Sons, which from 1885 made a range of fancy glass with applied fruit and flowers.

'Favrile' glass

The iridescent finish was developed by Louis Comfort Tiffany in the 1890s and simulated the effect of weathering on ancient glass.

■ Much of Tiffany's iridescent glass has a blue or amber background and is strikingly organic in shape, inspired by flowers and gourds.

■ Similar glass was made by the Steuben Glassworks, which used a slightly different formula to produce a brighter iridescence.

■ Most Tiffany pieces are signed. One genuine signature – L.C.T. – shown here has often been faked.

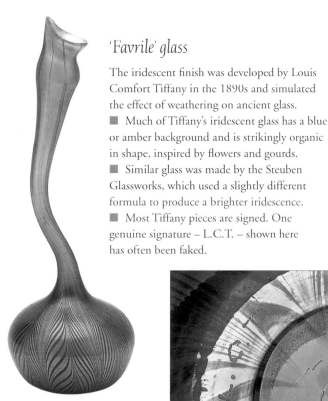

Tiffany sprinkler, *c.*1900 [C]

Carnival glass plate, *c.*1910 [O]

Carnival glass

Press-moulded glassware with an iridescent finish, known as 'carnival' glass, originated in the USA. This flat plate was made in Wheeling, West Virginia, by Harry Northwood, son of the British glassmaker John Northwood, and its pattern is now known as 'Northwood's Peacocks'. The term 'carnival' glass was used only from the 1950s.

■ This type of glass was made in many countries under different names from *c.*1880 to the 1940s. Production revived in the 1960s, using new moulds and designs, or reproducing glass using the original moulds.

Story of Enamelled & Gilded Glass

Bottle by Osvaldo Brussa, *c*.1730 [G]

ALTHOUGH ENAMELLING AND GILDING *were both used independently on early Roman glass, Islamic glassmakers from the 7th to the 15th century were the first to combine the two decorative techniques with spectacular results, producing high-quality vessels. They became particularly famous for magnificent enamelled and gilded mosque lamps that were to inspire generations of glassmakers of different nationalities.*

In mid-15th century Europe, Venetian glassmakers, inspired by contact with glassmakers from the Islamic world, first used enamelling to decorate the newly discovered *cristallo* glass. This was a clear, fine-walled glass that was too thin for cut and engraved decoration. Both enamelling (where colours in the form of metallic oxides mixed with glass and suspended in oil are painted onto the glass and fired) and gilding (where gold leaf, or gold paint, is applied to the surface of the glass) were particularly suited to *cristallo*. By the mid-to late 16th century enamelling was no longer fashionable in Venice, but the brightly coloured Venetian enamelled decoration of coats of arms, portraits and crests had inspired German and Bohemian glassmakers, who came to the fore in the late 16th century, using enamelled decoration on a wide variety of traditional drinking vessels. The hearty and robust Bohemian and German decoration employed political and imperial symbols, which were applied liberally to many trade guild vessels as well as to communal drinking bowls.

In the course of the 17th and 18th centuries, German *Hausmaler* (decorators who worked from home and not in a factory) developed new types of enamelling. Johann Schaper, a porcelain and glass decorator, who worked in Nuremberg from 1665, developed a technique that became known as *Schwarzlot* (black lead), using brown or black transparent enamels to decorate glass vessels, especially beakers.

Between 1762 and 1815, Samuel Mohn, a Dresden *Hausmaler* developed thin, transparent, coloured enamels, which were also used primarily on beakers with gilt borders. His son, Gottlob Samuel Mohn, took the technique with him *c*.1810 to Vienna, where he taught the technique to Anton Kothgasser, then a decorator at the Royal Porcelain Factory.

The elaborate enamelled decoration of the Imperial double-headed eagle identifies this traditional 16th-century cylindrical German drinking vessel as a Reichsadler Humpen (Imperial Eagle Beaker). It was designed to toast the Holy Roman Emperor, whose Empire is represented by the shields hanging from the eagle's outspread wings. [H]

Made in Syria or Egypt c.1330–45, this gilded and enamelled mosque lamp (left), carries an heraldic shield and an inscription of a verse from the Koran. It is an excellent example of the magnificent pieces that inspired late 19th-century Islamic-style glass. The loops on the side were used to suspend the lamp from the mosque ceiling. [A]

The engraved and gilded boar-hunting scene on this Zwischengoldglas beaker (c.1750) was a common design used by Bohemian glassmakers in the mid-18th century. The theme is continued even on the base, where a horse and stag are shown in a medallion. [H]

Kothgasser became one of the technique's best-known exponents. In Venice, the art of enamelling was revived by the workshop of Osvaldo Brussa and his son, Angelo. They used charming, naive depictions of birds and flowers to decorate a range of beakers, carafes, flasks and bottles.

In Britain, enamelling was comparatively rare before the mid-18th century, after which the Beilby family became famous for their enamelled wares. These were decorated with brightly coloured armorials as well as single-coloured naturalistic designs, some including gilding.

Although gilding was often combined with enamelling, usually in the form of decoration on the rim or feet of a vessel, it was also used on its own. During the late 17th and early 18th centuries, coloured and opaque white glass pieces were often decorated with gilding, most famously on 'Bristol blue' decanters, which had gilded labels and lettering that described their contents.

In the early 18th century, German glassmakers developed a technique known as *Zwischengoldglas*. Gold or silver leaf was applied to a clear drinking glass that was engraved with a design, then covered with a protective sleeve of plain glass to create a type of 'gold sandwich'.

In the 19th century, London's Great Exhibition of 1851 provided a showcase for the superbly decorated enamelled and gilded show pieces made by such British companies as W. H., B. & J. Richardson. This firm was also involved in patenting new decorative processes that included the use of transfer printing.

French glassmakers made some of the finest enamelled and gilded wares, in particular opaline vases with gilded rims and feet decorated with superbly painted enamelled birds, butterflies and flowers. Other French glass artists, such as Philippe-Joseph Brocard and I. J. Imberton, looked back to 13th- and 14th-century Islamic mosque lamps for inspiration, as did the Austrian firm of J. & L. Lobmeyr, whose elaborately enamelled and gilded Islamic-style glass won prizes at the Paris Exhibition of 1878.

The unification of Germany in 1871 made *Historismus* – glass made and decorated in historical styles – fashionable. Many drinking vessels, such as *Römers* and *Humpen,* were produced that were often decorated with enamelled coats of arms, copied from 16th- and 17th-century originals.

English 'Bristol' glass decanters were often decorated with gilding, either in the form of simulated labels, or, as on this amethyst wine decanter of c.1775, with a motif of grapes and vine leaves. This decanter's long neck and lozenge stopper is typical of Bristol glass. [K]

Rare armorial goblet (c.1765) by William Beilby [B]

The Beilby Family

In 1760, the gold- and silversmith William Beilby and his seven children moved from Durham to Newcastle-upon-Tyne, where he and his son William and daughter Mary, were to become the best-known enamellers in mid-18th century Britain. They decorated decanters and glasses, typically with thinly applied pink and bluish white enamel motifs, but their most famous pieces are rare, brightly coloured armorial goblets. The family is particularly known for the 'Royal Beilby' goblets that featured the feathers of the then Prince of Wales, later George III.

The bucket bowl of this rare armorial goblet (left) was decorated by William Beilby, with an elaborate, brightly coloured coat of arms, which has since been attributed to the Buckmaster family. The reverse side of the goblet carries a more typical Beilby motif of a fruiting vine, in opaque white enamel.

Types of Enamelled & Gilded Glass

Transparent enamelling

Decorated with transparent enamelling, this beaker has the waisted shape, introduced *c*.1815, favoured by Anton Kothgasser, who was one of the most prolific Viennese enamellers.

■ The thinly applied translucent enamels look like watercolours.

■ Beakers decorated with town and cityscapes, such as this one, were made as expensive souvenirs.

**Viennese *Ranftbecher*,
c.1815 [E]**

Polychrome enamelling

This opaque white vase, with superb gilding and enamelling of cascades of fruit, flowers and birds, is one of a prize-winning pair shown at the Great Exhibition of 1851 in London.

■ The extravagant combination of gilding and naturalistic designs was also very popular on 19th-century French opaline and opaque-coloured glass.

■ French and English glassmakers generally produced the finest examples of this type of decoration; although Bohemian glassmakers were more prolific, they tended to be less skilful enamellers.

Exhibition vase by Benjamin Richardson, *c*.1850 [C]

Opaque enamelling

This Bohemian tankard is made of cased glass (two or more layers of glass) combined with gilt and opaque enamelled decoration. Introduced *c*.1825, the tankard was found all over Europe by the mid-19th century.

■ Typical colour combinations are white over red, blue or green; recent Italian copies have over-bright colours and over-shiny gilding.

■ The best examples have fine brushwork on the painted panels.

**Bohemian tankard,
c.1850 [Q]**

Islamic-style enamelling

Inspired by early Islamic mosque lamps (*see* p.192), this thickly enamelled and gilded vase was made by the Austrian firm of J. & L. Lobmeyr (est. 1823), one of the finest practitioners of this technique, which was revived in the 1860s.

■ The combination of outlining and infilling with solid, vividly coloured enamelling closely resembles the *cloisonné* enamelling used on metalwork.

■ Typically, the elaborate, symmetrical decoration depicts stylized, scrolling foliage.

■ Other important craftsmen who used this technique include the French glassmaker Philippe-Joseph Brocard.

**Islamic vase by J. & L.
Lobmeyr, *c*.1880 [I]**

High-relief enamelling

This small posy vase with scrolled gilt feet was made by Ludwig Moser, whose Bohemian glassworks (est. 1857) specialized in high-relief decoration built up with multiple layers of enamelling.

■ Moser often bought in blanks (undecorated wares) that were then enamelled, typically with a colourful array of flowers and insects.

■ Animals and birds were often first painted in heavy grey enamel, then overpainted in bright colours and fired.

■ Moser's mark does not appear on all pieces and attribution can be difficult with unsigned pieces.

Posy vase by Ludwig Moser, c.1890 [L]

High-relief gilding

The high-relief gilding on this oriental-style vase is typical of the work of Jules Barbe, a French designer who worked for Thomas Webb & Sons in the 1880s.

■ The relief layers of gold paste required two to four firings to build up the decoration.

■ The form, colour and gilding reflected the fashion of the time for the Japanese style.

Vase by Thomas Webb & Sons, c.1890 [N]

'Mary Gregory' enamelling

A 'cranberry' body and white enamelled decoration distinguish 'Mary Gregory' glass, first made in the USA in the late 19th century.

■ When fired, the white or pinky white enamel looks like glass on glass; on later examples the enamelling may look like white paste.

■ Other body colours than reds exist, but the decoration is always of young boys and girls in Victorian dress.

'Mary Gregory' jug, c.1870–80 [N]

Transparent enamelling

Transparent enamelling, as seen on this liqueur glass decorated by the Bavarian firm of Theresienthal (est. 1836), was a particular feature of Austrian and German Art Nouveau bowls, as well as wine and champagne glasses.

■ The design was outlined in colour and then filled in with thin, transparent enamels.

■ Companies such as Moser and Lobmeyr (*see* above left and opposite left) produced similar glasses, which were largely unmarked and without pontil marks. The stems are of various colours (green is most commonly found) and have sharp, gilded rims.

Theresienthal liqueur glass, c.1900 [N]

Story of Engraved & Etched Glass

ENGRAVING WAS FIRST INTRODUCED *by early Roman glassmakers who adapted a gem-engraving technique to cut a shallow design into the glass suface using a flint, diamond or copper wheel. By the mid-17th century, engraving had developed into a sophisticated art and, two hundred years later, it was used in conjunction with the newly perfected use of acid to 'etch' designs on a whole range of glassware.*

Engraved jug, 19th-century [E]

This illustration, showing a glass engraver at work, is from Apsley Pellatt's Curiosities of Glass Making, *published in London in 1849.*

Roman glass was decorated with shallow wheel-engraved patterns from as early as the 1st century AD, and Roman glassmakers were also known to have used a form of diamond-point engraving, scratching shallow designs on glass, possibly with sharp flints. The Venetian *cristallo* glass developed in the 15th century was too fine and delicate for wheel engraving, but diamond-point engraving was used on the soda glass, even *façon de Venise* pieces produced in the Low Countries in the 16th and 17th centuries (*see* p.174).

Meanwhile, the technique of wheel-engraving was revived in Bohemia by Caspar Lehmann, a German gem engraver who, from 1588, worked at the court of Emperor Rudolph II in Prague. Lehmann adapted the wheel-engraving technique used on gems and rock crystal for use on glass and founded an engravers' school.

Jacob Sang, one of the most accomplished 18th-century Dutch engravers, worked in Amsterdam, where this signed goblet and cover was made in 1762. Like many of his contemporaries, he engraved glass imported from Newcastle in England, often with designs celebrating friendship or such subjects as marriage and birth. [H]

The Ancient and Medieval Art Exhibition, organized by the Royal Society in London in 1850, inspired a revival of Neo-classical decoration, such as the cornucopiae engraved on this two-handled amphora-like vase made by Thomas Webb & Sons. [J]

By the beginning of the 18th century, two important innovations had affected wheel-engraving. First, water power could now be used to drive the cutting wheels, and, second, a more robust type of glass had been developed that was suitable both for *Hochschnitt* engraving, where the design stands proud of the surface, and *Tiefschnitt*, or intaglio, where the design is cut into the glass surface. Over the next hundred years or so, wheel-engraving largely overtook the older diamond-point and stipple engraving methods.

The 19th-century passion for invention included attempts to use acid to create decorative patterns on glass. While engraved glass satisfied the higher end of the market, this expensive technique was gradually combined with, or – on less expensive pieces – superseded by, acid-etching, first patented in Britain in 1857 by Benjamin Richardson. Here the glass object is first covered in an acid-resistant coating and the design is cut or scratched on the glass. Then the piece is dipped into hydrofluoric acid, which corrodes or 'acid etches' the exposed design into the glass.

Stipple Engraving

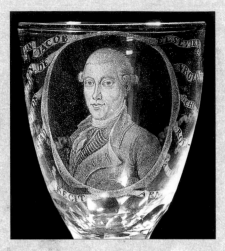

Stipple engraving was first introduced in Holland *c*.1620 by Anna Roemers Visscher, an amateur glass decorator. The technique was a variation of diamond-point engraving, at which Dutch engravers excelled. Basically, the engraver used a diamond-point stylus to tap the glass, creating a design built up from a series of dots. Two major 18th-century experts in this technique were Frans Greenwood and David Wolff, who were both Dutchmen. They used glass that was probably imported from Newcastle and better suited to stippling than the Dutch glass of the time. In the 20th century, stipple engraving was revived in England by Laurence Whistler.

The subtle tones possible with stipple-engraving are visible in this portrait (*c*.1785) by David Wolff. [D]

The etching's depth and texture is determined by the length of time it is exposed to the acid. Glassmakers such as John Northwood experimented with ways of controlling the depth of shading and relief using a less powerful 'white' acid, and outlined designs with the aid of templates. Engraving and acid-etching continued to be used separately and together (notably on cameo glass). In the 20th century, the technique of stipple engraving was revived, but sand-blasting superseded acid-etching.

Much of the decoration by the American company T. G. Hawkes & Co. was carried out on blanks (undecorated wares) supplied by other manufacturers, as was the case with this punch-bowl, made between 1903 and 1915, and engraved with the 'Renaissance' pattern. [L]

The English firm of J. & J. Northwood made such fine pieces as this acid-etched jug (c.1865–75). It was established in 1860 specifically to decorate acid-etched glass and made many major technological contributions to the development of the technique. [M]

Types of Engraved & Etched Glass

Wheel engraving: 18thC

Found in Britain from *c*.1720, this type of engraving used simple cuts.

■ The matt engraved areas should feel granular if you touch them.

■ The bowl of this plain-stemmed English wine glass is engraved with naturalistic flowers, which are typical of the period.

Wine glass, *c*.1730–40 [Q]

Wheel engraving: 19thC

Wheel engraving in the 19th century was generally more refined than in the 18th century. From *c*.1860, when new abrasives became available for the cutting wheel, a much finer finish could be achieved.

■ The matt engraving detailed below has a silky finish and the cut areas have been polished to provide extra definition.

Lemonade jug, 1870 [P]

Intaglio engraving

A complex and expensive technique, this method was first used for gem engraving and is particularly associated with 17th-century German and Silesian glass.

■ This champagne glass has an intaglio-engraved bowl, in which the design, although hollowed out, gives the appearance of standing proud of the surface.

Champagne glass by Thomas Webb & Sons, *c*.1900 [R]

Rock crystal engraving

Rock crystal engraving was revived by English glassmakers in Stourbridge. From the 1880s, the technique was used to make technically demanding, expensive pieces, such as this lavish wine glass.

■ The basic form is first shaped by cutting, then the piece is intaglio engraved, and finally given a distinctive all-over polish.

Wine glass, *c*.1890 [L]

Diamond-point engraving

In diamond-point engraving, hundreds of shallow scratches are made with a diamond point to build up a design. The scratches can be seen if you look closely – and you should be able to feel the shallow cuts.

■ The technique was first used in the 16th century, but was largely superseded by wheel engraving in the 18th century.

Mammoth goblet, *c.*1890 [J]

Stipple engraving

The design is built up from a series of dots, made by gently tapping the glass with a diamond-pointed stylus, to form areas of light and shade.

■ The finest examples of stippling use both the front and back of the glass to create depth and perspective.

■ This method, dating back to the 17th-century, is still used.

Goblet by Doug Burgess, 1985 [P]

Acid-etching

This English tankard is an example of the middle-range pieces produced using hydrofluoric acid from the mid-19th century until after World War I, when the dangers associated with the technique were recognized.

■ If you look closely at the surface of an acid-etched piece, you should be easily able to see the shiny grooves created where the acid has eaten into the surface of the glass.

Tankard, 1870–80 [R]

Acid-etching

Sophisticated acid-etching involved several additional stages in which the glass was engraved, 'polished' with acid, re-exposed to acid and re-engraved, to build up layers of matt and polished detail. This created a textured, three-dimensional effect.

■ These labour-intensive pieces have always been rare and expensive luxuries.

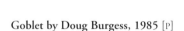

Dessert wine glass, *c.*1900 [S]

Story of Cameo Glass

John Northwood's replica of the Portland Vase (1876) [A]

THE INVENTION OF THE BLOWING IRON *around the 1st century BC led to the development of cased glass, comprising two or more layers of coloured glass. This innovation enabled the Egyptian and Roman glassmakers to produce the earliest cameo glass. The technique was not revived until the 19th century, when the initial supremacy of British cameo glass was eclipsed by superb French Art Nouveau artistry.*

One of the earliest surviving pieces of cameo glass is the Morgan Cup, a piece of dark blue Roman glass with an opaque-white frieze decoration carved in relief that is now in the Corning Museum of Glass, New York State. Dating from around the 1st century BC, this cup shows how Roman glassmakers adapted the cameo technique used by gemstone engravers to produce pieces made of two layers of differently coloured glass, often dark blue covered by opaque white. The outer layer was carved away, by hand or wheel, to leave the design standing proud on a different-coloured background.

The cameo technique was revived in Britain in the 19th century largely owing to the influence of the Portland Vase. This magnificent, translucent blue-black amphora-type vase, with opaque-white relief decoration, was thought to be of Roman origin, made between the 1st century BC and the 1st century AD. It was brought to London by Sir William Hamilton, Ambassador to the Court of Naples and a keen collector. He, in turn, sold the vase to the Dowager Duchess of Portland (hence its name) before 1785. In 1810, the 4th Duke of Portland lent the vase to the British Museum,

English cameo glass usually retained the formal shapes and white design on a coloured background of early Roman glass. This vase by George Woodall, made c.1890 uses a characteristically late-19th century interpretation of a classical motif. [C]

where it remains to this day. When it was first shown, it created a sensation and started a fashion for cameo glass in classical shapes and with classical decorations. Initially, British glassmakers led the way in developing the technique. The firm of John Northwood in Stourbridge, J. & J. Northwood, became a leading producer of fine acid-etched glass. It seems very probable that a combination of acid-etching and hand-carving was used in the course of Northwood's 20 years of meticulous experiments that eventually resulted, in 1876, in his exact copy of the Portland Vase.

Stourbridge in Worcestershire became the centre of English cameo glass. George and Thomas Woodall, the leading names in the next generation of British cameo glassmakers, were apprenticed to John Northwood, and neighbouring glassworks, such as Thomas Webb & Sons and W. H., B. & J. Richardson, also produced fine

Made c.1900 in the studios of the American firm of Tiffany, this superb cameo bowl was probably a special order. It may well have been a collaboration between Tiffany's jewellery and glassmaking craftsmen as the finely carved, applied green and pink glass poppy decoration is echoed in the silver mount. [C]

pieces, in the then fashionable Neo-classical shapes, usually in two colours with opaque-white decoration. The Stourbridge glassmaker Joseph Locke also made a copy of the Portland Vase that was exhibited at the Paris Exhibition of 1878. About four years later, he emigrated to the USA, where he introduced the technique to American glassmakers.

In Bohemia, glassmakers readily adopted the cameo technique, which was very similar to that used in the heavily cut cased glass in which they had led the field. They produced a whole range of glass, from hand-carved exhibition pieces to acid-cut 'commercial' or *faux* (fake) cameo, with typical Bohemian designs such as hunting scenes.

Producing cameo glass was labour-intensive, and in order to reduce costs, speed up production and meet increased

George Woodall carving a cameo vase

George Woodall

George Woodall (1850–1925) was one of the most celebrated British artists working in the cameo technique. After an apprenticeship with John Northwood, he and his brother Thomas were employed by the Stourbridge factory of Thomas Webb & Sons. There they produced some of the finest 19th-century British cameo glass. Pieces made by George Woodall usually have a coloured background with white relief decoration of intricately handcarved designs. These were often inspired by classical or oriental motifs, many with a slightly erotic content. Wares such as plaques and vases made by the brothers between 1889 and 1899 are signed 'T & G Woodall'.

demand, the top layer (or layers) of glass were made thinner and cut away with a wheel rather than by hand. Sometimes a combination of the two techniques was used. From the mid-19th century, acid was increasingly used to etch away the surface, either in combination with wheel and hand-carving, or on its own.

In the hands of the late 19th-century French glassmakers, *faux* cameo was elevated to a true art form, produced by leading factories such as Baccarat and, more notably, Daum Frères at Nancy and the supreme cameo artist, Emile Gallé. His Art Nouveau cameo-glass pieces, which have as many as five different layers of coloured glass and often combine acid-etching, engraving and hand-carving, represent the most superb examples of the technique.

This English cameo vase (left), made c.1910 and attributed to George Woodall, is an interesting combination of acid-etching and hand-carving. It uses subtle gradations of colour and texture to recreate the Antarctic landscape, giving a three-dimensional quality. [B]

French cameo glassmakers were adventurous with colour and technique. On this vase by Emile Gallé, c.1895, a frosted amber ground is overlaid in burgundy and then mould-blown to create a relief decoration of plums, which has been further etched to provide texture and colour. [D]

A CLOSER LOOK *Cameo Glass*

This glass can be divided into two main types: hand-carved and acid cameo. The most exclusive and expensive examples are one-off cameo pieces, often made of several layers of coloured glass, with intricate hand-carved details. As the demand for cameo glass increased during the 19th century, acid (usually hydrofluoric), rather than hand- or wheel-carving, was used to eat away the layers of glass to create the design. This 'commercial' or *faux* (fake) cameo was employed to create more regular, less complicated forms, that have fewer, thinner layers of coloured glass and less intricate designs. From the late 19th century, many pieces combine techniques such as hand-carving and wheel-engraving with acid-etching. It is often difficult to distinguish one technique from another.

Cameo vase, c.1880–90
With its formal shape and naturalistic decoration in white on a coloured background, this vase, made by John Northwood, is typical of late 19th-century English cameo glass. [K]

Cameo vase, c.1900
This organic-shaped piece was made by Daum Frères, a leading maker of Art Nouveau cameo glass in Nancy, France. Tiny foil-backed pads of glass have been applied, having been first wheel cut to look like snails. [G]

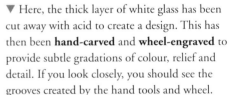

▼ **Acid** has been allowed to eat into the layers of this vase to varying degrees to create a **speckled surface** that is rough and pitted and has a very handmade feel. The shimmering effect has been achieved by using five layers of glass of different thicknesses.

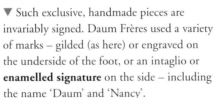

▼ Such exclusive, handmade pieces are invariably signed. Daum Frères used a variety of marks – gilded (as here) or engraved on the underside of the foot, or an intaglio or **enamelled signature** on the side – including the name 'Daum' and 'Nancy'.

▼ Here, the thick layer of white glass has been cut away with acid to create a design. This has then been **hand-carved** and **wheel-engraved** to provide subtle gradations of colour, relief and detail. If you look closely, you should see the grooves created by the hand tools and wheel.

Acid cameo wine glass, c.1890
Unlike the other pieces on these pages, this English wine glass consists of one layer of clear glass only. The flower-and-leaf decoration reflects the interest in designs taken from nature in Europe and the USA at the end of the 19th century. [S]

▶ **Acid cameo** (or cutback), is where the background is eaten away to leave a very **sharp, shiny edge** to the design. This is the exact opposite of acid-etching (*see* p.196). The design is then further engraved and the object dipped into acid to produce the detail seen here.

▶ The layers of glass are very thin in mass-produced cameo. Here **acid-etching** and **wheel-engraving** have both been used to give a soft **blurred edge** and subtle gradations of colour. Unlike the white layer on the Northwood vase opposite, the shallow layers are more difficult to detect.

▼ The **Gallé** signature appears in many different versions on cameo glass – reproductions are often marked 'Tip Gallé'. Feel the area around the signature to make sure the word 'Tip' hasn't been ground away in order to deceive the potential buyer.

Cameo vase,
c.1920
The darker colours seen on this acid-etched and wheel-engraved commercial cameo vase are typical of Gallé pieces made after World War I. [H]

Bibliography

Furniture

Agius, Pauline *British Furniture, 1880–1915* (Woodbridge, 1978)

Allwood, Rosamond *Victorian Furniture 1837–1887* (Woodbridge, 1999)

Andrews, John *Victorian and Edwardian Furniture* (Woodbridge, 1998)

Barquist, David I. *American Tables and Looking Glasses* (New Haven, Connecticut, 1992)

Beckerdite, Luke, ed. *American Furniture* (New England, 1997)

Cathers, David M. *Furniture of the American Arts and Crafts Movement* (New York, 1996)

Chinnery, Victor *Oak Furniture* (Woodbridge, 1986)

Collard, Frances *Regency Furniture* (Woodbridge, 1983)

Comstock, Helen *American Furniture* (New York, 1962)

Cooper, Jeremy *Victorian & Edwardian Furniture & Interiors* (London, 1998)

Cooper, Wendy *The Classical Taste in America 1800 to 1840* (New York, 1994)

Dell, T. *Furniture in the Frick Collection* (New York, 1992)

Edwards, Ralph *The Shorter Dictionary of English Furniture* (London, 1964)

Edwards, Ralph and Jourdain, Margaret *Georgian Cabinet-Makers* (London, 1946)

Fastnedge, Ralph *Sheraton Furniture* (London, 1962)

Fitzgerald, Oscar *Three Centuries of American Furniture* (New York, 1982)

Forman, Benno M. and Norton, W.W. *American Seating Furniture, 1630–1840* (New York, 1988)

Gilbert, Christopher *Furniture at Temple Newsam House and Lotherton Hall* (London, 1978)

Hayward, Helena, ed. *World Furniture* (London, 1990)

Hechsher, Morrison H. *American Furniture at the Metropolitan Museum of Art: Late Colonial Period, Queen Anne and Chippendale* (New York, 1985)

Jervis, Simon *Victorian Furniture* (London, 1968)

Kane, Patricia E. *300 Years of American Seating Furniture* (New Haven, 1976)

Kenny, Peter *Honoré Lannuier: Cabinetmaker from Paris* (New York, 1998)

Kjellberg, Pierre *Le Mobilier français du XVIIIe siècle* (Paris, 1989)

Musgrave, Clifford *Regency Furniture: 1800 to 1830* (London, 1970)

Symonds, R. W. and Whinneray, B.B. *Victorian Furniture* (London, 1987)

Thornton, Peter *Seventeenth Century Interior Decoration in England, France and Holland* (London, 1978)

Ward, Gerald W.R. *American Case Furniture* (New Haven, 1988)

Watson, Francis *The History of Furniture* (London, 1976)

Ceramics

Atterbury, Paul and Batkin, Maureen *Dictionary of Minton* (Woodbridge, 1990)

Battie, David, ed. *Sotheby's Concise Encyclopedia of Porcelain* (London, 1990)

Boger, Louise Ade *The Dictionary of World Pottery and Porcelain* (London, 1971)

Carswell, John *Chinese Blue and White and its Impact on the Western World* (Chicago, 1985)

Charleston, Robert, J., ed. *World Ceramics* (London, 1982)

Cushion, J.P. *Handbook of Pottery and Porcelain Marks* (London, 1996)

Dawes, Nicholas M. *Majolica* (New York, 1990)

Frelinghuysen, Alice Cooney *American Porcelain: 1770–1920* (New York, 1989)

Garner, Harry *Oriental Blue and White* (London, 1970)

Godden, Geoffrey *British Pottery: An Illustrated Guide* (London, 1974)

Godden, Geoffrey *Mason's China and Ironstone Wares* (Woodbridge, 1980)

Godden, Geoffrey *Staffordshire Porcelain* (London, 1983)

Godden, Geoffrey *Ridgway Porcelain* (Woodbridge, 1985)

Godden, Geoffrey *An Illustrated Encyclopaedia of British Pottery and Porcelain* (Leicester, 1992)

Godden, Geoffrey *New Handbook of British Pottery and Porcelain Marks* (London, 1999)

Kovel, Ralph and Terry *Kovel's New Dictionary of Marks: Pottery and Porcelain 1850 to the Present* (New York, 1986)

Langham, Marion *Belleek* (London, 1993)

Lewis, Griselda *A Collector's History of English Pottery* (Woodbridge, 1999)

Lockett, Terence and Godden, Geoffrey *Davenport: China, Earthenware, and Glass* (London, 1989)

Macintosh, Duncan *Chinese Blue and White Porcelain* (Woodbridge, 1994)

Medley, Margaret *The Chinese Potter* (Oxford, 1976)

Menzhausen, Ingelore *Early Meissen Porcelain in Dresden* (London, 1990)

Messenger, Michael *Coalport* (Woodbridge, 1996)

Pugh, P.D. *Staffordshire Portrait Figures* (London, 1990)

Reilly, Robin *Wedgwood* (London, 1989)

Roberts, Gaye Blake *Mason's: The First Two Hundred Years* (London, 1996)

Rondot, Bertrand *Discovering the Secrets of Soft-Paste Porcelain at the Saint-Cloud Manufactory* (Yale, 1999)

Sandon, Henry *Royal Worcester Porcelain* (London, 1995)

Sandon, John *Dictionary of Worcester Porcelain* (Woodbridge, 1993)

Savage, George and Newman, Harold *An Illustrated Dictionary of Ceramics* (London, 1992)

Savill, Rosalind *The Wallace Collection Catalogue of Sèvres Porcelain* (London, 1988)

Schiffer, Nancy *Japanese Porcelain, 1800–1950* (West Chester, 1986)

Vainker, S.J. *Chinese Pottery and Porcelain* (London, 1997)

Van Lemmen, Hans *Tiles: A Collector's Guide* (London, 1979)

Watney, Bernard *English Blue and White Porcelain* (London, 1973)

Watney, Bernard *Liverpool Porcelain of the Eighteenth Century* (Shepton Beauchamp, 1997)

Whiter, Leonard *Spode* (London, 1978)

Wilson, Timothy *Italian Maiolica* (Oxford, 1989)

Wojciechowski, Kathy *Nippon Porcelain*
(West Chester, 1992)
Yates-Owen, Eric and Fournier, Robert *British
Studio Potters' Marks* (London, 1999)

Silver

Blair, Claude, ed. *The History of Silver*
(London, 1987)
Brett, Vanessa *The Sotheby's Directory of
Silver* (London, 1986)
Clayton, Michael *The Collector's Dictionary of
Silver and Gold of Great Britain and North
America* (Woodbridge, 1985)
Hartop, Christopher *The Huguenot Legacy*
(London, 1996)
Langford, Joel *Silver: A Practical Guide to
Collecting Silverware and Identifying
Hallmarks* (London, 1991)
Newman, Harold *An Illustrated Dictionary of
Silverware* (London, 1987)
Pickford, I., ed. *Jackson's Silver and Gold
Marks of England, Scotland and Ireland*
(Woodbridge, 1989)
Truman, Charles, ed. *Sotheby's Concise
Encyclopedia of Silver* (London, 1993)

Glass

Battie, D. and Cottle, S., eds. *Sotheby's
Concise Encyclopedia of Glass*
(London, 1991)
Bickerton, L.M. *Eighteenth Century English
Drinking Glasses: An Illustrated Guide*
(Woodbridge, 1986)
Boggess, Bill and Louise *Identifying American
Brilliant Cut Glass* (West Chester, 1991)
Dawes, Nicholas M. *Lalique Glass*
(New York, 1986)
Grover, Ray and Lee *Carved and Decorated
European Art Glass* (Rutland, 1970)
Koch, Robert Louis C. *Tiffany's
Glass-Bronzes-Lamps* (New York, 1971)
Revi, Albert Christian *American Art Nouveau
Glass* (Camden, NJ, 1968)
Tait, Hugh, ed. *Five Thousand Years of Glass*
(London, 1991)

Value Codes

Beside every antique featured is a value code, which gives the approximate value of the item. These are broad price ranges and should only be seen as a guide, as prices for antiques vary depending on the condition of the piece, where it is sold and market trends.

The codes are as follows:

[A]	Over £30,000	[H]	£2,000–3,000	[O]	£250–350
[B]	£20,000–30,000	[I]	£1,500–2,000	[P]	£200–250
[C]	£10,000–20,000	[J]	£1,000–1,500	[Q]	£150–200
[D]	£7,500–10,000	[K]	£750–1,000	[R]	£75–150
[E]	£5,000–7,500	[L]	£550–750	[S]	Under £75
[F]	£4,000–5,000	[M]	£450–550		
[G]	£3,000–4,000	[N]	£350–450		

General

*Bulfinch Illustrated Encyclopedia
of Antiques, The* (London, 1994)
Cathers, Beth and Volpe, Tod *Treasures of
the American Arts and Crafts Movement:
1890–1920* (New York, 1987)
Duncan, Alastair *American Art Deco*
(London and New York, 1986)
Duncan, Alastair *Art Deco* (London, 1988)
Fleming, John and Honour, Hugh *The Penguin
Dictionary of Decorative Arts*
(London, 1989)
Fusco, Tony *Art Deco Identification and Price
Guide* (New York, 1993)
Klein, Dan, McClelland, Nancy A., and Haslam,
Malcolm *In the Deco Style* (London, 1991)
Montgomery, Charles F. and Kane, Patricia E.,
eds. *American Art: 1750–1800 Towards
Independence* (Boston, 1976)
Turner, Jane, ed. *Dictionary of Art*
(London, 1996)
Wright, Michael, ed. *Reader's Digest
Treasures In Your Home* (London, 1993)

A–Z of People & Places

All the most important designers and crafts-people are listed here for handy reference, as well as the major manufacturers and centres of production. Major marks are also included as well as the dates when they were in use.

A

Adam, Robert (1728–92) Scottish architect and designer of interiors, textiles, furniture and silver. He developed the light and elegant interpretation of the Neo-classical style that bears his name and was enormously influential both in Britain and Europe in the late 18th century.

Ashbee, Charles Robert (1863–1942) English architect and designer. In 1888, he founded the Guild of Handicraft in London, an Arts & Crafts group to which he contributed his successful designs for silver, often incorporating enamel and semi-precious stones.

B

Bacchus, George & Sons (1840–) English glasshouse based in Birmingham, West Midlands. One of the first companies to use transfer printing, it is now known for its opaque white glass with transfer-printed enamel decoration.

Barlow family English family of ceramic decorators. Hannah (1851–1916) and her sister Florence (d.1909) were employed by the nearby DOULTON art pottery while students at the Lambeth School of Art, London. They decorated a range of buff or grey stoneware, often using muted colours and incised decoration.

Bateman, Hester (d.1794) English gold- and silversmith who, although virtually illiterate, ran a flourishing family business in London from 1760–90, producing elegant silverware.

Beilby family English of glass decorators, based in Newcastle-upon-Tyne, Northumberland. William (1740–1819) and his sister Mary (1749–97) established the family's reputation as the leading 18th-century enamellers of English wine glasses, goblets and decanters, usually in white and bluish white enamel, more rarely in bright colours.

Belleek Porcelain Factory (1857–) Irish ceramics factory in Co. Fermanagh, N. Ireland, which produced stoneware and earthenware but is best known for its decorative porcelain vases, sweetmeat dishes and openwork baskets, often decorated with applied flowers.

1891–

Belter, John Henry (1804–63) American furniture designer and manufacturer. Belter is known for his extravagant Rococo Revival chairs and sofas. Their extraordinary shapes and wealth of elaborate carved and pierced decoration were made possible by his patented technique for bending and laminating rosewood.

Bérain, Jean (1640–1711) French designer. One of the most important and influential designers, his major contribution was a type of decoration known as grotesque, where symmetrical arrangements of animals, swags, scrolls and other Baroque motifs were given a fantastical treatment and applied to silver, ceramics, textiles and interior decoration.

Berlin Porcelain Factory (1751–7; 2nd factory 1761–) German factory bought by Frederick the Great in 1763 and taken over by the State in 1918. The finest pieces included those in the Neo-classical style where the porcelain became a canvas for superb hand-painted decoration, and Rococo pieces with relief trelliswork and pierced decoration.

KPM

1832–

Bing, Samuel (1838–1905) German art dealer and gallery owner. In Paris, he opened a gallery in 1885 called *La Maison de l'Art Nouveau*, from which the Art Nouveau style probably took its name. The gallery became a showcase for work by TIFFANY, GALLE and LALIQUE.

Boch, Jean-François (1735–1817) German ceramics manufacturer. He inherited two family ceramics factories, where he introduced transfer printing. He established a Belgian ceramics factory, Boch Frères, in 1767, which is now best known for its Art Deco ceramics. In 1809, he founded a factory at METTLACH, which later became Villeroy & Boch.

Böhm, August (1812–90) Bohemian glass engraver, one of the most outstanding of the Biedermeier period (c.1820–40) and known for his figurative decoration.

Boston & Sandwich Glass Co. (1826–88) American glasshouse established on Cape Cod, Massachusetts, famous for its inexpensive pressed domestic glass, especially the popular 'Lacy' glass.

Böttger, Johann Friedrich (1682–1719) German inventor of European hard-paste porcelain. Böttger's experiments resulted first in a red stoneware (c.1708) and then hard-paste porcelain (1710), both of which carry his name.

Boucher, François (1703–70) French painter. One of the leading artists of the Rococo period, Boucher's paintings of idyllic pastoral scenes inspired the painted landscape decoration used on porcelain produced at factories such as SEVRES, FRANKENTHAL and CHELSEA.

Boulle, André-Charles (1642–1732) French cabinet-maker and designer. While employed as chief cabinet-maker at the court of Louis XIV, he made monumental commodes and armoires and developed a type of elaborate marquetry combining brass and tortoiseshell that is now known as 'Boulle'or 'Buhl' work.

Bow (1744–76) English porcelain factory. It produced soft-paste porcelain figures, with plain mound bases in the 1750s and Rococo bases in the 1760s, Chinese-inspired blue-and-white wares and *blanc-de-Chine* white porcelain.

c.1762–76

Bristol City and port in the west of England famous for glass and delftware. Bristol delftware, usually decorated with oriental-inspired designs, was produced from c.1650 to the last quarter of the 18th century by five factories in Bristol and others from the surrounding area. Numerous 17th- and 18th-century factories produced a range of bottles and window glass, opaque white glass and coloured 'Bristol' glass.

Brocard, Philippe-Joseph (d.1896) French glassmaker. Inspired by 13th- and 14th-century mosque lamps, he is best known for his elaborately enamelled and gilded Islamic-style glasswares made throughout the 1860s for which he won first prize at the 1878 Paris Exhibition.

Brussa workshop (c.1750–1800) Italian glass workshop in Murano, Venice, where Osvaldo Brussa and his son Angelo revived the Venetian art of glass enamelling.

Bustelli, Franz Anton (1723–63) Porcelain modeller, born in Locarno, Switzerland. He worked at NYMPHENBURG between 1754 and 1763 where he created a series of outstanding Rococo porcelain figures, notably 16 figures from the Italian *commedia dell'arte*.

C

Cafe English family of silversmiths. The reputation of John Cafe (active 1740–57) and his brother William (d.1802) is based on the candlesticks, snuffer trays and candlestick accessories in which they specialized at their London workshops.

Cantagalli (1878–) Pottery factory established in Florence by Ulysse Cantagalli (1839–1901), famous for its copies of early maiolica.

Capodimonte Porcelain Factory (1743–59) Italian ceramics factory near Naples. It produced soft-paste porcelain with stippled designs and a range of figures modelled by Guiseppe GRICCI.

Carder, Frederick (1863–1963) English glassmaker and designer who emigrated to the USA where he co-founded the STEUBEN glassworks and produced innovatory glass in fashionable contemporary styles.

Chantilly Porcelain Factory (c.1725–1800) French factory established when Louis-Henri de Bourbon was exiled to his estate at Chantilly. Early soft-paste wares had a distinctive milky white tin glaze and copied East Asian porcelain, such as KAKIEMON, and even MEISSEN interpretations of Japanese porcelain. From c.1755 the factory produced *blanc-de-Chine* wares decorated with applied sprigs of flowers.

Chelsea Porcelain Factory (1744–84) English soft-paste porcelain factory established in Chelsea, London, by Nicholas SPRIMONT. Its production is generally divided into five periods based on the five different marks used by the factory; the early 'Triangle' period (c.1744–49), the Raised Anchor period (c.1749–52), the Red Anchor period (c.1752–56), and the Gold Anchor period (c.1756–69). In 1770 the factory was sold to William Duesbury, owner of DERBY, and a 'Chelsea-Derby' mark was used.

Chippendale, Thomas (1718–79) English cabinet-maker. One of the leading names in British furniture-making. His enormous influence is largely due to the designs published in *The Gentleman and Cabinet-Maker's Director*, first published in 1754, which illustrated a range of 'household furniture in the Gothic, Chinese and modern taste' and inspired Chippendale-style furniture throughout Britain and the USA. His son Thomas Chippendale (1749–1822) took over the family firm c.1777.

Cliff, Clarice (1899–1972) English ceramic designer and decorator. Her name is synonymous with English Art Deco ceramics on which she made an indelible mark with her 'Bizarre' and 'Fantasque' earthenwares, hand-painted with dramatic, bright colours and geometric decoration.

Coalport Porcelain Factory (c.1780–1926) English ceramics factory based at Coalport, Shropshire, from 1796. Its hard-paste porcelain mostly imitated Chinese and French pieces, but most typical are the elaborate Rococo-style pieces, covered with applied floral decoration that were known as 'Coalbrookdale' or 'English Meissen'.

c.1810–25

Cole, Henry (1808–82) English civil servant and designer. He played an important role in British design, organizing a series of exhibitions, which included the Great Exhibition of 1851 in London; overseeing newly formed schools of design and setting up a museum that became the Victoria & Albert Museum in South Kensington, London.

Cologne German city on the River Rhine and a centre for the production of silver in the 16th century. From the Middle Ages, it was also an important centre for the production of stoneware and in the late 18th century three faience factories made tea and dinner services and other everyday wares.

Cooper, Susie (1902–95) English ceramic designer and decorator. From the early 1930s, she had her own Crown Works production unit at Wood & Sons, Burslem, Staffordshire. There she designed several ranges of attractive domestic earthenware, with stylized, understated floral decoration, often applied by the transfer-printing technique that she perfected.

Corning Glass Works (1851–) American glass works established in Cambridge, Massachusetts, then relocated in 1868 to Corning, New York. Initially known for providing high-quality 'blanks', in 1918 it took over the STEUBEN Glassworks, and under the art director Frederick CARDER produced a range of technically innovative glass.

Cressent, Charles (1685–1768) French cabinet-maker and sculptor. He was the leading furniture-maker during the Régence and the reign of Louis XV, for whom he made commodes with superb veneering. He is best known for the extravagant Rococo ormolu mounts that became his trademark, which he cast and gilded himself.

D

Daum Frères (1875–) French glassworks in Nancy, acquired and run as a family firm by Jean Daum (1825–85). His sons Jean-Louis Auguste (1853–1909) and Jean-Antonin (1864–1930) were responsible for establishing the factory as a leading producer of high-quality Art Nouveau glass, particularly cameo glass vases and lamps. All Daum pieces are signed, but the signature has changed over the years.

1875–

Davenport Factory (1794–1887) English pottery and porcelain factory in Staffordshire. It first produced hard-paste porcelain c.1810 and became a highly prolific factory specializing in tea and dinner services, with coloured backgrounds and hand-painted decoration similar to pieces produced by ROCKINGHAM and RIDGWAY.

Davidson, George & Co. (1867–) English glassworks established in Gateshead, Northumberland. The company pioneered

several notable lines of glass, including 'Cloud', launched in 1922, which used swirling colours to create a distinctive effect.

c.1880–90

Delft Town in the Netherlands famous from the mid-17th century as a centre of production of tin-glazed earthenware. Some 30 workshops were set up in former breweries and enjoyed a golden age from c.1640–1740, producing wares inspired by imported oriental porcelain.

Derby Factory (1750–1848) English soft-paste porcelain factory. Although some pieces of Derby were made from c.1748, production took off under the directorship of William Duesbury, under whom the factory became one of the leading manufacturers of figures. It has been known as the Royal Crown Derby Porcelain Co. Ltd from 1890.

Dixon, James & Sons (1835–) English firm of silversmiths, one of the largest in SHEFFIELD, Yorkshire. It is known for domestic silverware, especially the claret jugs with minimal decoration designed by Christopher DRESSER.

Doccia Porcelain Factory (1737–1896) Italian factory established by Marchese Carlo Ginori (1702–57). Bronzes from his collection were copied as large groups and figures in hard-paste porcelain by the factory's modellers. Doccia decorative wares and tablewares can be recognized by their distinctive decoration, such as oriental-style iron-red peonies and red and gold cockerels.

19th century

Doulton & Co. (1815–) English ceramics factory based initially in Lambeth, London. Money made from the highly profitable manufacture of sanitary and laboratory fittings in the 1840s funded an art pottery in the 1860s, which specialized in the production of Arts & Crafts-inspired salt-glazed stoneware with blue decoration. In 1877, the firm set up a factory in Burslem, Staffordshire, which produced bone-china tablewares and, in the 1920s and 1930s, a successful range of Art Deco female figures.

c.1902–36

Dresden German city, capital of Saxony, and centre of ceramics production. The porcelain factory of MEISSEN was established nearby in 1710. Some 40 porcelain workshops were in operation in and around the city from the mid-19th century.

Dresser, Christopher (1834–1904) Scottish designer of glass, ceramics and metalwork. One of the most versatile designers of the late 19th century, he worked for James DIXON, among others. After a visit to Japan, his designs took on a strong Japanese influence, resulting in simple, elegant but innovative shapes that anticipate the minimalism of the Modern Movement.

E

Eberlein, Johann Friedrich (1693–1749) German modeller and sculptor, employed at MEISSEN from 1735, where he collaborated closely with Johann Joachim KÄNDLER on a range of figures and tablewares.

Egermann, Friedrich (1777–1864) Bohemian glassmaker and factory owner, best known for his invention of Lithyalin glass and the technique of colouring glass by staining.

Elers, David (1656–1742) and **John Philip** (1664–1738) English potters. Their major contributions include the introduction of sprigged red stoneware to Staffordshire and plaster of Paris moulds for casting slipware.

F

Fabergé, Peter Carl (1846–1920) Russian goldsmith and jeweller whose workshops in St Petersburg supplied the Imperial court with fabulous jewellery, silver and decorative objects, including the famous Imperial Easter eggs.

Feilner, Simon (1726–98) German master modeller at FURSTENBERG and HOCHST, where he created a range of realistic porcelain figures of miners (both painted and unpainted), and a range of *commedia dell'arte* characters.

Frankenthal Porcelain Factory (1755–99) German factory near Mannheim. Its hard-paste porcelain figures, recognized by their slightly stiff modelling and doll-like faces, were second only to MEISSEN figures, and the factory is also known for outstanding hand-painted tea and dinner services.

1762–93

Frye, Thomas (1710–62) English painter whose long-term collaboration with the potter Edward Heylyn (1695–c.1758) eventually resulted, c.1744, in a patent for a porcelain used at BOW.

Fulham Pottery (est. 1672) English pottery workshop in London where some of the earliest English stoneware was made in the mid-17th century. The stoneware jugs, mugs and tankards with applied relief decoration and two-tone brown glaze were made throughout the 18th and 19th centuries. In the Fulham workshop, John Dwight (d.1703) was one of the first to produce salt-glazed stoneware.

Fürstenberg Factory (1747–) German ceramics factory established by the Duke of Brunswick. Hard-paste porcelain was made from 1753 and used for tablewares with distinctive decoration of birds and landscapes, and superb statuettes modelled by Simon FEILNER, including *commedia dell'arte* figures.

c.1800–

G

Gallé, Emile (1846–1904) French designer of glass, ceramics and furniture. One of the founder members of the Nancy school of Art Nouveau, in 1867 Gallé established his glasshouse in Nancy, where he produced some of the very finest Art Nouveau art glass, especially cameo vases and lamp bases, often in organic shapes and decorated with motifs drawn from nature.

1870s

Gillows of Lancaster (1730–) English furniture company, established in Lancaster by Robert Gillow and later directed by his sons. One of the best-known English furniture manufacturers, the company's reputation was based on its high-quality household furniture. In 1900, the company amalgamated with Waring and became known as Waring & Gillow.

Godwin, Edward William (1833–86) English architect and furniture designer best known for his elegant, ebonized Aesthetic furniture.

Goldscheider (1885–1954) Austrian ceramic manufacturing company based in Vienna and famous for its fine Art Deco figures and brightly coloured earthenware wall masks.

Gorham & Co. (1831–) American silver manufacturer established in Providence, Rhode Island, by Jabez Gorham. One of the leading companies in the late 19th century, it is best known for novelty pieces and Art Nouveau silver decorated with flowers and fruit.

Martelé
950-1000 FINE
1898–1905

Greenwood, Frans (1680–1762) Dutch amateur glass engraver who signed and dated many of his pieces, which were the first to be decorated exclusively with stipple engraving. Designs included fruit, flowers and contemporary prints.

Gricci, Giuseppe (1700–1770) Italian sculptor and chief modeller between 1743 and 1759 at the factory of CAPODIMONTE, outside Naples. He designed a fine range of distinctive figures, with unusually small heads painted with muted pastel decoration.

Griffen, Smith & Hill (1867–1902) American ceramics manufacturer. Established in Phoenixville, Pennsylvania, the factory was famous for its fine-quality majolica wares, which were called 'Etruscan'.

H

Hamada, Shoji (1894–1978) Japanese potter. One of the major potters of the 20th century, Hamada was largely responsible for the cross-cultural influence between Japanese and English ceramics through his friendship with Bernard LEACH, with whom he worked at St Ives, Cornwall, on a range of stoneware pots that reflected the Japanese folk craft tradition.

Hawkes, T. G. & Sons (1880–1962) American glassworks established at Corning, New York, by an immigrant Irish glassworker, Thomas G. Hawkes (1846–1913). The factory is best known for its high quality cut-and-engraved 'Brilliant' crystal tablewares.

1895–c.1960

Heintz American factory, known for its Arts & Crafts ceramics.

Hepplewhite, George (d.1786) English cabinet-maker and furniture designer. Hepplewhite's posthumous *Cabinet-Maker and Upholsterer's Guide* (first published 1788) was the first major pattern-book to follow the *Director* by Thomas CHIPPENDALE. Its Neo-classical designs, including the distinctive shield-back chair, had a far-reaching influence in the USA and Europe.

Hicks & Meigh (1806–22) English ceramics factory established at Shelton, Staffordshire, that produced fine earthenware and stone china dinner services in a similar style to MASON'S ironstone.

Hirado Porcelain Factory (est. c.1760) Japanese factory near Arita known for its small, refined white and blue-and-white hard-paste porcelain.

Hoare & Co., J. (1853–1920) American glassworks established in New York by an immigrant Irish glassworker, John Hoare (1822–96), and famous for its 'Brilliant' style cut glass.

1895–1920

Höchst Porcelain Factory (1746–96) German ceramics factory. It first made faience, but is best known for hard-paste porcelain made from 1750 in a range of figures by leading modellers such as Simon FEILNER and Johann Peter MELCHIOR, and tablewares decorated with landscapes.

1762–96

Hope, Thomas (1769–1831) English furniture designer. Hope, together with George Smith, was largely responsible for the English version of Neo-classicism that became popular in the early 19th century. Rams' heads, lions' heads and hairy cloven feet are just some of the revived classical motifs typically associated with his designs published in his *Household Furniture and Interior Decoration* (1807).

Höroldt, Johann Gregorius (d.1775) German chemist and painter. From 1720, he was technical director at MEISSEN, where he expanded both the range of wares and enamel colours. He is also known for his chinoiserie designs and scenes of landscapes and harbours.

I

Imberton, I. J. (active mid-19th century) French glassmaker. A contemporary of Philippe-Joseph BROCARD, he produced Islamic-style glassware with superb enamelled decoration.

J

Jensen, Georg (1866–1935) Danish silversmith. One of the most influential 20th-century designers, he produced a wide range of silverware and jewellery, but is perhaps best known for his distinctive restrained cutlery with a timeless appeal. Many of his designs are still produced today.

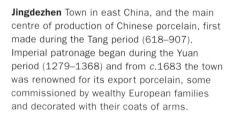

1933–44

Jingdezhen Town in east China, and the main centre of production of Chinese porcelain, first made during the Tang period (618–907). Imperial patronage began during the Yuan period (1279–1368) and from c.1683 the town was renowned for its export porcelain, some commissioned by wealthy European families and decorated with their coats of arms.

Jones, George & Sons (1862–1951) Staffordshire pottery specializing in the production of majolica. Established in Stoke-on-Trent, it concentrated on making useful wares rather than ornamental pieces. These included ashtrays, oyster plates, sardine boxes and tureens.

1862–1951

K

Kakiemon, Sakaida (1596–1666) Japanese porcelain decorator and member of a dynasty of potters after whom 'Kakiemon' ware is named. The best known hard-paste porcelain wares are of hexagonal or octagonal shapes, decorated with asymmetrical designs in iron red, blue-green, light blue and yellow. They were widely copied by European factories.

Kändler, Charles (active 1727–73) English silversmith of German birth. After a partnership with James Murray, he was later joined by Charles Frederick Kändler, a nephew or cousin. He is known for elaborately decorated Rococo silver, including a magnificent wine cooler.

Kändler, Johann Joachim (1706–75) German porcelain modeller. From 1733, he was chief modeller at MEISSEN, where he made a remarkable range of brightly coloured animals and birds as well as an outstanding series of humorous *commedia dell'arte* figures.

Kent, William (1685–1748) English architect and designer. His flamboyant giltwood furniture and silver designs, incorporating seahorses, dolphins and, in particular, eagles, set a new fashion in England and resulted in many aristocratic commissions.

Kinkozan Japanese family of potters, based in Kyoto. From the late 19th century they produced earthenware vases, bowls and jars decorated with scenes of everyday life, birds and flowers.

Kirk & Sons (1815–) American silver firm. Established in Baltimore, Maryland, by Samuel Kirk, it produced quality silver that reflected contemporary styles. The company enjoyed a reputation for fine craftsmanship that gained it commissions from the White House.

Kok, Juriaan (1861–1919) Dutch potter. He worked at ROZENBURG, where he developed a new type of eggshell-thin, slipcast porcelain with hand-painted decoration that contributed to the factory's distinguished Art Nouveau ceramics production.

Kothgasser, Anton (1769–1851) Austrian ceramics and glass decorator. He was a painter at the Royal Porcelain Factory in VIENNA when Gottlob Samuel MOHN introduced him to the thin, transparent enamels he subsequently used to decorate glass beakers with romantic, watercolour-like landscapes and cityscapes.

Kunckel, Johann (1630–1703) German chemist and glassmaker. While director of the Potsdam Glass Factory, he invented a new type of ruby-coloured glass – *Goldrubinglas* – by adding gold.

L

Lalique, René (1860–1945) French designer of glass and jewellery. His stunning Art Nouveau jewellery often combined silver, enamelling and semi-precious stones. In 1921, he acquired a glassworks in Alsace where he made a huge range of glass, usually clear with a frosted surface, that established him as the foremost producer of Art Deco glass.

Lannuier, Charles-Honoré (1779–1819) French cabinet-maker. In 1803, Lannuier emigrated to New York, where he became a leading furniture-maker, introducing elements of the French Empire style – classical decorative motifs and the use of gilt-bronze mounts – into American furniture. His furniture is referred to as American 'Classical'.

Leach, Bernard (1887–1979) English studio potter. One of the most influential potters of the 20th century, he combined the ideas of the English Arts & Crafts Movement with the Japanese craftsman-potter tradition that he gained via his friendship with Shoji HAMADA. His handmade pots produced in St Ives, Cornwall, revived traditional English medieval shapes.

Leeds English town in West Yorkshire famous for its production of creamware, produced from c.1760. Typical wares include baskets with twisted handles and pierced decoration. Items were often left unpainted but sometimes used transfer-printed designs.

Lehmann, Caspar (d.c.1622) German gem-engraver. While employed at the Prague court of the Holy Roman Emperor Rudolph II, he adapted the technique of wheel-engraving on semi-precious stones for use on glass, which transformed the range of decoration available to Bohemian glass engravers.

Lenci (1919–) Italian ceramics factory in Turin, known for its range of Art Deco female figures with matt and glossy glazes.

Liberty & Co. (1875–) English retail store, established in Regent Street, London, by Arthur Lasenby Liberty. The shop acted as a vanguard for the newly fashionable Arts & Crafts, Art Nouveau and Aesthetic styles, and commissioned and sold jewellery, furniture, textiles and silver from many distinguished designers.

Limoges City in central France, famous for hard-paste porcelain production. It was home to many distinguished factories from c.1771 because of the brilliant white porcelain made from local china clay deposits. In the late 19th century, following the development of the railway system, it was the most important centre of French porcelain production.

1797–

Linke, François (1855–1945) French cabinet-maker, famous for his fantastic cabinets and armoires in the Louis XVI Revival style.

Liverpool English city and port on the north west coast famous for ceramic production in the 18th and 19th centuries. At this time, its factories produced all types of ceramics from delftware to porcelain for both the home and export markets. The last ceramics factory closed in 1840.

Lobmeyr, J. & L. (1823–) Viennese glasshouse. Founded in 1823 by Josef Lobmeyr (1792–1855) and registered as J. & L. Lobmeyr in 1860 by his sons Josef and Ludwig. It became famous for cut and engraved glass and prize-winning enamelled 'Islamic' glassware.

Locke, Joseph (1846–1936) Versatile and innovative English glassmaker who emigrated to the USA where he worked for several leading glass companies, including NEW ENGLAND GLASS CO., for which he developed a range of highly successful shaded coloured glass.

Longton Hall Porcelain Factory (c.1750–60) English soft-paste porcelain factory founded in Staffordshire by William Littler. The factory made figures and tableware, but is probably best known for its blue-and-white wares with a streaky, but rich, underglaze blue known as 'Littler's blue'.

Lowestoft Porcelain Factory (1757–1802) English factory in Suffolk famous for its blue-and-white soft-paste porcelain tablewares with naive decoration, and inscribed souvenirs.

Ludwigsburg Porcelain Factory (c.1759–1824) German factory established by the Duke of Württemburg, now best known for a range of hard-paste figures – a particular passion of the Duke's – with rather stiff modelling and precisely painted decoration.

1759–1824

Lund's Bristol (c.1749–52) English porcelain factory in Bristol established by Benjamin Lund. Its porcelain recipe included soapstone, which made the factory's blue-and-white wares more durable. The factory and the formula were bought by WORCESTER in 1752.

M

Mason's (1796–) English ceramics factory. In 1813, in Fenton, Staffordshire, the firm of Charles James Mason (1791–1856), son of Miles Mason, took out a patent for ironstone. A range of wares was made in ironstone, including pot-pourris, huge vases and dinner services. Wares were decorated in imitation of Japanese Imari porcelain in red, gold and blue. The factory also made blue-and-white transfer-printed pieces.

Medici Porcelain Factory (1575–87) Italian porcelain factory in the Bomboli Gardens, Florence, founded by Francesco I de' Medici. It was the first factory in Europe to produce soft-paste porcelain. Very few pieces – all with blue decoration – are known to exist.

Meeks, Joseph, & Sons (1797–1868) American furniture manufacturer based in New York and famous for fine-quality Rococo Revival furniture in the 1850s and 1860s.

Meissen (1710–) German porcelain factory established in the Albrechtsburg Palace in Meissen. The earliest and one of the most famous factories in Europe, it is probably best known for an outstanding range of 18th-century hard-paste figures by leading modellers such as J. J. KÄNDLER, and tablewares and services with superb hand-painted decoration that were widely copied by many other European factories.

Melchior, Johann Peter (1742–1825) German ceramics modeller. One of the leading figure modellers of his day, Melchior worked at HOCHST, FRANKENTHAL and NYMPHENBURG, producing figures, often of children, in biscuit porcelain.

Mennecy Porcelain Factory (1734–1806) French factory established in Paris by François Barbin, which relocated to Mennecy in 1749. The factory produced soft-paste figures, typically with rockwork bases, and tablewares decorated with flowers, often in red and puce.

Mettlach Factory (1809–) German ceramics factory established near Saar by Jean-François BOCH and best known for its stoneware tankards and dishes decorated with historical themes.

Minton & Co. (1793–) English ceramics factory in Stoke-on-Trent, Staffordshire, from 1968 part of DOULTON. The factory enjoyed a golden age in the 19th century when, during the 1820s and 1830s, it was one of the most important English porcelain factories, producing finely decorated and gilded table wares, which won prizes at the international exhibitions, and enjoying the patronage of Queen Victoria. From 1849, it was equally well known for its majolica tablewares, figures and, in particular, tiles. In the 20th century, it readily adopted the fashionable Art Nouveau and Art Deco styles.

Mohn family German glass decorators. Samuel Mohn (1762–1815) was the first to use thin, transparent enamels to transform glass beakers into expensive tourist souvenirs decorated with topographical scenes. His son, Gottlob Samuel Mohn (1789–1825), used the technique in VIENNA, where he introduced it to Anton KOTHGASSER.

Morris, William (1834–96) English painter, writer and designer of furniture, textiles and ceramics. One of the major influences on design in the late 19th century, Morris's belief in the value of the tradition of the medieval craftsman who conceived and created his own work from start to finish, using local materials and traditional designs and decoration, inspired the Arts & Crafts Movement.

Moser, Ludwig (1833–1916) Bohemian glass engraver. In 1857, he established a glass factory in Karlsbad (now Karlovy Vary, Czech Republic) that produced fine enamelled, cased and Art Nouveau glass.

1880s–

N

Nabeshima Type of Japanese hard-paste porcelain, mainly plates and bowls, produced at the kilns of the same name from 1650s–c.1870. Such wares were typically decorated with multicoloured designs, often based on textiles.

Nantgarw Porcelain Factory (1813–20) Welsh ceramics factory established by the ceramics painter William Billingsley (1758–1928) near Cardiff. The factory is known for its soft-paste porcelain plates with ornate hand-painted decoration on richly coloured backgrounds.

New England Glass Co. (1818–90) American glass factory founded in East Cambridge, Massachusetts, which developed the first glass-pressing machine and is known for a range of coloured glass developed by Joseph LOCKE.

Nigg, Josef (active 1800–43) Austrian porcelain decorator. He worked at the VIENNA factory and is best known for his superbly detailed paintings of flowers and botanical subjects.

Noritake (est. 1904) Japanese ceramics factory established in Nagoya by Icizaemon Morimura

and now renowned for its hard-paste porcelain export tablewares, in particular those by such leading designers as Frank Lloyd WRIGHT.

Northwood English family of glassmakers. After apprenticeships with several well-known STOURBRIDGE glasshouses, John Northwood (1836–1902) and his brother Joseph founded J. & J. Northwood Glassworks in 1860. John was responsible for many technical innovations but is probably best remembered for his copy of the cameo Portland Vase, which took him over 20 years to complete.

Nuremberg German city in Bavaria. In the 15th and 16th centuries, it was one of the greatest artistic centres in Europe, famous for silver. By 1514, there were 129 gold- and silversmiths producing outstanding pieces for local patrons.

Nymphenburg Porcelain Factory (est. 1747) German hard-paste porcelain factory established in Neudeck and relocated c.1761 to the Nymphenburg Palace, Munich. It produced tablewares, but is best known for its figures, particularly those by Franz Anton BUSTELLI.

19th century

O

Osler, F. & C. (1807–c.1940) English glasshouse established in Birmingham. A leading Victorian company, it was best known for magnificent cut glass, including candelabra and chandeliers and an elaborate glass fountain for the Great Exhibition of 1851 in London.

Ott & Brewer Porcelain Factory (1863–93) American ceramics factory in Trenton, New Jersey, best known for its 'American Belleek' – a type of gilded and painted ivory biscuit porcelain produced in the 1880s under the directorship of William Bromley from BELLEEK, and parian ware.

Owen, George (1845–1917) English potter employed at WORCESTER where he made remarkable wares that imitated pierced ivory.

P

Pairpoint & Co. (1880–1958) American company in New Bedford, Massachusetts, named after Thomas J. Pairpoint, a leading silversmith and designer, who joined the company from GORHAM & Co. and helped establish its reputation as one of the largest American manufacturers of silver-plated domestic wares.

1880–

Paris Capital city of France, by 1784, home to some 15 hard-paste porcelain factories, which enjoyed a golden age between 1797 and 1830. Among the most famous are Nast (1781–1834) and Honoré (1794–1824), with reputations that gained them commissions for dinner services for the White House, Washington, DC.

Pellatt, Apsley (1791–1863) English glassmaker and owner of the Falcon Glassworks, London, who patented a technique for making sulphides – 'cameo incrustations' – in 1819. His fascination with the technical aspects of glass production are reflected in his highly respected book *Curiosities of Glass Making* (1894).

Petit, Jacob (1796–1865) French porcelain painter and owner of factories in Belleville and Fontainebleau where he produced richly decorated hard-paste porcelain novelty items and clockcases in elaborate revival styles.

Phyfe, Duncan (1768–1854) American cabinet-maker. One of the leading New York cabinet-makers of the early and mid-19th century, his fine furniture with sabre legs, paw feet and other Neo-classical decoration was so influential that 'Phyfe' style is used to describe much American Neo-classical furniture.

Plymouth Porcelain Factory (1768–70) English factory established by William Cookworthy, where he produced the first commercial hard-paste English porcelain and made wares decorated with Chinese-influenced designs. In 1770, the factory moved to Bristol.

Potschappel (1872–) German hard-paste porcelain factory near Dresden established by Carl Thieme. It specialized in high quality and prolific imitations of MEISSEN porcelain.

Powell, James & Sons (*see* WHITEFRIARS GLASSWORKS)

Pratt family English family of potters. Founded c.1755 by William Pratt, the factory at Lane Delph, Staffordshire, was taken over by his eldest son Felix Pratt (1780–1859) in 1810. It produced earthenware teapots, jugs and figures in bright ochres, blues, greens and browns known as Prattware.

Q

Quimper French town in Brittany famous for faience, pipes and tobacco-boxes with brightly coloured naive decoration and, in the 19th and 20th centuries, souvenirs decorated with *scènes bretonnes* (Breton figures and landscapes). Important factories include that of Antoine de la Hubaudière and Fougeray, which made copies of 18th-century wares.

HB

1872–

R

Ramsden, Omar (1873–1939) Sheffield-born silversmith. He set up a London studio with Alwyn Carr and specialized in Arts & Crafts silver based on medieval, Gothic and Renaissance designs and prestigious commissions for church silver. The partnership was dissolved in 1919 and Ramsden continued alone.

Raphael (1483–1520) Italian painter, one of the greatest European artists, whose narrative paintings and designs for 'grotesque' decoration were spread by prints and had a profound effect on decorative arts throughout Europe in the 16th century. They were revived as part of the Neo-classical style of the late 18th century.

Ravenscroft, George (1632–83) English glass merchant turned glassmaker who first produced, in 1676, the lead glass for which he is now best known. From 1677, his glass was marked with a raven's head seal.

Reed & Barton (1840–) American firm established in Taunton, Massachusetts, by Henry G. Reed and Charles E. Barton. Early plated silverware was gradually replaced in the late 19th century by sterling cutlery and domestic wares such as coffee sets in 'historical' styles.

Reinicke, Peter (1715–68) German modeller at MEISSEN, where he worked from 1743 modelling figures both independently and as assistant to Johann Joachim KÄNDLER.

Richardson, W. H., B. & J. (1836–) English glasshouse at Wordsley, near Stourbridge, Worcestershire, established by three brothers – William Haden, Benjamin and Jonathan – known for its prize-winning gilded and painted opaque white glass vases, and for technical innovations such as iridescent glass and shaded glass.

Ridgway (1792–1848) Family firm of ceramic manufacturers, based in Cauldon Place, Staffordshire, where the factory produced transfer-printed wares for export to the USA and a range of teawares similar to those of SPODE, ROCKINGHAM and WORCESTER.

Riedel, Josef (active 1830–48) Bohemian glassmaker who used uranium to develop a new type of green and yellow coloured glass.

Ringler, Joseph Jakob (1730–1804) Viennese chemist who was a primary developer of hard-paste porcelain at HÖCHST, STRASBOURG, NYMPHENBURG and LUDWIGSBURG.

Rockingham Porcelain Factory (1826–42) English ceramics factory, known as Rockingham after its relocation to the Wentworth estate of the Marquess of Rockingham and best known for its hard-paste flower-encrusted Rococo Revival tea services.

Rockingham Works Brameld

c.1826–30

Rohlfs, Charles (1853–1936) American cabinet-maker and furniture designer, working in Buffalo, New York State, where he produced high-quality Arts & Crafts furniture in solid oak. Many of his pieces were decorated with the characteristic Art Nouveau 'whiplash' decoration resembling a flailing cat-o'-nine-tails.

Rookwood Pottery (1880–1960) American ceramics factory established in Cincinatti, Ohio, by Maria Longworth Nichols. It is best known for its glossy 'standard' glaze wares, in particular vases decorated with muted browns, yellows and greens with hand-painted portraits of native American Indians. A matt glaze known as 'vellum' was patented in 1904.

Rouen French town in Normandy known for its production of faience from the mid-16th century. In the 17th century, the factory of Edmé Poterat made blue-and-white wares decorated with lacy designs. It became one of the most important centres for the production of French multi-coloured faience in the 18th century.

Royal Winton (1885–) Trade name of the firm Grimwade Ltd, an English company based in Stoke-on-Trent, Staffordshire. The company produced a range of moulded earthenware and, in the 1930s, a range of popular domestic wares decorated with pretty floral transfer prints, known as 'chintzware'.

Rozenburg (1883–1916) Dutch ceramics factory established in The Hague by Wilhelm Wolff von Gudenberg and best known for its Art Nouveau hard-paste porcelain by such distinguished designers as Juriaan KOK.

Ruskin, John (1819–1900) English writer, art critic and painter. Ruskin was one of the most influential figures in the 19th-century British art world. His rejection of the mechanization, materialism and decorative excesses of the Victorian period in favour of a return to the purity and spirituality of medieval art and the medieval craftsman strongly influenced William MORRIS and underpinned the Arts & Crafts Movement.

S

Saint-Cloud (1666–1766) French soft-paste porcelian factory near Paris. Early experiments with porcelain were perfected c.1695, after which the factory specialized in pot-pourri jars and white wares with sprigged decoration.

Samson, Edmé & Cie (1845–1969) French ceramics company established by the potter Edmé Samson (1810–90) in Paris specializing in high-quality reproductions including copies of 18th-century SEVRES, CHELSEA and DERBY porcelain that have often deceived collectors.

1845–

Sandwich Glass Co. (*see* BOSTON & SANDWICH GLASS CO.)

Sang, Jacob (*d*.1783) Dutch glass engraver based in Amsterdam who specialized in decorating commemorative goblets and glasses. He worked with his brother Simon Jacob and they may have originally come from Germany.

Satsuma Important Japanese centre of ceramics production, best known for its cream-coloured export wares with enamelled and gilded decoration made from the mid-19th century.

Sèvres (1756–) French ceramics factory based in the chateau of Sèvres, near Paris. Under the patronage of Louis XV and his mistress Madame de Pompadour, the factory produced Rococo soft-paste porcelain tablewares and large decorative pieces and figures. Hard-paste porcelain introduced from 1800 resulted in larger Neo-classical wares, and more elaborate backgrounds on early 19th-century wares.

Seymour American family of cabinet-makers. In 1794, the British cabinet-maker John Seymour (*c*.1738–1818) set up in business with his son Thomas (1771–1848) in Boston, where they produced high-quality furniture in the Federal style.

Sheffield English city in West Yorkshire and major centre of production of silver from the mid-18th century, when it was home to many independent cutlers. The development of Sheffield plate in the 1750s and 1760s further enhanced the city's importance until, in the 1840s, the electroplating process was developed.

Sheraton, Thomas (*c*.1751–1806) English furniture designer. Few pieces can be attributed to him but his pattern books – *The Cabinet-Maker and Upholsterer's Drawing Book* (1791–4) and the *Cabinet Dictionary* (1803) – were enormously influential both in Europe and the USA, introducing a style, often in satinwood and with painted and inlay decoration, that was revived in the late 19th/early 20th century.

Siegburg German town, near Bonn, that gave its name to a type of off-white stoneware first made in the 15th century. The most famous Siegburg wares are the 16th-century *Schnellen* (tankards), decorated with strapwork and other types of decoration based on Renaissance prints. Siegburg tankards were much copied during the 19th century.

Spode (1776–) English ceramics factory established in Stoke-on-Trent by Josiah Spode I (1733–97). The firm is known for its fine bone-china tablewares decorated with Imari patterns as well as blue-and-white transfer-printed wares with the famous 'Willow' pattern.

Spode
Felspar porcelain
c.1815–27

Sprimont, Nicholas (1716–71) English silversmith and porcelain manufacturer. He made both Rococo silver and, in 1744, turned his hand to ceramics as manager of the CHELSEA factory.

Steuben Glassworks (1903–) American glassworks founded by Frederick CARDER and Thomas G. HAWKES in Corning, New York State. Taken over by CORNING in

1903–

1918, it remains one of leading producers of American glass, best known for its elegant, clear Art Deco style with engraved decoration.

Stevens & Williams (1846–) English glasshouse at Brierley Hill, near Stourbridge, Worcestershire, known for its cut-glass table services and Art Nouveau cameo glass. Its cut-glass 'Royal Brierley' range received a warrant from George V, and distinguished freelance designers working for the company include John NORTHWOOD.

1890s

Stickley, Gustav (1857–1942) American architect and designer. Probably the best-known designer of American Arts & Crafts furniture, Stickley set up his own company in 1898 in Eastwood, New York, where he produced the 'Craftsman' range of oak furniture using traditional 17th-century shapes and joinery techniques.

Stinton English family of porcelain decorators. John Stinton (1854–1956) and his son Harry (1883–1968) were employed at the WORCESTER factory, where they specialized in scenes of Highland cattle in Scottish landscapes.

Storr, Paul (1771–1844) English silversmith. One of the leading Regency silversmiths, Storr was a subsidiary partner in the firm of Rundell, Bridge and Rundell, London. He received several royal commissions and produced high-quality silver in both Neo-classical and Regency styles.

Stourbridge English town in the West Midlands famous as a centre of glass production. The first glass was made there in the 16th century, since it has been home to many minor and major English glassworks.

Strasbourg French town in north-east France. It was the centre for several faience factories, the best known of which was owned by the Honnong family. The factories produced table services and other pieces hand-painted with a floral design known as *fleurs de Strasbourg* that was widely copied by other centres of production.

Stuart & Sons (1881–) English family glasshouse established in Stourbridge in the West Midlands by Frederick Stuart (1817–1900). It was renowned for its Art Deco cut glass, in particular pieces by such leading designers as Ludwig Kny and Eric Ravilious.

T

Thieme, Carl (*see* POTSCHAPPEL)

Tiffany & Co. (1837–) American silver, jewellery and glass company founded by Charles Louis Tiffany (1812–1902) in New York. He opened a branch in London in 1868 and the company was inherited in 1902 by his son Louis Comfort Tiffany (1848–1933), an established

glassmaker and founder of Tiffany Studios (est. 1900). The company was the supreme manufacturer of American Art Nouveau (often referred to as the 'Tiffany' style), producing jewellery and silver, but is best known for its outstanding cameo, coloured and iridescent glass.

TIFFANY & Cº
MAKERS
STERLING-SILVER
925-1000
M
1875–91

Tournai Factory (1751–1891) Belgian ceramics factory established by François-Joseph Peterinck. The factory's everyday ceramics were decorated with multicoloured flowers in the *fleurs de Strasbourg* style; its most distinctive luxury porcelain was decorated with gold and landscapes in shades of purple.

Tucker, William Ellis (1800–32) American ceramics manufacturer. His company (1826–38) in Philadelphia, Pennsylvania, produced hard-paste porcelain that blended the fashionable French and English styles, until forced to close because of increased competition from Europe.

Turners & Co. (*c*.1762–1806) English ceramics factory established in Lane End, Staffordshire, by John Turner, whose name was given to a type of white stoneware and patented earthenware.

U

Union Porcelain Works (1863–*c*.1922) American porcelain factory founded in Brooklyn, New York, which produced hard-paste continental-style porcelain, often with decorative relief modelling. It specialized in the production of oyster plates.

V

Vauxhall China Works (*c*.1752–64) English soft-paste porcelain factory, established in London by Nicholas Crisp. It was a short-lived factory and best known for its blue-and-white tablewares based on Chinese export porcelain and delftware.

Vienna Porcelain Factory (1718–1864) Austrian factory that first produced hard-paste porcelain *c*.1719. It made figures and table-wares in the Rococo style, but enjoyed a golden age from 1784– *c*.1830 thanks to its Neo-classical pieces with superb decoration and gilding.

1749–80

Vienna Workshops (1903–32) Workshops in Vienna, modelled on C. R. ASHBEE's Guild of Handicraft, that produced metalwork, ceramics, furniture and glass designed by such distinguished craftsmen as Josef Hoffmann and Kolo Moser.

Vincennes (1740–56) French porcelain factory. established at the chateau of Vincennes, known for its early Meissen-influenced wares and later Rococo pieces, including figure groups and painted decoration influenced by the work of François BOUCHER. In 1756 the factory relocated to the chateau of SEVRES.

Visscher, Anna Roemers (1583–1651) Dutch amateur glass decorator. She worked in Amsterdam and decorated beakers and *Römers* with diamond-point engraving and developed the stippling technique.

W

Waring & Gillow (*see* GILLOWS OF LANCASTER)

Webb, Thomas & Sons (1837–) English firm of glass manufacturers near Stourbridge, Worcestershire, established by Thomas Webb I (1802–69), which operated a number of different glassworks. It is best known for the cameo glass made by the WOODALL brothers from the late 1870s as well as a range of coloured and iridescent glass.

1880–

Wedgwood (1759–) English ceramics factory, established in Burslem, Staffordshire, by Josiah Wedgwood (1730–95). A household name, the firm owes its success to both the quality and variety of its wares. The firm is best known for its fine creamware called 'Queensware', pearlware, black basalt, blue jasper wares, majolica and Art Deco wares by such designers as Keith Murray. In 1986, the firm merged with the Irish glass firm to become Waterford Wedgwood.

Weller Pottery (1872–1948) American ceramics founded in Zanesville, Ohio, by Samuel Weller. It produced wares that were closely based on ROOKWOOD ceramics.

Westerwald Region in the Rhineland, Germany, famous for its grey salt-glazed stoneware jugs and tankards often with a blackish-blue glaze decoration that have been produced from the 17th century to the present day.

Whieldon, Thomas (1719–86) English potter, one-time partner of Josiah Wedgwood and founder of the Whieldon factory in north Staffordshire in 1740, known for its lead-glazed tortoiseshell ware.

Whistler, Laurence (*b.*1912) English writer, poet and glass engraver who revived the art of diamond-point and stipple decoration on 20th-century glass. He engraved many pieces with views of country houses.

Whitefriars Glassworks (*c.*1680–1980) English glassworks founded in London, acquired in 1834 by James Powell and known as James Powell & Sons until it reverted to Whitefriars Glass Ltd in 1962. The company has played an important part in the development of modern English glass under the directorship of Harry Powell (1853–1922), who had a passion for historical glass, his son Barnaby (1871–1939) and the designer Geoffrey Baxter, who were responsible for the textured and brightly coloured glass produced in the 1950s and 1960s.

Wickes, George (1698–1761) English silversmith. Appointed goldsmith to Frederick, Prince of Wales in 1735, he became one of the leading craftsmen, working in the lavish Rococo style and receiving many aristocratic commissions.

Wincanton English town in Devon and a leading centre for the production of English delftware from the 1730s.

Wistar, Caspar (1696–1752) American glass manufacturer. A German immigrant, in 1739 he founded the Wistarburg Glassworks, one of the earliest American glassworks, in Salem County, New Jersey, which produced window glass, bottles and vials and a small range of tablewares, some in pale blue and green. The factory closed in 1780.

Wolff, David (1732–1798) Dutch glass engraver, a talented exponent of diamond-point and stipple engraving, usually of portraits, on goblets and wine glasses.

Wood, Ralph (1715–72) English potter, active in Burslem, Staffordshire, and best known for his finely modelled figures and Toby jugs.

Woodall family English family of glass decorators. Thomas Woodall (1849–1936) and his brother George (1850–1925) were trained at the firm of John NORTHWOOD and worked at Thomas WEBB & SONS making very fine cameo glass. Thought to have been the more talented of the two, George's most outstanding work is a plaque called 'The Moorish Bathers', now in the Corning Museum of Glass, Corning, New York State.

Worcester (1751–) English porcelain factory founded in Worcester by Dr John Wall and William Davis. Mass production of blue-and-white wares followed the factory's discovery, in the 1750s, of blue-and-white transfer printing, and by 1770 it was the most successful porcelain factory in Britain. Fortunes slumped briefly to revive under the directorship of John Flight (1783–92), who abandoned blue-and-white wares in favour of gilded porcelain and armorial tea and dinner services for which the factory is probably best known. From 1862 the factory was called the Royal Worcester Porcelain Co.

Wright, Frank Lloyd (1867–1959) American architect and designer of furniture, metalwork and ceramics. During the 1920s, he designed ranges of Art Deco porcelain tableware for the Japanese firm NORITAKE.

Glossary

A

acanthus classical ornament in the form of thick, scalloped leaves of the Mediterranean acanthus plant, used as a decorative motif particularly on RENAISSANCE and Neo-classical wares.

acid etching process of corroding a design on to a glass object by exposing it to hydrofluoric acid.

air-twist decorative spiral patterns in the stems of wine glasses, produced by twisting a glass rod embedded with thin columns of air.

alabastron small cylindrical flask made of core-formed glass.

amberina type of late 19th-century ornamental American glass, ranging from pale amber to ruby.

Annagelb/Annagrün yellowish green (*Annagelb*) or greenish yellow (*Annagrün*) glass produced by adding uranium to the BATCH. First made in Bohemia in the 1830s.

anthemion classical ornament roughly resembling a honeysuckle flower, and a particularly popular motif in the late 18th century.

apostle spoon type of ornamental spoon with a cast figure of one of the twelve apostles as the FINIAL. First made in continental Europe, they were made in England from the late 15th century.

apron ornamental 'skirt' beneath the seat rail of a chair or settee, or below the underframe of a cabinet-stand, side table, chest-of-drawers or COMMODE.

arcading continuous decorative motif of linked arches, often featured on medieval chests.

armoire tall, free-standing French closed cupboard used for storage.

armorial wares porcelain or glass decorated with coats of arms or crests.

assay mark town mark confirming that a piece of silver has been assayed (tested) for purity.

astragals (*see* GLAZING BARS).

B

background solid colour used on ceramic wares.

ball and claw carved ornamental foot for furniture legs, composed of a bird's claw or animal foot clasping a ball. First used in the early 18th century.

baluster bulbous shape inspired by classical vases and used from the RENAISSANCE on goblet stems, coffeepots, chair backs and candlesticks.

balustroid type of light BALUSTER wine glass with an elongated stem, developed in England in the mid-18th century.

banding decorative veneered edge of contrasting wood to the main veneer and used on table tops, drawer fronts or panelling. Crossbanding is cut across the grain, straight banding along the grain, and featherbanding at 45 degrees to the grain.

barley twist spiral-turned wood giving the effect of a twisted column, used on chair and table legs, as well as chair backs, from the late 17th century.

basalt type of black, fine-grained unglazed STONEWARE developed by Josiah Wedgwood in the mid-1760s, used for vases, busts and plaques.

batch the ingredients used to make glass. Also known as the mixture.

Bellarmine (*Bartmannskrüg*) bulbous, narrow-necked stoneware jug from the Rhineland, Germany, with a moulded mask of a bearded man. Made from the 15th century, it takes its name from Cardinal Roberto Bellarmino.

bergère French upholstered wing armchair with a rounded back and wide seat, with caned or upholstered sides, first made in the early 18th century. Known as an 'easy' chair in England.

birdcage mechanism platform support used on a TILT-TOP TABLE from *c*.1740 to allow the top to swivel and tilt upright.

biscuit porcelain porcelain fired only once and left unglazed. It has a texture similar to white marble and is used mainly for figures and busts.

blanc-de-Chine French term for white, translucent, thickly glazed Chinese porcelain made from the Ming dynasty at Dehua in south-east China and widely imitated by European factories in the 18th century.

blue-dash charger English delftware dish, first made in the late 17th century, the edge decorated with blue dashes and boldly painted figures or scenes.

bocage modelled leaves and flowers, generally including a shrub or small tree, forming a support for, and background to, a porcelain figure or group.

body material (type of clay) from which a ceramic object is made.

bone china type of SOFT-PASTE PORCELAIN developed in England in the 18th century that includes ground-up animal bones in the paste.

bonheur du jour French term for an 18th-century lady's small writing table containing tiered shelves, drawers, cupboards and pigeon holes.

boulle work type of MARQUETRY using inlaid tortoiseshell or horn combined with metal, usually brass. Developed by the French cabinet-maker André-Charles Boulle in the late 17th century, it was known as 'buhl' work in 19th-century England.

bracket foot flat, simple-shaped foot diagonally projecting from the floor to the CARCASS, used on case furniture from the late 17th century and especially popular in the 18th century.

breakfront term applied to the central section of a bookcase, sideboard, COMMODE or cabinet, that protrudes slightly in front of the side sections.

bright-cut engraving type of faceted ENGRAVING on silver that produces a glittering effect, particularly popular on Neo-classical and Federal silver.

Britannia Standard silver standard (95.8 per cent pure) that had a higher content of pure silver than sterling silver. It was made the legal standard in 1697. A hallmark with the figure of Britannia was used. STERLING SILVER was reintroduced as the legal standard in 1720.

bun foot flattened ball foot introduced in the mid-17th century and commonly used on chests-of-drawers and bureaux.

bureau writing table or desk made from the mid-17th century distinguished by a sloping front that falls forward to reveal an interior fitted with drawers and pigeon holes and a base containing drawers.

bureau Mazarin type of late 17th-century French bureau with BOULLE WORK decoration and eight scrolled legs joined by flat STRETCHERS. Named after Cardinal Mazarin, chief minister to Louis XIV.

burr wood dense swellings on a tree, most commonly walnut, elm and yew, that when cut reveal decorative markings. Popularly used from the early 18th century for VENEERING.

C

cabinet cup beaker-shaped cup usually with one handle, often with high-quality painting and GILDING, intended primarily for display in a cabinet. Particularly popular during the late 18th century and early 19th.

cabriole leg curving leg modelled on the hind leg of an animal that tapers inwards towards a club, hoof, bun, paw, ball-and-claw or scroll foot. Used on tables and chairs from the late 17th century.

cameo glass decorative glass with two or more different coloured layers, the outer layers cut to leave the design standing proud against the background colour. First made during Roman times.

canapé French term for a type of settee or sofa.

caneware yellow or buff-coloured STONEWARE usually decorated in relief and developed in the Staffordshire region in the 1770s.

carcass main body or structure of a piece of furniture on to which veneers can be applied.

carnival glass PRESSED GLASS made in purple, red, blue-green and orange. First made between *c*.1895–*c*.1940, pieces were given as prizes at American fairs and carnivals. Copies are still made today.

cartouche ornamental frame in the form of a scroll, surrounding crests, inscriptions or pictorial decoration.

case furniture items of storage furniture, including chests-of-drawers, wardrobes and BUREAUX.

cassone Italian marriage chest made from the 15th century; usually lavishly decorated in relief with mythological or religious scenes.

casters small, swivelling wheels attached to furniture legs and usually made of brass, porcelain or wood.

celadon refined Chinese STONEWARE with a bluish green semi-translucent glaze. The very best were made during the Song dynasty (960–1279).

chaise longue French term for an upholstered, elongated chair, often called a day bed.

chamberstick small portable candlestick set on a plate-shaped base with a scroll or ring handle.

chasing technique of decorating the front surface of a piece of silver by punching it with small tools. Unlike ENGRAVING, no silver is removed.

chest-on-chest two-sectioned chest-of-drawers. Also called a double chest-of-drawers or sometimes a tallboy in the USA.

chiffonier French term for a decorative side cabinet with a cupboarded front topped with shelves, which are sometimes backed with a mirror.

china clay fine, white clay, which is mixed with china stone and quartz to form HARD-PASTE PORCELAIN. Also known as kaolin.

china stone essential ingredient for making HARD-PASTE PORCELAIN. Also known as petuntse.

chinoiserie European imitations of Chinese designs with fanciful motifs including pagodas, FRETWORK, mandarins, birds, landscapes and rivers.

cloisonné method of enamelling where ENAMEL colours are poured into small compartments called cloisons, which are created by soldering thin wires on to a metal surface.

commedia dell'arte traditional Italian theatre, whose characters were especially favoured for 18th-century porcelain figures such as those made by J. J. Kändler at Meissen and F. A. Bustelli at Nymphenburg.

commode French chest-of-drawers, often a *bombé* (swollen) shape, originally meant for the drawing-room rather than the bedroom.

crawling fault caused by the glaze on a ceramic BODY pulling back from the clay during firing.

creamware thin, lightweight, cream-coloured lead-glazed earthenware, developed in Staffordshire in the 1740s and used for standard domestic tablewares during the 18th century. Josiah Wedgwood called his version 'Queensware' in honour of his patron Queen Charlotte.

credenza Italian term for a type of D-shaped sideboard with open storage or display shelves at either end. The form was particularly popular in England during the Victorian period.

cristallo type of SODA GLASS made with the ashes of plants and manganese oxide, producing a colourless glass resembling ROCK CRYSTAL. It was first developed in Venice in the 15th century.

crizzling defect in glass characterized by a network of very fine cracks. It is caused by inaccurate proportions of the ingredients in the BATCH, particularly an excess of alkali, which makes the glass decompose and crumble.

cut-card decoration technique of decorating silver by soldering patterns cut from rolled sheets of silver on to another silver object. The method was much favoured by Huguenot silversmiths in the late 17th and early 18th centuries.

D

Davenport type of small compact desk with a sloping lid above a series of drawers at each side. First introduced during the Regency period and supposedly named after a Captain Davenport for whom the first desk was made.

deutsche Blumen ('German flowers') naturalistically painted flowers, derived from botanical prints, popularly used on 18th-century European faience and porcelain.

device heraldic or emblematic figure or design.

diamond-point engraving method of ENGRAVING on glass using a diamond. A popular technique used throughout Europe from the 16th century.

doucai Chinese term for porcelain enamelled with colours that neatly dovetail together. Pieces are characterized by UNDERGLAZE BLUE outlines and OVERGLAZE enamels.

dovetailing method of joining two pieces of wood at right angles by interlocking wedge-shaped mortises and tenons.

drawer lining side of a drawer.

duchesse brisée French term for an 18th-century CHAISE LONGUE with a rounded back.

E

ebonizing staining or colouring inexpensive wood to resemble ebony. Popular during the Aesthetic Movement at the end of the 19th century.

egg and dart classical moulding incorporating egg and 'v' shapes used to enrich Neo-classical wares.

electroplating process by which an electrical current is used to deposit a thin layer of silver on a base metal, usually copper or nickel. The method was patented in England in the 1840s by Elkington & Co.

enamel opaque or translucent glass paste coloured with metallic pigments that can be fused to metal, glass or ceramics for decorative effects.

engraving method of decorating metal or glass by cutting narrow furrows into the surface.

escritoire FALL-FRONTED writing desk fitted with drawers. Made from the 16th century, it was originally portable, but in the 17th century was placed on a chest-of-drawers or a stand.

escutcheon metal plate that protects and decorates the edges of a keyhole in a piece of furniture.

etching method of creating a design on glass or metal using hydrofluoric acid, which 'bites' into the surface of the object to produce a pattern.

F

façon de Venise ('in the Venetian style') French term used to describe glass influenced by 15th-century Venetian glass; made throughout Europe in the 16th and 17th centuries and revived in the late 19th.

faience French name for TIN-GLAZED EARTHENWARE.

fall front flap of a BUREAU or desk that pulls down to create a flat writing surface.

famille rose and verte Chinese porcelains, made mainly for export to Europe, decorated with distinctive 'families' of opaque enamels: *famille rose* is dominated by a rose-pink; *famille verte* by a brilliant apple green.

fauteuil French term for an open armchair with an upholstered back and seat.

favrile glass type of iridescent glass developed by Louis Comfort Tiffany from 1892. It was made in imitation of excavated Roman glass.

festoon ornament in the form of a garland or chain of fruit, flowers and ribbons suspended in a loop. Popularly used on Rococo and Neo-classical wares.

figuring natural decorative pattern created by the grain in wood.

finial top or end ornament that can take many forms, including ball, flame, flower, acorn or vase.

firing process of exposing a ceramic BODY to various temperatures in a kiln in order to harden the clay, to

melt the glaze so that it adheres to the surface and to fuse the colours and gilding to the surface. Also used for fixing colours to glass and enamels to metal.

flatback pottery figure with a flat, undecorated back, intended to stand on a mantelpiece and produced mainly in Staffordshire from the 1840s.

flatware general term for cutlery.

fluting shallow, concave, parallel grooves running vertically on a column or other surface; popular for use on the legs of tables and chairs.

flux alkaline substance (potash or soda) that is an essential ingredient in the glass BATCH to aid fusion.

fly bracket neat bracket for supporting a flap on a small table such as a Pembroke table.

folded foot stable foot on a wine glass with its rim turned under to make a thick double layer of glass.

frame and panel type of basic furniture construction with shaped or rectangular parts framed by horizontal rails, vertical STILES and MUNTINS.

fretwork band of pierced geometrical ornament consisting of intersecting straight, repeated vertical and horizontal lines. Popularly used on mid-18th century CHINOISERIE furniture.

frieze horizontal band often used to decorate the underframe of tables or benches.

G

gadrooning decorative relief pattern consisting of a series of parallel, alternating convex or concave lobes. Used on furniture, ceramics and silver.

gateleg table drop-leaf table with a square, oval or circular top and flaps supported on pivoting 'gates' that are hinged to the central section.

gilding ornamental finish made of gold leaf or gold dust, used for decorative effect on furniture, porcelain, and in the case of silver, to protect it from the damaging effects of salt, egg or fruit juices.

glazing bars decorative semi-circular wood mouldings used for supporting glass in cabinets and bookcases. Also known as astragals.

Goldrubinglas ('gold-ruby glass') German term for a type of deep ruby-red glass.

grotesque light decorative motif, based on ancient Roman wall paintings, incorporating fantastic animals and birds. Widely popular during the RENAISSANCE and Neo-classical periods.

guilloche classical motif of undulating lines forming a continuous figure-of-eight pattern; popular for decorating silver and furniture from the 16th century and especially during the Neo-classical period.

H

hard-paste porcelain also known as 'true' porcelain. Composed of china stone (petuntse) and china clay (kaolin); developed in China from the 7th century.

Hausmaler ('home painter') German term for an independent decorator who painted glass or porcelain outside the factory during the 17th and 18th centuries.

highboy American term for a high chest-of-drawers.

Historismus German term coined in the late 19th century referring to the preoccupation at that time with revivalist styles, and the especial interest in capturing the spirit of bygone days.

Hochschnitt ('high relief') German term for glass cutting where the design stands out in relief. A common type of glass decoration in late 17th-century Bohemia and Germany. Opposite of *TIEFSCHNITT*.

honey gilding decorative technique using gold leaf that has been ground up and mixed with honey. It usually has a warm, reddish tinge.

Humpen German term for a type of tall, cylindrical glass beaker, usually for beer, sometimes with elaborate enamelled decoration; popular in central Europe in the mid-16th century.

I

incising scratching on a ceramic vessel, as decoration or to record a name, inscription or date.

inlay decorative technique on furniture that involves creating a pattern by laying pieces of ivory, glass, precious metals, mother-of-pearl or wood into carved-out recesses in the CARCASS.

istoriato ('story painted') Italian term for biblical, mythological or historical subjects decorating Italian MAIOLICA from the 15th century.

J

japanning term used to describe a variety of European methods imitating oriental LACQUER decoration, by the application of coats of varnish or paint to furniture from the 1660s.

jasper ware type of very fine-grained STONEWARE sprigged with white classical figures and motifs. Made by Josiah Wedgwood from the 1770s. The most usual colour was sky blue.

Jaspisporzellan hard red STONEWARE, made in the early 18th century at Meissen, and so called owing to its likeness to the semi-precious stone jasper.

K

kakiemon style of decoration derived from the work of a Japanese family of potters called Kakiemon working in Arita. The decoration is sparse and is executed in a palette of red, blue, green, yellow and black. The style was copied by European factories in the 18th century.

kaolin (*see* CHINA CLAY).

karakusa ('octopus scrollwork') band of scrolled foliage, derived from Chinese vine scrolls, which was a favoured decorative pattern for late 17th- and 18th-century Japanese porcelain made in Arita.

knop decorative bulge on the stem of a glass in a variety of shapes, either hollow or solid; a FINIAL decorating teapots and vase lids, or the terminals of spoons.

kraak ware late Ming Chinese blue-and-white porcelain exported to Europe by Dutch traders in ships known as 'carracks'.

L

lacquer oriental varnish, used for decorating furniture and decorative wares, made from tree gum with a high gloss finish that became fashionable in Europe in the 17th century and was copied in JAPANNING. Wares were frequently inlaid with mother-of-pearl, coral or metals to create a decorative effect.

latticino Italian term for a type of clear glass decorated with embedded threads of white glass to form an intricate lacy pattern.

lattimo ('milk') Italian term for opaque white glass made from the mid-14th century in Venice and coloured by adding bone ash or tin oxide to the BATCH and sometimes by adding antimony or zinc.

Laub-und-Bandelwerk German term meaning 'leaf and bandwork'. A type of Baroque ornament.

lead glass type of glass containing a quantity of lead oxide, first made by George Ravenscroft in 1676 as a remedy for CRIZZLING. It is more brilliant than *CRISTALLO*, and well suited to cutting.

lead glaze thick, transparent ceramic glaze containing lead oxide that can be coloured with metallic oxides.

loaded method of strengthening and stabilizing hollow metal objects, such as candlesticks or candelabra, with an iron rod secured inside the shape with pitch or plaster of Paris.

M

maiolica Italian term for earthenware covered with an opaque white tin glaze and painted with multicoloured decoration. The earliest maiolica was made in the late 14th century.

majolica type of tin-glazed earthenware decorated with brightly coloured LEAD GLAZES, loosely based on early Italian MAIOLICA and lead-glazed wares by the 16th-century French potter Bernard Palissy. Popular in Europe and the USA from the 1850s.

marquetry type of decoration on furniture whereby shaped pieces of differently coloured (often exotic) woods are applied as veneers to the surface, often in very decorative floral patterns.

mercury gilding dangerous process by which a combination of gold and mercury is applied to a metal or ceramic object. When heated it leaves a film of gold on the surface as the mercury evaporates. The effect is more brilliant and brassy than HONEY GILDING.

metal term generally used to describe molten (and also cold) glass.

molinet silver stick inserted through the top of a chocolate pot to stir the liquid inside.

monopodia type of classical chair or table support in the form of an animal's head and a single leg and foot; favoured by Neo-classical designers.

mortise-and-tenon joint used from the 16th century in which a rectangular cavity (mortise) in one section receives the projecting tongue (tenon) of the other, which is glued or held firm by a wooden peg.

mote spoon type of pierced spoon used to skim tea leaves off the surface of a cup of tea.

muntin vertical central bar between panels on a piece of furniture of FRAME AND PANEL construction. The end bar is called a STILE.

O

ogee continuous shallow double curve in the shape of an 'S' used primarily for mouldings, arches and BRACKET FEET.

opaline translucent glass made opaque by the addition of ashes of calcined bones and coloured with metallic oxides.

ormolu French term for gilt-bronze.

overglaze painted or printed decoration applied on top of the glaze of a ceramic object.

P

palmettes fan-shaped decorative motifs resembling palm leaves, originating in antiquity and revived during the RENAISSANCE and Neo-classical periods for decoration of ceramics, metalwork and furniture.

parcel gilt decoration on silver or furniture that is partially covered in gold, creating a contrast between the GILDING and the material beneath.

parian ware unglazed, fine-grained translucent porcelain popular for making imitation marble figures and busts in the 19th century.

parquetry variant of MARQUETRY where the veneers are placed symmetrically on the carcass to create geometric designs.

paste mixture of different clays and other materials used to make a ceramic BODY.

pâte-sur-pâte ('paste-on-paste') French term for an elaborate and expensive technique of relief decoration made by gradually building up layers of SLIP on a coloured, unfired porcelain BODY to simulate the effect of a cameo.

patera circular or oval motif, frequently decorated with ACANTHUS leaves or FLUTING, popular during the Neo-classical period.

patination attractive and desirable surface sheen on furniture and silver resulting from years of handling, polish and dirt.

pearlware type of earthenware with a bluish pearly glaze, introduced by Josiah Wedgwood in 1779 in an effort to improve on his CREAMWARE.

pediment triangular gable on a classical temple, frequently appearing at the top of CASE FURNITURE.

Pembroke table type of small occasional table with two drop leaves supported on hinged brackets. Introduced in Europe in the mid-18th century.

petuntse (*see* CHINA STONE).

pietre dure ('hardstones') Italian term for an expensive type of INLAY using a variety of semi-precious stones; perfected in Italy in the early 17th century.

pontil mark rough circular mark left when the pontil iron, used to manipulate a glass during shaping and finishing, is broken off the finished item.

potash glass type of hard glass containing potash, derived from plant ash, and suitable for cutting.

pressed glass type of glass made from the 1820s shaped by placing a gather of molten glass in a metal mould and then pressing it with a metal plunger to form the external shape and decoration.

prunt decorative blob of glass, usually applied to the stem or bowl of a glass object.

Q

quarter veneering type of VENEERING using two pairs of matching slices of wood placed on to the CARCASS to create a decorative pattern.

quatrefoil four-lobed Gothic motif resembling a four-leaf clover. Popularly used on 19th-century Gothic Revival furniture.

Queensware (*see* CREAMWARE).

R

rail horizontal piece of wood that runs above and below a panel in a frame-and-panel construction or between the STILES on a chair back.

Ranftbecher German term for a type of beaker with a tapering or waisted shape standing on a thick-cut base, frequently decorated with transparent enamelling and GILDING.

reeding parallel, convex moulding derived from the decoration on classical columns, often used on chair and table legs.

Renaissance period and style in Italy in the early 14th century to the end of the 16th. Inspired by classical motifs such as ACANTHUS leaves, SWAGS, PEDIMENTS, PATERAE and FESTOONS. The style was revived in the 19th century.

ribbonwork carved decoration resembling rippled ribbons tied in loose bows, usually featured on the SPLATS of chair backs and most associated with the designs of Thomas Chippendale.

rock crystal transparent, colourless quartz that is very hard and usually carved into decorative objects.

Römer German term for an early type of glass drinking vessel with an ovoid bowl, a hollow cylindrical stem decorated with PRUNTS and a spreading foot. Made in *WALDGLAS*.

rosewood dense, heavy wood with dark purplish-brown FIGURING. Generally used as a veneer, particularly on Regency furniture.

S

sabre term for leg shaped like a sabre and gently tapering outwards, as seen on the ancient Greek 'Klismos' chair. Particularly associated with Regency and Federal chairs and sofas.

salt glaze type of hard-wearing, glittery glaze on STONEWARE made by throwing salt into the kiln during firing. Often creates a pitted surface.

sancai **ware** ('three-colour') Chinese earthenware, first made during the Tang dynasty (618–907) decorated with thick, treacly LEAD GLAZES in green and brown/amber. The 'third' colour was the cream earthenware BODY.

Satsuma ware type of 19th-century Japanese earthenware featuring lavish enamelling, a finely crackled glaze and heavy GILDING.

scale-blue background pattern of UNDERGLAZE BLUE overlapping scales, first used at the English factory of Worcester in the 1760s.

Schnelle tall tapering tankard usually made in salt-glazed STONEWARE in the 16th century in the Rhineland, often with vertical panels decorated in relief with biblical or mythological subjects.

Schwarzlot ('black lead') German term for a type of painting in black, imitating engraving. Used on glass, FAIENCE and porcelain and mainly executed by German *HAUSMALER*.

sconce type of decorative wall plaque with a projecting arm or arms for holding candles and a polished surface to reflect the candlelight.

seaweed marquetry type of intricate MARQUETRY decoration on a walnut background usually composed of holly or boxwood. The pieces are arranged to look like seaweed.

secretaire writing cabinet with a hinged mock drawer front that lets down to create a writing surface and reveals hidden pigeon holes.

Sheffield plate substitute for silver made by fusing a layer of silver to an ingot of copper and rolling it to form a sheet. Developed by Thomas Boulsover in the 1740s it was used commercially during the second half of the 18th century and first half of the 19th.

shou Chinese symbol signifying good luck, long life, happiness and riches.

slip creamy mixture of clay and water used to decorate pottery, cast hollow figures or attach relief moulded decoration to a ceramic BODY.

slipware ceramics decorated with SLIP, either by dipping the article into the slip, or by trailing slip across the surface to create decorative effects.

soda glass type of glass in which the alkali in the BATCH is obtained from soda (sodium carbonate).

soft-paste porcelain type of porcelain BODY developed in Europe in the 16th century, made from materials such as CHINA CLAY, glass, soapstone or bone ash, in an attempt to make HARD-PASTE PORCELAIN. Also known as 'artificial' porcelain.

soldering method by which various parts of a piece of silver are joined together using an alloy.

splat flat, upright back support between a chair's seat and TOPRAIL.

sprigging small, low-moulded ceramic relief decoration applied (sprigged) on to the BODY and attached with thin SLIP.

Stein German term for a cylindrical STONEWARE beer or ale mug with one handle and a hinged lid, usually ornamented with relief decoration.

sterling silver standard of silver where the silver content is 92.5 per cent pure silver.

stile upright supporting post on a piece of furniture.

stipple engraving technique of tapping a glass surface with a sharp implement such as a diamond point to produce a pattern made up of tiny dots. Introduced in Holland in the 1620s.

stoneware non-porous ceramic BODY, usually grey, brown or off-white, made from clay combined with sand or flint, which is fired at a high temperature. Often covered with a SALT GLAZE.

stretcher strengthening or stabilizing rail that runs horizontally between furniture legs.

striations irregularities in a glass object created when it was shaped using various tools.

swag decorative ornament of suspended garlands of fruit, foliage or flowers, ribbons or drapery, found particularly on furniture, ceramics and silver of the RENAISSANCE and Neo-classical periods.

T

tallboy (*see* CHEST-ON-CHEST).

tambour desk type of desk with a roll front formed from thin strips of wood glued to a canvas backing. Popular from the 19th century.

taperstick holder for holding a taper- or candlestick, used for lighting pipes and melting sealing wax.

tear drop-shaped air bubble most frequently enclosed within the stem of a wine glass or goblet.

Tiefschnitt ('deep carving') German term for ENGRAVING where a design is wheel engraved below the surface of a glass object, in order to produce an image in relief where the background is the highest plane. Opposite of *HOCHSCHNITT*.

tilt-top table popular form of pedestal table from the 1740s where the top is hinged to the base and can be tilted vertically when not in use.

tin-glazed earthenware type of low-fired earthenware covered with a glassy, opaque white glaze made by

adding tin oxide to a clear glaze. Usually painted with blue or multicoloured decoration. The most common types include MAIOLICA, FAIENCE and DELFTWARE.

tongue and groove straight or right-angled joint made by cutting a groove in one piece of wood into which fits the projecting tongue of another.

toprail uppermost horizontal RAIL on a chair back.

transfer printing method of mass producing printed decoration on ceramics, by transferring a design from an inked copper plate on to a ceramic surface.

turning decorative technique for shaping wood by cutting it while revolving it on a lathe.

U

underglaze blue ceramic decoration whereby cobalt blue is painted on the BODY, glazed and finally fired to fix it to the surface.

uranium glass greenish opaline glass made by adding uranium oxide to the batch. First made in Bohemia in the 19th century.

V

vaseline glass type of glass made with a small amount of uranium, which imparts a yellowish green or greenish yellow colour and has a 'greasy' appearance resembling vaseline. First made in Bohemia in the 1830s.

veneering furniture-making technique that consists of fixing a thin layer or long strips of fine woods, such as mahogany, rosewood, satinwood or walnut, to cover or decorate the surface of a less expensive, coarser CARCASS, such as pine or oak.

vent hole small hole in the base or back of a ceramic figure or bust, which allows air to escape during firing thus preventing it from exploding.

verre de fougère ('fern glass') early type of greenish POTASH GLASS, produced in France after the Roman period. The alkali ingredient was provided by potash made from burnt fern or bracken.

Vitruvian scroll classical ornament of repeated spiral scrolls, generally on a frieze; frequently used on early Georgian furniture.

W

Waldglas ('forest glass') German term for an early type of POTASH GLASS with a greenish tinge, where the flux in the batch consists of the ashes of burnt wood or bracken. Made from the Middle Ages.

Wellington chest type of tall chest with seven drawers named after the Duke of Wellington.

wheel engraving technique of ENGRAVING into the surface of glass by holding a rotating wheel of stone or metal against it.

wucai Chinese 'five colour' palette where the design is drawn in underglaze cobalt blue and filled in with black, red, yellow, green and brown enamels.

Y

Yixing type of hard red Chinese STONEWARE often decorated with sprigged designs such a plum blossom. Wares were copied in the 18th century at Meissen and by the Elers brothers in Staffordshire.

Z

Zwischengoldglas ('gold sandwich glass') German term for a decorative technique used on Bohemian glass in the mid-18th century. Gold leaf applied to the outer surface of a glass vessel was engraved and protected by another glass casing or sealed with transparent varnish.

Index

Acknowledgments

The publishers would like to thank the following people and organizations for supplying pictures for use in this book or for allowing their pieces to be photographed.

ADAGP Société des Auteurs dans les Arts Graphiques et Plastiques **AKG** AKG London **AJ** A & J Photographs **ASH** Ashmolean Museum, Oxford **AL** Andrew Lineham Fine Glass, The Mall, Camden Passage, London N1 **AR** Artemis **BD** Barry Davies Oriental Art Ltd., 1 Davies Street, London W1 **BAL** The Bridgeman Art Library, London **BH** Broadfield House Glass Museum, Kingswinford, West Midlands **BM** British Museum **BV** Barbara Veith **CC/ME** Clive Corless/Marshall Editions **C&D** Cathers & Dembrosky, 43 E10th Street, New York **CHG** Trustees of the Cecil Higgins Art Gallery, Bedford **C** Christie's **CI** Christie's Images Ltd. 1999 **CM** Chrysler Museum, Norfolk, Virginia **CMG** Photographic Services, Office of the Registrar, Corning Museum of Glass, Corning, NY **CO** Corbis Images **DACS** Design and Artists Copyright Society, Parchment House, 13 Northburgh Street, London EC1 **DS** David Seidenberg, 836 Broadway, New York **ETA** ET Archive, London **FL** Fay Lucas, 50 Kensington Church Street, London W8 **GA** Gem Antiques, 1088 Madison Avenue, New York **GR** Graham Rae **GV** Grosvenor Antiques, 27 Holland Street, London W8 **IS** courtesy of Israel Sack, Inc., New York **JB** Jill Bace **JH** Jeanette Hayhurst, 32a Kensington Church Street, London W8 **JHO** Jonathan Horne 66c Kensington Church Street, London W8 **JM** Judith Miller **KB** Karl Bartley **LK** Leigh Keno, 980 Madison Avenue, New York, NY **LN** Lillian Nassau, 220 E57th Street, New York **MG** Maison Gerard, 53 E10th Street, New York **ML** Marion Langham, 41a Lower Belgrave Street, London SW1 **NB** Nic Boston, Kensington Antiques Centre, 58–60 Kensington Church Street, London W8 **ND** Nicholas M. Dawes, 67 E11th Street, New York **OH** Osterley House **PA** Phillip's Fine Art Auctioneers **RN** Raymond Notley **RR** Robin Rice **S** Sotheby's **SF** Silver Fund, 40 Bury Street, London SW1 **SPL** Sotheby's Picture Library **SS** Simon Spero, 109 Kensington Church Street, London W8 **ST** Steve Tanner **STR** Stradlings, 1225 Park Avenue, New York **TC** Tim Clinch **TMG** Terrence McGinniss **TM** The Toledo Museum of Art, Toledo, Ohio; purchased with fund from the Libbey Endowment, gift of Edward Drummond Libbey **V&A** Victoria & Albert Museum Picture Library, London **VH** Valerie Howard, 2 Campden Street, London W8 **WE** Josiah Wedgwood & Sons Ltd.

Key
b bottom; **c** centre; **l** left; **r** right; **t** top

1 VH; **2** tl KB/S, tr AJ/C, bl AJ/C, br AJ/S; **3** b TMG/LN; **4** t AJ/S; **5** t TMG/DS, bl AJ/NB, br AJ/AL; **6** CI; **7** t AJ/C, b KB/S; **8** tl Prado, Madrid/ETA, tr CC/ME, bl SPL, br Musée de Versailles, France/ETA; **9** tl & tr SPL, bl CI, br V&A; **10** t & cl CI, cr IS, b CI; **11** t private collection/BAL, bl CI, br AJ/GV; **12** tl TC/OH, tr CI, b CC/ME; **13** t ETA, c Brand Inglis Ltd/BAL, b CI; **14** tl Museum of Fine Arts, Texas, USA/BAL, tr, bl & br IS; **15** tl & tr IS, bl CI, br IS; **16** t ETA, c SPL, b CI; **17** tl AJ/JH, tr CC/ME, c CI, b V&A; **18** tl CI/BAL, tr SPL, c AJ/AL, b ND; **19** tl AJ/JH, tc & tr TMG/ND, c ETA, b TMG/ND; **20** tl ETA, tr SPL, bl C&D, br TMG/ND; **21** tl TMG/ND, tr SPL, c C&D, b V&A; **22** tl ETA © DACS 2000, tr CI, bl V&A, br CI; **23** tl & tr CI, c AKG © ADAGP, Paris and DACS, London 2000, b SPL; **24** tl Oldham Art Gallery, Lancs/BAL, tr CC/ME, bl PA, br SPL; **25** t CC/ME, b SPL; **26** tl private collection/Stapleton Collection/BAL, tc CC/ME © Estate of Eric Ravilious 2000. All rights reserved, DACS, tr TMG/ND, bl SPL, br RR/MG; **27** tl TMG/MG, tr ETA, cl AJ/JH, cr CI; **28–9** AJ/S; **30** t CO, c CI, b CC/ME; **31** CI; **36** tl CI, tr ETA, bl & br SPL; **37** t SPL, c SPL, b CI; **40** AJ/S; **41** AJ/S; **42** tl, tc & tr SPL, c SPL, bl CI, br SPL; **43** tl SPL, tr CI, bl & bc SPL, br CC/ME; **44** AJ/S; **45** AJ/S; **46** AJ/S; **47** TMG/LK; **48** tl & tr CI, bl LK, br private collection/BAL; **49** tl CI, tc & tr CC/ME, bl CC/ME, br CI; **52** AJ/S; **53** TMG/LK; **54** SPL; **55** tl CI, tr SPL, bl & br CC/ME; **56** AJ/S; **57** t & cl AJ/S, cr SPL, b AJ/S; **58** tl SPL, tr CI, bl SPL, br CI; **59** tl CI, tr SPL, bl CI, br SPL; **60** TMG/C&D; **61** tl, tr & c AJ/S, b CC/ME; **62** tl & tr SPL, bl CI, br LK; **63** tl CI, tr SPL, bl & br CI; **64** tl & tr CI, c Blackburn Museum & Art Gallery/BAL, b CI; **65** t CI, c LK, bl Bonhams/BAL, br SPL; **66** AJ/S; **67** tl, tr, cl & cr AJ/private collection, bl SPL, br AJ/private collection; **68** AJ/S; **69** AJ/S; **70** tl SPL, tr Wallace Collection/BAL, bl SPL, br LK; **71** tl & tr SPL, bl & br CC/ME; **72** tl & tr CI, bl SPL, br CI; **73** tl SPL, tr CI, bl SPL, br CI; **74** AJ/S; **75** t AJ/S, c & b SPL; **76** SPL; **77** tl CC/ME, tr CI, bl & br SPL; **78** tl & tr SPL, c private collection/BAL, b SPL; **79** SPL; **80** AJ/S; **81** tl, tr, cl, cr & bl AJ/S, br CC/ME; **82** tl & tr CI, bl SPL, br CI; **83** tl CI, tr SPL, bl SPL, br CI; **84–5** KB/S; **86** t & c SPL, b ND; **87** CI; **88** SPL; **89** tl & c CC/ME, bl ND, br AJ/VH; **90** t, cl, cr, & bl KB/S, bl & br ASH; **91** tl SPL, tr, cl, cr, bl & br KB/S; **92** tl & tr JHO, c & b ETA; **93** tl GR/JHO, tr SPL, bl JHO, br CC/ME; **94** GR/JHO; **95** GR/JHO; **96** tl CC/ME, tr JHO, bl JHO, br SPL; **97** t SPL, c WE, bl SPL, br CC/ME; **98** KB/S; **99** KB/S; **100** AJ/NB; **101** t, c & bl TMG/ND, br AJ/NB; **102** tl & tr CC/ME, bl & br SPL; **103** tl SPL, tr CC/ME, bl TMG/LN, br TMG/GA; **104** tl & tr SPL, c CI, b JHO; **105** SPL; **106** KB/S; **107** tl KB/S, tr SPL, bl & br KB/S; **108** tl CC/ME, tr JHO, bl & br SPL; **109** tl & tr CC/ME, bl SPL, br CI; **110** AJ/VH; **111** t, c, bl, bc AJ/VH, br SPL; **112** tl SPL, tr V&A, bl & br SPL; **113** tl SPL, tr TMG/BV, bl CI, br CC/ME; **114** KB/S; **115** tl KB/S, tr SPL, c, bl & br KB/S; **116** KB/S; **117** KB/S; **118** SPL; **119** SPL; **120** AJ/BD;

121 AJ/BD; **122** tl, tr & bl SPL, br CC/ME; **123** CC/ME; **124** tl KB/S, tr CI, bl SPL, br CC/ME; **125** tl & tr SPL, b CI; **126** tl, tc & tr KB/S, c KB/S, bl CI, br KB/S; **127** KB/S; **128** KB/S; **129** KB/S; **130** tl SPL, tr AJ/JB, bl AJ/SS, br SPL; **131** tl SPL, tr KB/S, bl & br SPL; **132** KB/S; **133** AJ/JM; **134** tl PA, tr SPL, bl PA, br SPL; **135** tl & tr PA, bl CI, br SPL; **136** AJ/GV; **137** TMG/STR; **138** tl CI, tr SPL, bl V&A, br SPL; **139** tl CI, tr CC/ME, bl & br CI; **140** AJ/ML; **141** AJ/ML; **142** tl & tr SPL, bl CI, br SPL; **143** tl CC/ME, tr TMG/GA, bl SPL, br PA; **144–145** AJ/C; **145** AJ/C; **146** t & c CI, b SF; **147** CI; **148** t AJ/FL, rest AJ/C; **149** br TMG/DS, rest AJ/C; **152** tl CI, tr AJ/C, cl, cr & b CI; **153** CI; **154** AJ/C; **155** AJ/C; **156** AJ/C; **157** AJ/C; **158** tl, tr & c CI, b V&A/ETA; **159** t, c & bl CI, br V&A/BAL; **160** AJ/C; **161** TMG/DS; **162** AJ/C; **163** AJ/C; **164** tl AJ/C, tr & b CI; **165** tl AJ/C, tr CI, b CI; **166** AJ/C; **167** AJ/C; **168** AJ/C; **169** AJ/C; **170–71** AJ/C; **172** t AJ/JH, c & b SPL; **173** t AJ/JH, b CM; **174** tl CI, tr SPL, b AJ/JH; **175** t CHG, bl SPL, br AJ/AL; **176** ST/JH; **177** ST/JH; **178** AJ/JH; **179** AJ/JH; **180** tl AJ/JH, tr V&A, bl CM, bc KB/S, br BM; **181** t CM, c & b AJ/JH; **182** ST/JH; **183** tl ST/JH, tr TMG/STR, bl, bc & br ST/JH; **184** AJ/JH; **185** tl, tr & bl AJ/JH, br TMG/ND; **186** tl & tr CI, b AJ/JH; **187** tl & tr BM, bl TM, br CI; **188** AJ/AL; **189** t CI, c AJ/AL, bl & br AJ/AL; **190** tl AJ/JH, tr AJ/AL, bl AJ/AL, br AJ/JH; **191** tl AJ/JH, tr AJ/AL, bl TMG/LN, br RN; **192** tl SPL, tr CI, b BM; **193** tl SPL, tr AJ/JH, b SPL; **194** tl & tr SPL, bl AJ/AL, br SPL; **195** tl AJ/AL, tr AJ/JH, bl & br AJ/AL; **196** tl SPL, tr AJ/JH, bl V&A, br BH; **197** t CI, bl CMG, br JH; **198** tl & tr, ST/JH, bl & br AJ/JH; **199** tl AJ/JH, tr ST/JH; bl & br ST/JH; **200** tl CMG tr & b PA; **201** t BH, bl CM, br CI; **202** tl AJ/AR, tr AJ/AL, bl & bc AJ/AR, br AJ/AL; **203** tl & tr ST/JH, c, bl & br AJ/AR.

The publishers would like to thank the following for all their invaluable help and experience in putting the book together:

Nic Boston, Cathers & Dembrosky, Barry Davies Oriental Art Ltd., Gem Antiques, Charles Hajdamach, Jonathan Horne, Valerie Howard, Leigh Keno, Marion Langham, Andrew Lineham, Fay Lucas, Maison Gerard, Lillian Nassau, Raymond Notley, Israel Sack and Simon Spero.

If the publishers have unwittingly infringed copyright in any illustration reproduced, they will pay an appropriate fee on being satisfied as to the owner's title.

Antiques are delicate objects and should always be handled with care.